D1507477

The Writer's Voice:
Lessons In Composition

Lynne Dozier

Paperback Edition
Second Edition includes updates for Career and College Readiness Standards
and Writing Across the Curriculum.

Printed in the United States of America
ISBN-13: 978-1484899229
ISBN-10: 1484899229

Library of Congress Number: 2013909037

Cover Design: Don Dozier and Chris Miller
Aquilae Stilus logo: Yolim Khoo
Clip art purchased iclipart.com

We have made a great effort to contact the students whose works appear in this book. I regret any oversights that have occurred and will be happy to rectify them in future printings.

For more information, please contact:

Lynne Dozier
http://teacherweb.com/Dozier
D& L Global Consulting, Inc.
Houston, Texas 77066

Acknowledgements

Several years ago, Don, my husband, insisted I complete this book so he offered to help by ordering take-out pizzas "online" while I worked on it at our kitchen table. Our four children and eight grandchildren have waited patiently for me to finish it so they could buy it at their local bookstore, check it out from the library, or read its words on the screens of their tablets or laptop computers.

My father, Dan Drew, loved language, and, typing with two fingers, he wrote hundreds of letters, notes and memos on a used Smith Corona typewriter. Saved in shoeboxes and stored on a closet shelf, they wait for the time when I can organize them for his great, great grandchildren to read. A self-educated man, he would have enjoyed reading my essays, stories and poems—and those of my students, but he would never have understood the power of technology and the Internet.

If I've made a difference at all in thirty years of teaching, it's because of the ideas and inspiration of several great teachers: Mrs. Jenkins, a fifth grade teacher, who appreciated the poems I wrote when I finished quizzes early; Mr. Cole and Ms. Glasscock, the only English teachers at the high school in Hayti, Missouri, who encouraged me to write stories in addition to traditional book reports; Dr. Bierk, my first college English professor, who challenged me to write better than I thought I could; Dr. Grauel, chairman of the English Department at Southeast Missouri State University, who showed me the subtlety and humor of the English language and Dr. Joyce Carroll, noted author, professor, former director of the New Jersey Writing Project and Abydos Learning International, the first person who called me, "writer."

Finally, I want to thank the student writers whose "voices" have helped our school's literary magazine, *Aquilae Stilus,* rank as one of the best in Texas for almost twenty years. Through them, I learned that writing, revising and editing a book takes time, hard work, dedication to purpose, and a strong focus on the needs of readers. One of those students, the art/manuscript editor of the 1997-98 edition, Dr. Stephen Tsui, now an Assistant Professor in the Physics Department at California State University San Marcos, provided his editorial skills, technical expertise and important feedback as we worked to complete this edition. I also deeply appreciate the creative design and formatting assistance of former student:

Christopher Miller
aggie2016@hotmail.com
http://christheITpro.com

Table of Contents

Preface

After an especially frustrating week watching my students struggle with their writing processes and my assignments, I stood by the door of my classroom waiting impatiently for the bell to ring at the end of the school week. My student writers had wanted an easy way—a quick road to an "A" on their compositions. However, I insisted that they could develop their own unique voices, share the power of their ideas, and understand the English language, so I had continued to encourage—and push—them to:

- Make every word count like Frost and Sandburg;
- Craft sentences like Hemingway, Steinbeck and Fitzgerald;
- Use evidence to defend their positions like Jefferson and King;
- Express their individual voices in stories like Cisneros and Wright;
- Listen to the "beat of a different drummer" like Thoreau.

On their way out the door that particular Friday, I heard one of them grumble, "You know, it's not the writing in Dozier's class that bothers me. It's the thinking that's killing me." I smiled, walked back to my desk, and thought, "Maybe this week, I made a difference after all."

A few years later, some of my students asked, "Why don't you staple all your handouts together so we can keep up with them for the whole year?" That summer, I began to organize my lessons into "A Guide For Students." The next year, they asked me to add a table of contents. The next year, they wanted graphics and charts to "break up the all the words," and then, with their permission and encouragement, I added students' poetry and prose as examples, and they suggested a title: *The Writer's Voice.* Since the beginning, students in my junior English classes and the editors of our school's literary anthology, *Aquilae Stilus* (Latin for "the eagle's pen"), made suggestions, helped edit, revise and proofread this project. As we worked together to discover the writing process through a variety of assignments, they have challenged me to think about the effectiveness of my lessons and to reach beyond the obvious and the ordinary. I appreciate their honest help, thoughtful criticism and unusual patience.

This book, produced with the help of a former student, Chris Miller, compiles personal essays, student models, and mini-lessons created, developed and used throughout thirty years of teaching language and composition to young, developing writers. I believe we have created a "kid-friendly" guide—easy to follow, helpful to use and moderately entertaining to read.

Once, Hemingway wrote, "There is nothing to writing. All you do is sit down at a typewriter and bleed." I have left some blood on these pages, but it hasn't been the writing that bothered me. It was the thinking that nearly killed me.

Dedication

To all the student writers in my classroom whose "voices"
made the lessons in this book possible.

LESSON 1.
GETTING STARTED:
FINDING YOUR "VOICE"

"A Sense of Humor Is a Sign of Intelligence."

"Think Outside the Box."   "Avoid the Obvious."

"Create Velcro Phrases."   "Be Specific."

                                            "Show. Don't Tell."

"Write Tight."

"Parallelism: Remember the Rule of Three."

"Use   Action Verbs and Concrete Nouns."

"The 5 P's: Prior Planning Prevents Poor Performance."

"The **best** thing about writing   is making decisions.
The **worst** thing about writing is making decisions."

A Letter: "Becoming a Writer"

Dear Friends,

Everyone can learn to write convincing, correct and concise prose required in school and the working world. Learning to write well, like learning a sport, involves four components: instruction, practice, evaluation and performance. For example, when you learned to play baseball, your coach showed you how to throw a ball and swing a bat and then, you spent hours and hours practicing. During practice, your coach, teammates, and sometimes parents, pointed out that you needed to step into the pitch, keep your eyes on the ball or change your stance. When you felt confident, you stepped up to the plate, took a signal from your coach, and swung for the fences.

Most people can learn the craft of writing. Reading good literature can help you see how others accomplish the task of writing. However, you can watch baseball players hit, field and throw, but unless you get on the field, swing a bat, throw the ball, and run around the bases, often and with enthusiasm, your progress as an athlete will be slow. Athletes—and writers—also listen to the opinions of coaches and teammates. When you think about it, you hear opinions expressed many times a day about such simple things as style of clothing. For example, when a friend asks you if a shirt and pants go together, you might look at the two, notice that although the colors are complementary, the patterns are not, and try to suggest a different combination. The same process works when you evaluate the effectiveness of a piece of writing

A Writer's Notebook provides a place for you to practice writing each day. Your teachers, friends, classmates—and you— will analyze your compositions and share ideas about your audience, purpose, message and tone. Readers can decide quickly if a composition or essay contains well-organized, clearly stated ideas and appropriate language. Then, they might ask questions like these: How do you form paragraphs? How does word choice make ideas and events vivid? How do figures of speech, details and imagery help communicate meaning? How does the evidence support the thesis? What transitions improve fluency? How will this piece of writing affect readers' emotions? Intellects? Ethics? What is the writer's purpose, and how did the writer achieve it?

Finally, your readers will come to some conclusions: "Yes, this essay persuades because...." "I think you could improve this description by...." "I was confused in this narrative when..." Notice that suggestions follow each of these comments. Saying, "I liked it," or "It didn't work for me" is not enough. You must say why you think as you do and offer suggestions for improvements.

As you write your way through this book, you will receive instruction, practice and opportunities for evaluation at each step in the process. An instructor, your friends, parents, and your own self-evaluation will help you monitor and rate your performance. If you are willing to experiment, start over and revise until you achieve your purpose and meet the needs of your audience, then you will discover how to write from a position of strength and achieve a maturity of style.

Sincerely,

Lynne Dozier

How Do I Use This Book?

Each of the lessons begin with an essential question that helps guide the writing process, information that answers that question and an example or "model" for you to follow. A "Your Turn" assignment follows the lesson so that you have a chance to practice the skills in the examples and information provided. Occasionally, pieces of writing by students that connect to an idea, topic or theme of the essay and/or the section of the lesson, and published in our school's award winning art/literary anthology, *Aquilae Stilus* (the "eagle's pen"), will provide more ideas. The *Aquilae Stilus* logo will indicate essays and poems written by students.

You should also remember to save all your compositions, essays, poems, including your drafts in a Writer's Notebook. As you write responses to the "Your Turn" assignments included in each lesson, you should save them in folders on your computer. **Always save drafts in at least two different places: "N" drive, hard drive, desktop folder or "flash drive" just in case the wonderful world of technology should "crash and burn." At the end of the course, you can choose your best pieces to revise for your FINAL PORTFOLIO.** At the end of the book, or end of the class, whichever comes first, you will review your pieces of writing and choose the ones you want to revise, edit and include in a Final Portfolio.

The most important thing you should remember is to relax and have fun. Each of the lessons in this book help you get started, and then take you through revision, methods and techniques, style, vocabulary and finally, how to create a portfolio. So, enjoy! See you at the end of the book!

Publishing Process

The book lies face down on the desk,
waiting for the next page,
the next chapter.
The words stare and we pick them up
and we turn them over,
review lessons.
We want to complete the story,
watch a few sentences
find paragraphs,
turn new ideas into chapters,
and come to an ending.
Tonight we thought
we found a tidy conclusion
but fresh chapters unfolded.
A new story
surfaced, grew and now we wonder
if we live in the book
or the book lives in us.
    ~Lynne Dozier

Your Turn:
Write a letter to a future grandchild about your experiences with becoming a writer. Use these questions to help generate ideas: Who has influenced your ability to write? Who usually reads your writing? What problems do you experience when writing an essay or composition? Where and when do you write? What kinds of writing do you enjoy? Dislike? Why did you purchase this book? What do you hope to accomplish as a writer? When you have finished, save it as the first entry in your Writer's Portfolio. Feel free to add more ideas as you progress through the "Your Turn" exercises in this book.

How Do I Keep a Writer's Notebook?

Setting Up a Writing Routine

Just like practicing music, football, or dancing, you will improve your skills and abilities if you practice writing every day in a Writer's Notebook. As with any activity or sport, you need to establish a time and place for practice. Here are a few suggestions:

1. Write several different times a day until you find one that you like best. Then, try to write at that same time so writing becomes a strong and positive habit.

2. Write in several different places until you find one that is comfortable. Then try to write at that same place every time you write.

3. Listen to music while you write. Alternatively, study some painting, photograph, or poster. Look out of a window—seek sunshine or the moon and stars or clouds and rain. Try to avoid facing a blank wall.

4. Record dates for each entry. Like an artist's sketchbook, a Writer's Notebook will provide a place for you to record your ideas, details and impressions on a regular basis. Treat your notebook like a trusted friend. Give your Writer's Notebook a name or title.

What to Include in a Writer's Notebook

1. Lists (people you talk to, items in a grocery cart or locker, things you remember from childhood, objects you see while walking or driving, types of commercials you see, places you want to visit);

2. Bits of conversation you overhear;

3. Reactions to news stories you read in newspapers, magazines or on the Internet, or hear on television or radio;

4. Interesting or unusual words or phrases you find in newspaper headlines, advertisements, on bathroom walls;

5. Records of your dreams, doodles, drawings and " mind maps;"

6. Questions you have that might help generate ideas about topics and issues;

7. Notes and summaries of movies you have seen, songs you love, and books you read.

Your Turn:

For a week, write for thirty minutes in your Writer's Notebook before you go to sleep, or for thirty minutes each morning before the day starts. Date each entry. At the end of the week, circle ideas, strong words and sentences that you enjoy reading aloud because they "sound good," or that you think might develop into an essay, poem, story, or other composition.

How Do I Create a Motto?

A motto is a short statement of beliefs, values and ideals that can serve as a slogan that summarizes or advertises those ideas you believe have significance in your life. Knowing who you are and what you believe in can help you develop a "voice" that others want to hear.

> **My Motto**
> "Teach what I know and reproduce what I am."

My Core Beliefs

I promise that I will—
Talk about good health to people I meet,
Show family and friends they are important,
Think optimistically,
Grow intellectually and spiritually,
Strive for excellence,
Enjoy the success of others as much as my own,
Stay so strong that nothing disturbs my peace of mind,
Learn from past mistakes and work toward
    Greater achievements in the future,
Smile—and laugh—often,
Spend so much time improving myself
    That I have no time to criticize others,
Remain too noble for anger, too strong for fear,
    And too happy to permit the pressure of worry.

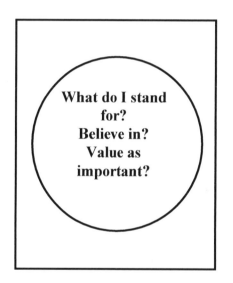

What do I stand for?
Believe in?
Value as important?

Your Turn:
What code do you live by? What do you value? What promises do you make to yourself every morning? How can you make your life meaningful and successful? How would you define "success"?

List your most important beliefs and then create your own motto. Write them on the first page of your Writer's Notebook where they can provide inspiration and encouragement throughout the year. Feel free to revise and rewrite your motto and your list of Core Beliefs as the year progresses and you reflect on your strengths and weaknesses, accomplishments and failures, plans and process of growing as a writer and as a person.

How Do I Create a Mission Statement?

When people say, "I'm on a mission," they give the impression of a total, single-minded focus towards a worthwhile goal. A Statement of that Mission helps guide and focus decisions by answering these questions: Why am here? What is my purpose? Where am I going in my life? What do I want to accomplish?

My Mission Statement is to:
Develop student writers whose "voices" show they understand the power
of language and composition.

A Mission Statement has three components:
1. the identification of an **organization or person;**
2. **a function**—what tasks you intend to perform, your purpose, job, and roles you will fulfill;
3. **a distinction**—how you will perform the function, the level of skill, the standard that sets you apart from others.

Organization	Function	Distinction
Klein Forest High School	To instill leadership and purpose	in every voice.
Aquilae Stilus student literary magazine staff	To create an anthology of prose, poetry and art that reflects	the most creative minds of Klein Forest students.
Facebook	To give people	the power to share and make the world more open and connected.

Your Turn:
Draft a personal mission statement for your Writer's Notebook that shows your purpose as a student writer. Use the following questions to help generate ideas:
- What do you value, or believe is important, about learning?
- What do you want to accomplish as a result of acquiring an education?
- What kind of leader do you want to become?
- What are your specific talents and abilities?
- What do you want to have achieved by the end of the school year?

Suggestions for Revision:
  1. Use "action" verbs found in the list in Lesson 2.
  2. Eliminate all adverbs and most adjectives.
  3. Eliminate indefinite pronouns (thing, anyone, everyone, anything, and someone)
  4. Eliminate the 2nd person pronoun, "you."
Save your Mission Statement for your Final Portfolio.

How Do I Write Goals?

A goal is a time-limited measurable target. Setting goals can help you decide where you want to go in life, what you want to achieve, and they help you focus your efforts so you accomplish your mission. They can strengthen your self-confidence and motivate you to spot the distractions that might take you off course.

A meaningful goal is **SMART**[1]

Specific
Measurable
Action Oriented
Realistic
Time Limited

My Goals

1. **Prepare** students to reach commended levels on state tests and exceed the national average on SAT and Advanced Placement standardized tests administered during the spring semester.
2. **Complete** the final draft of *The Writer's Voice* by August 2012.
3. **Design, Format and Submit** a digital version for publication by December 2012 and a "print copy" by June 2013.

Your Turn—Part 1:
Draft SMART Goal statements for 2-3 of the following tasks:
- ♦ Something you want to learn;
- ♦ Something you want to achieve;
- ♦ Some record you want to set (or break);
- ♦ Something you want to create;
- ♦ A book you want to read, an essay, story or poem you want to write;
- ♦ A leadership position you want to attain.

Your Turn—Part 2:
Write your SMART goal sentences inside the cover of your Writer's Notebook. Use the model goal statements provided above to help you begin each goal sentence with an action verb (page 8). As you review your writing assignments throughout the year, use your goals to check, measure and evaluate your progress.

How Do I Write Objectives?

An objective—a precise, simple, declarative sentence—shows the steps or actions you plan to take that will help you achieve a specific goal. An objective statement includes three parts: **an action verb, a topic** and **details**. For example, my #1 goal when I taught AP Language and Composition was to:

> "**Prepare** students to reach commended levels on state tests and exceed the national average on SAT and Advanced Placement standardized tests administered during the spring semester," (*The Writer's Voice*, 14).

Three objectives—actions or steps—I took to meet that goal included:

	Action Verb	+	A Topic	+	Details
	Teach		students to self-evaluate		by using evaluation rubrics for every assignment.
	Improve		students' organizational skills		by checking Writer's Notebooks weekly;
	Increase		students' reading speeds		by using specific reading strategies to teach comprehension skills.

ACTION VERBS TO USE IN OBJECTIVE STATEMENTS

Achieve	Install	Evaluate	Communicate
Coordinate	Perform	Collect	Create
Develop	Simplify	Plan	Establish
Make	Inspire	Reduce	Recommend
Participate	Transmit	Unite	Schedule
Resolve	Compile	Institute	Initiate
Train	Replace	Research	Promote
Supervise	Improve	Read	Explain
Classify	Build	Write	Describe
Supervise	Synthesize	Review	Interview
Verify	Assemble	Triple	Schedule
Prepare	Maintain	Argue	Prove

> **Your Turn:**
> In your Writer's Notebook, on the same page as your Motto, Mission Statement, and Goals, write an objective for each one of your goals for the year. As you write, remember to begin each objective with an action verb. The list of verbs will help you write objectives for your goals.

How Do I Create a Résumé?

Most people treat a résumé as a personnel file, job application, or a detailed list of jobs. However, a résumé—a concise introduction or advertisement for yourself—should open doors, provide an overview of your abilities, and encourage a reader to want to invite you for an interview. The most important quality needed in a resume, besides accuracy, neatness and clarity, is that your individuality and personal accomplishments shine.

The audience for your final portfolio might be a college admissions director, a scholarship chairperson, a possible employer, or a member of the community whom you want to impress. **Your résumé will be the first page of a final portfolio and serve as an introduction, not only to you, but also to your unique skills and abilities as a writer.** You can find a template for a full resume on Microsoft Word. Go to "File—New--Résumés" and select the template that works for you, but work with the template to make it reflect your creativity. As you "write" through the next few months, update your résumé to reflect any changes in the categories of information that it provides.

Sample Outline for Student Résumé

- Contact Information: name, address, phone number and email address;
- Objective: a concise statement that indicates how you will achieve your goals;
- Extra-curricular Involvement and Leadership Positions;
- Work/Volunteer/Community Service Experiences;
- Honors/Awards/Recognitions/Publications;
- Areas of Special Interests/Skills/Languages:
- Personal References

The Six Biggest Résumé Mistakes:

1. Personal information about sex, race, weight, height, religion or health;
2. Unfocused, vague and general objectives and unclear goals;
3. Exaggerated, overblown and overwritten job descriptions and titles;
4. Little or no extracurricular activities, volunteer or community service involvement;
5. Vague descriptions of duties, skills and leadership roles.
6. Spelling/grammatical mistakes, illegible handwriting

Your Turn:

In your Writer's Notebook, draft a brief résumé that contains the information included in the outline above. Make sure you continue to "update" your resume throughout the year to reflect changes in your achievements and accomplishments. Prepare to use your résumé as the first page of your Writer's Portfolio when you have completed the lessons in this book.

Why Are Writing Groups Important?

Writers rarely work alone. Working with other student writers on an assignment can help all writers, especially young writers, solve problems, hear the true "voices" of other writers, and improve the ability to write for a "real" audience.

Your Turn:
Interview six classmates, or friends, about their reading/writing experiences. Record their names, email addresses and responses in your Writer's Notebook for future reference. The information will help you realize how much you have in common with other people who sometimes struggle with putting their ideas on paper.

Classmate # 1: Earliest memories What is your earliest memory of reading/writing? What specific books do you first remember reading?	**Classmate # 2: Summarizing Text** Tell me about the best book you read this summer. How did you find out about this book? Why was it interesting to you?
Classmate #3: Informational Text Tell me about something important you learned from reading a book, magazine or newspaper. How did you find out about it? Why was in interesting?	**Classmate #4: Favorite Author** Who is your favorite author? What does he/she do as a writer that you enjoy? How did you discover this author?
Classmate # 5: Future Plans for Writing Do you know, right now, something you would like to write about this year? Why do you want to write about this topic?	**Classmate #6: General Writing** What do good writers do when they write? What are some things that get you excited about writing? What do you like most about writing?

Student Voices

Cross Legged

He sat cross-legged on the table,
every few moments
taking the time to pop a knuckle
or two.
He smiled through Asian eyes
and spoke of pop culture,
existential nihilism,
the destruction of ethics,
the loss of morals,
dispersing a few quotes here
and there.
He liked Andy Warhol,
and as Andy did,
he warned us that our
fifteen minutes of fame had
dwindled to at least
fourteen.
And we believed him,
all of us looking at our watches.
~Jessica Moore (1998:85)

Your Turn:

Write at least 100 words that create a picture of a friend, teammate or a student in your class. Use the suggestions below to help generate details for your description:

1. Do **not** use the person's full name.
2. Include a major goal of the person.
3. Create at least two similes.
4. Use details to describe appearance—distinguishing characteristics of eyes, skin, facial features, mouth, nose, hair.
5. Share person's likes, dislikes, opinions
6. Actions like way of talking, walking, habits like nail biting, hair twirling)
7. Describe the person's backpack, locker, bedroom, favorite place to hangout
8. How does the person's personality, mannerisms, voice and gestures   affect others?

A Poem for Doug

My desk is the one
in the back of the classroom,
beneath the burned out
fluorescent fixture with only one tube
that glows a dull purple.
Sometimes it hums.
my desk wobbles,
because the back right
stud foot is missing.
My name is always the one
my teachers has to look up
to remember.

At least I can lean my head against
the white cinder block wall and sleep.
Nobody really notices.
The halls are a maze,
swirling with clouds of humanity,
through which I pass unnoticed.
The seat across from me
at lunch is always empty.
That's O.K.
I read a book.
Sometimes I have things I'd like
to talk about,
but the book
doesn't listen.
~ Heath Hofmeister (1995:42)

What Should I Think About When I Write?

1. **Ideas**—the ability to show that I understand a subject, have opinions and can take a position. I intend to develop a confident and convincing tone so my readers will be interested in what have to say. My readers should not have to struggle to understand vagueness, generalities and ambiguities of my words and ideas. **I anticipate questions that my readers might have about my subject when I write.**

2. **Organization**—the capability of forming a central idea, theme or thesis and presenting examples, illustrations, facts and other material logically so they support my ideas. I will provide my readers with a sense that I have a well, thought-out plan from beginning to end, and that I understand my purpose in writing. **I have a purpose when I write.**

3. **"Voice"**—the sound of the real "me" talking to a real reader. All effective writing conveys the sound of someone talking to someone else, but a writing "voice" should also suit the subject, occasion, audience and purpose. Just as I change speaking or dress styles, when moving from informal to formal situations, my writing "voice" creates the relationship and connection, that I, as a writer, want to establish with my readers. **I anticipate reactions my readers might have to my words and phrases when I write.**

4. **Word Choice**—the use of specific and precise words and phrases. Important, too, in developing a tone of confidence and conviction is economy. I eliminate all unnecessary words, repetitions and redundancies so that every word, sentence and paragraph contributes to my meaning. **I edit when I write.**

5. **Sentence Fluency**—the rhythm, flow, cadence and the sound of language. I understand that readers read, not only with their eyes, but also with their ears. I rarely achieve all the previously discussed characteristics during a first draft. Revision—painful and time consuming—is the key to my success. I read everything I write aloud several times to make sure it sounds "right." If it does not, I fix it. **I revise thoughtfully when I write.**

6. **Conventions**—the willingness to spell and punctuate correctly, check word meanings, connotations and grammatical relationships before I share my compositions with readers. I know that an error in mechanics can make my writing look unprofessional, hurried, and incomplete. **I proofread carefully when I write.**

7. **Presentation**—the way my compositions look on the page. I indent paragraphs when I change topics, speakers, ideas, and time, or as a visual aid to my readers. My manuscripts will follow a structure: poems will look like poems; essays will look like essays; stories will look like stories and dramatic scripts will look like dramatic scripts. I will follow guidelines for spacing, font size and type and write legibly when I cannot use a computer. **I take pride in my manuscripts when I write.**

LESSON 2.
THE PROCESS OF REVISION:
THE "VOICE" OF AN EDITOR

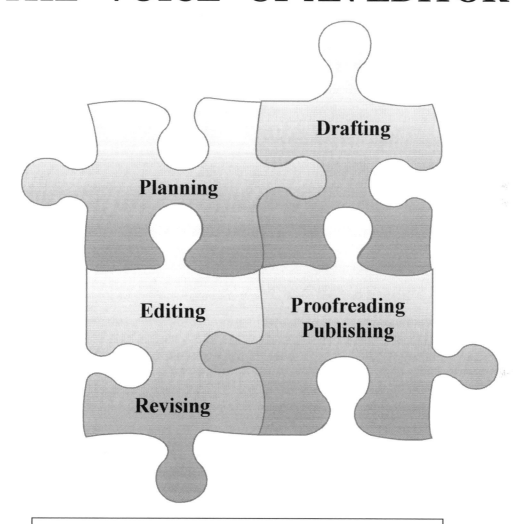

> "If you can think it, you can say it.
> If you can say it, you can write it.
> If you can write it, you can read it."
> **Dr. Joyce Carroll,**
> Abydos Learning Center
> New Jersey Writing Project

What Is Revising and Editing?

If you do not allow enough time during the process of writing for the most important steps—revision and editing—then you will never know how effective or well-written your prose or poetry could have been. Below, two writers—a student and a professional—have defined "revision" and "editing." Read and compare the two definitions. How does each writer view the process of revision? What differences do you see between the responses of the student and the polished, more experienced writer? Which writer best describes the way you revise your pieces of writing? What is the difference between "revising" and "editing?"

Student Writer

Revising means reviewing every word and making sure that everything is worded right. I check to see if I am rambling, and I look to see if I can put a better word in or leave one out. Usually when I read what I have written, I say to myself, "that word is so bland and boring," and then I go and use my Thesaurus to find a bigger, or more important sounding word. Then, I cross out words and put different ones in. I write one draft and make changes on that draft. If I have time, I check punctuation and spelling. I like to write by inspiration, and if I feel inspired, then I don't need to cross out many things.

Experienced Writer

Revising and editing means on one level, finding my purpose, and on another level, changing language to make my purpose more clear. When revising, I try to obey a cardinal rule: never fall in love with what I have written in a first or second draft. I don't trust an idea, sentence, or even a phrase that looks "catchy "until I have clearly defined my purpose. Every choice of words, phrases, sentences and techniques must support my goals as a writer. I constantly question my ideas, and respond to those questions. I read aloud, or silently in my head, so I can hear the sound of my voice on paper. If something does not sound right, I fix it. I think of my reader and try to determine which ideas I need to develop by providing more examples. I constantly chisel, polish and change as I revise.

Estimated Time Spent in Stages of The Process of Writing

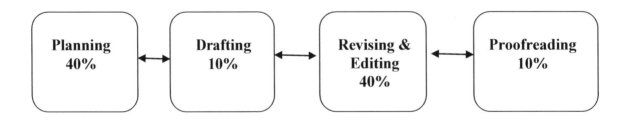

| Planning 40% | ⟷ | Drafting 10% | ⟷ | Revising & Editing 40% | ⟷ | Proofreading 10% |

Your Turn:
What does revision and editing mean to you? Write a brief definition in your Writer's Notebook, and then compare your definition with the responses of both the student and the experienced writer above.

Essay: A Teaching Philosophy[1]

I have a simple teaching philosophy. On a bookcase in my classroom, a plaque reads, "A teacher has a special way of making learning fun/ finding joy in every day and the best in everyone." In kindergarten, I loved hearing a school bell, smelling new books, watching an ink pen scratch words across a blank page, and feeling chalk dust on my skin. More than sixty years later, I still do.

I was born to teach. My first students—my brothers, our dog and my dolls—sat on the floor and listened while I read stories from my favorite books to them. I taught my brothers how to spell words from *The Golden Book Dictionary* and organized groups of neighborhood kids into performances of mini-dramas in our garage. When we played softball in the field behind our house, or "horse" on our basketball driveway, I pretended these games were our "recess."

Years ago, when I tutored less able students in the small town high school I attended, and as a senior, substituted in the neighboring elementary school, I formed attitudes and a teaching style that have encouraged student success.

First, lessons should respect students' minds and individual learning styles. They must engage students and help them want to persist. Learning activities should relate to their lives and experiences. I want young people to believe that "the best learning   is self-inflicted."

> A principal once told me, "You could sell snow to Eskimos."

Secondly, students learn from each other; conversation helps develop literacy skills. Some part of each lesson should include time for students to interact with each other to solve problems, debate questions, analyze ideas, share tasks, and evaluate their efforts and those of others.

Finally, teaching students to ask the "right" questions is as important as helping them find the "right" answers. As a young teacher who did not know many of the answers to students' questions, I said, "That's a good question. Who thinks they have an answer?" or "Good question. Now, how can we find an answer?" Today, when I know most of the answers, I still ask my students the same kinds of questions, and try to help them extend their answers long after they usually think an answer is adequate.

I encourage students to take responsibility for their learning, show them how to evaluate and keep track of their goals and learning processes. I am a guide, a facilitator and a coach—not a performer or fountain of wisdom.   Like Hestia, the spirit of hearth and home, I am a place for children to gather round, a point of balance, a stillness in a noisy world. In a rhythmic circle, my students and I should learn from each other.

A principal once told me, "You could sell snow to Eskimos."   I learned salesmanship techniques from my father, a sales representative for a major oil company. Every week, he drove miles in a car that had a card taped to dashboard that read, "Find the need. Show them why. Ask them to buy." Selling students on the need to read, write, think critically and use language that can communicate across borders and boundaries in a global economy continues to challenge educators.

In the movie, "Teachers," the actor, Nick Nolte, portrays a burned out teacher who needs a "wake-up" call from the school secretary to   encourage him to come to school. Throughout the course of the film, he finds renewal when he helps a struggling teen finally learn to read.   At the end of the movie, Nolte stands on the high school's front steps and shouts an   answer to the people who have told him, "The job is too tough, and you're crazy to go back in the building." He replies, "I'm a teacher. Of course, I'm crazy." So am I.

~Lynne Dozier

<u>Your Turn:</u>
In a few paragraphs, show how you feel about the importance of education. Use these questions to help plan and generate ideas: What is the point of school?   What is the difference between "training" and "education?" What type of learning occurs in school? Outside of school? What is the purpose of college? How is "teaching" connected to "learning?" What kinds of activities help you learn the most effectively? What kinds of experiences have you had in school that you could use as examples to support your opinions? Make sure you plan, draft, revise and edit your paragraphs.

Why Is An Audience Important?

As you revise, you need to consider the needs of the audience you will address—the people who will read your compositions. For example, if you write a description of a place you visited, you would present details in a different way for your grandfather than you would for an eight-year old cousin. If you write an essay about stem cell research for a biology teacher, you might add more scientific words than if you were writing a letter to an editor of a newspaper about the same topic. If you were writing a "blog," a Facebook, or "text" message you might not follow the rules of punctuation and spelling required for a formal paper for a teacher.

As you write, you should always make sure the **tone** of your voice and the **subject** is appropriate for the **occasion** that prompts it, the **audience** who will receive it and the **purpose** of the message you intend to communicate. When you consider these factors as you compose your ideas, you will show maturity and help you develop "style" and competence, and your readers will respect your abilities.

These questions will help you think about your audience:
1. Who will read my work? How old are they? Adults? Teenagers? Children? Male? Female? Friends? Relatives? Unknown?
2. What is their educational background? High school? College? Advanced degree? Socio-economic status?
3. What do I want them to know, or understand, about my topic?
4. What knowledge do they already have about my topic?
5. What information can I provide that is new for them? What kind of language would help them to see my subject in a new and fresh way?
6. What interests and opinions do they already have? What values and principles do they consider important? Do they have biases?
7. What beliefs and values can I expect them to have already? Are they liberal? Conservative? Progressive? Moderate?
8. How can I convince them to accept my ideas as reliable and valid? Will they respond more to emotional, logical, and ethical appeals or a combination?

Your Turn:
Write a paragraph that describes an action movie, or a video game, you've just seen or played, to your best friend. Then, write a paragraph that describes it for your mother. Next, write a paragraph that describes it to a leader in your church, synagogue or mosque.

What changes do you make in your paragraphs when you change your readers? How do you change your paragraphs? Do you leave out some details for one reader? Add more details for another? How does your language change? Do you use more formal words for one reader? Informal words for another? How does your purpose change when you change the audience?

How Do I "Show Not Tell?"

Immature writers often "pad" their prose with empty adjectives like "pretty," "nice" and "big" and adverbs like "usually," "quickly" and "really." *They* often emphasize their own personal responses—feelings and emotions—instead of focusing on the characteristics of an object, person, or place that make it special.

To write well, writers have to do more than <u>tell</u> that something is great, exciting, or scary; they have to <u>show</u> the special characteristics that create interesting, exciting, or scary pictures for their readers. Action verbs, direct words and concrete details—the facts that writers gather through their powers of observation—help readers imagine the subject of the description and see ideas more clearly.

How to put "flesh" on "bare bones" of a sentence —

Tell: The dog was mean.

<u>Use Action Verbs.</u> The dog bared his teeth and growled—a low rumble in his throat.

<u>Insert   Conversation   and   Quotations.</u>. "Don't open that gate," my neighbor warned, "that dog will bite."

<u>Provide Concrete Details.</u> A small river of saliva formed at the corner of the dog's mouth, now drawn into a tight, red line.

**Putting It All Together—
Revising to "Show. Don't Tell."**

Tell: The dog was mean.

Show: A small river of saliva formed at the corner of the dog's mouth, now drawn into a tight, red line. The dog bared his teeth and growled—a low rumble in his throat. "Don't open that gate," my neighbor warned, "that dog will bite."

<u>Note:</u>   You can change position of sentences in a paragraph, but the picture remains clear, correct and concise.

<u>Your Turn</u>:
Use action verbs, conversation and quotations, and concrete details to "show," or   create pictures for your readers, for each of these "telling" sentences below. Avoid the use of the pronoun, "I" as you write to keep the focus on your topic.
- ◆ The kid was a brat.
- ◆ He's always showing off.
- ◆ He had terrible table manners.
- ◆ The old house looked scary.
- ◆ The teacher was old and crabby.
- ◆ Find a paragraph that "tells" in your Writer's Notebook, and add action verbs, details, and direct thoughts and words so that it "shows," instead of "tells."

How Do I Make Writing More Vivid?

As a writer, you should choose words that transmit your personality to the written word, but you also have an obligation to help your readers understand your meaning. As you write, read your piece aloud often so that you can hear the sound of your "voice"—the valid and true "I" behind the words on the page. Change anything that does not sound natural, lively and interesting. Ask yourself, "What do I want my readers to see? To think about? What am I trying to show them? How do I want them to react to my words and ideas?"

In this section, you will find different descriptions of the same scene. Read each and ask yourself, "How does a writer make the scene more vivid?" Pay particular attention to the use of nouns and verbs. Notice the limited use of adjectives and adverbs.

Dull—It got cold. The sun disappeared from the grey sky. There was snow and slush in the streets. There were hundreds of evictions. I walked down the street between the tenement walls. The slush went through my shoes. The wind blew in my face. Furniture stood outside one of the apartment buildings.

Vivid—Life froze. The sun vanished from the death-grey sky, and the streets oozed with slush and muddy rivulets of water. Hundreds of evictions had emptied apartments. I walked down the street between dripping tenement walls. The slush seeped through my shoes; the wind scraped my face. A stack of furniture stood in front of a door: tables, chairs, a washtub packed with crockery and bedclothes, a broom, a dresser, a lamp.

Dull—People who had been pleasant became sad. Douglas tried but could not eat the food, and neither could Tom and Dad. Some people just did not like the meal.

Vivid—Smiling people stopped smiling. Douglas chewed one bite for three minutes; he watched Tom and Dad do the same. Guests swished the food together, making roads and patterns, drawing pictures in the gravy, forming castles of potatoes, passing meat chunks under the table to the dog.

Dull—The signal from the pitcher was clear. I was ready to catch the ball at least two feet outside the plate, but when he threw the ball, I was surprised.

Vivid—He signaled a fast breaking curve, and I expected the ball to break at least four inches outside the plate. Then he wound up and let it go, and I watched the ball come whistling right down the groove, heading for the center of the plate.

Your Turn:
Choose a "dull" paragraph from your Writer's Notebook and revise it so that it becomes "vivid." To help you do this, use action verbs, eliminate adjectives and adverbs, and add details that help create pictures in your readers' minds. When you finish, exchange your rewritten version with a partner. Ask your partner to draw a picture of the scene you just created.

Why Should I Edit Passive "be" Verbs?

Most student writers display an addiction to using the passive verb, "be." Any form of that "irregular" verb—**am, is, was, were, are, be, being,** and **been**—can suck energy from a sentence. Inexperienced and immature writers destroy English sentences when:

1. They forget that only two kinds of words matter: nouns and verbs. Everything else just adds window dressing and smothers ideas. Adverbs cling to verbs; adjectives clump around nouns. Conjunctions and prepositions string these clumps together.
2. They use passive forms of the "be" verb that bleed the life out of strong, action verbs.

Look at these two examples:

Weak: They shall go up exceedingly rapidly in the sky like night birds of prey with magnificent wingspans. They will move quickly and get really tired. When they walk slowly, they won't get too tired."

(A student writer trying to fill the space on a test)

Strong: "They will soar on wings like eagles; they will run and grow weary; they will walk and not feel faint."

Isaiah, 40: 31 (*New Standard Version Bible*)

Use these 4 techniques to eliminate "be" verbs:

♦ Substitute an "action" verb for a passive "be" verb.
    John was on the driveway. **(weak)**
    John <u>stood</u> on the driveway. **(stronger)**

♦ Use a conjunction to join adjectives and form an appositive.
    Ken is tall and strong and plays tennis. **(weak)**
    Ken, <u>tall and strong,</u> plays tennis. **(stronger)**

♦ Substitute simple verb forms for progressive forms.
    Ken was hitting the tennis ball. **(weak)**
    Ken <u>hit</u> the tennis ball. **(stronger)**

♦   Use active voice rather than passive voice verb forms.
    The gift was opened by Sue. **(weak)**
    Sue <u>opened</u> the gift. **(stronger)**

Your Turn:

Find a paragraph in your Writer's Notebook and use one or more of the revision techniques above   to eliminate all forms of the "be" verb. Which version sounds stronger? More mature? The original or your revised version?

Why Should I Avoid Clichés?

Writers use clichés because they communicate easily; readers enjoy clichés because they do not demand much thought. Today, in an age of "political correctness," clichés discourage the use of imagination, critical thinking and controversy whether they're used in a column in the school paper, a composition assigned in class or a truly impassioned speech by a politician about real problems affecting the lives of citizens today. Clichés, used by lazy writers, make immature readers feel comfortable.

No administrator has ever threatened a valedictorian with expulsion for writing a bland speech that repeats tired clichés about how commencement means "a new beginning." We do not boo and hiss at politicians because they say, "We'll put people first." Ending a speech with the line, "No dream is beyond our reach," is certainly more comforting—and less honest—than "we have real problems that we may not be able to solve, but we can sure as hell try."

Read the following sentences that contain clichés:
1. At their first meeting, she fell for his charms hook, line and sinker.

2. Losing his job and making other bad financial decisions put him behind the eight ball.

3. We took a three-week whirlwind tour of the United Kingdom.

4. No matter what happened during the game, she remained as cool as a cucumber.

5. My advice about writing fell on deaf ears, especially before a holiday.

6. We will fight for our rights as women until the bitter end.

7. I told her not to cry over spilled milk, to build a bridge and get over it.

8. The winds of change have affected the decisions of the voting public.

9. The shocking pink dress she wore made her stick out like a sore thumb at the funeral.

10. The understudy was chomping at the bit to take over the lead role.

11. When proofreading, I try to leave no stone unturned.

12. Books about how to improve writing are selling like hot cakes.

13. All writers find themselves in the same boat when they begin an assignment.

14. The teacher's negative comments nipped her enthusiasm for writing in the bud.

15. The doorbell rang, and the mailman delivered the package in the nick of time.

Your Turn:
1. Underline the clichés in these sentences, and rephrase them so that they have a feeling of freshness, innovation and imagination.
2. Make a list of 10 trite expressions you overhear in conversations in classrooms, lunchroom, athletic field, television, newspaper headlines, advertising, political speeches.

Remember, if you have heard a phrase many times before, it is probably a cliché.

Why Should I "Write Tight?"

As writers create meaning, they should consider the necessity of each word carefully. We can shorten—and improve—compositions without sacrificing style or content by searching out unnecessary words, editing them and then rewriting the sentences. Less is often more when writers try to add "punch" and "voice" to a poem, a story, letter, or an essay. As you edit, consider eliminating these eight unnecessary words in language and composition:

- **Is** and the rest of the "be" family of verbs (am, is, was, were, are, be, being, been).
    Smith will be tried in court today. **(Weak)**
    Smith's trial begins today. **(Strong)**

- **There, it.** Nearly every time you see "there," or "it," a "be" verb will follow. Get rid of both for a stronger sentence.
    There is something strange here. It is scary in the dark. **(Weak)**
    Something strange and scary lurks here in the dark. **(Strong)**

- **To.** Sometimes "to" adds baggage writers don't need to carry.
    She is starting to get sick. **(Weak)**
    She started feeling sick. **(Strong)**

- **And.** Consider the alternatives, then decide what meaning works best.
    She looked at me and laughed. **(Weak)**
    Laughing, she looked at me. **(Strong)**

- **By.** I found this example when I edited this section.
    It will be followed by a "be" verb. **(Weak)**
    A "be" verb follows. **(Strong)**

- **His** and similar possessive pronouns.
    He turned, his eyes glowing. **(Weak)**
    He turned, eyes glowing. **(Streak)**

- **The.** You'll need it most times, but read closely to make sure.
    The windows slammed shut behind me. **(Weak)**
    Windows slammed shut behind me. **(Strong)**

<u>Your Turn:</u>
Choose another paragraph from your Writer's Notebook, and circle all the unnecessary words from the list above that you find. Then, following the models provided, edit them to make stronger sentences. Notice that "be" verbs influence the use of most of them. When you eliminate extra words, which burden writing, you will start to discover your own unique and individual style.

How Can A Revision Checklist Help Me?

Taking time to revise enables you to critically assess your purpose as a writer, evaluate your use of techniques and strategies, and then make changes that will improve your compositions. A piece of writing is not finished until you have revised, edited and proofread several times before submitting it to an audience of readers. This book, for instance, has experienced eight revisions, and it may need another one before a final publication. If you do not take time to revise a piece of writing, you will never know how effective, interesting and entertaining you could have made it.

General Questions That Help Guide Revision

As you work through the "Your Turn" exercises and choose the pieces you want to revise for a teacher, an employer, or other readers, refer to these questions to help make sure you have achieved your purpose and goals as a writer.

1. What was my purpose for writing? How have I accomplished it?
2. Have I identified my audience, chosen a topic, words and images that will interest, inform and entertain them?
3. How do my title, "lead" and opening paragraphs capture the attention of my readers?
4. Do I develop my ideas logically and include enough details, examples, illustrations, and other forms of evidence so that my readers understand my thoughts and attitudes? Do I "show" rather than "tell?"
5. Do I write a strong conclusion that leaves my readers with an idea to think about?
6. Do I stick to my topic, or do I stray and include unnecessary information?
7. Does each paragraph contribute to the thesis, central idea, message or theme I want to communicate?
8. Have I eliminated weak "be" verbs, vague nouns, dull adjectives, useless adverbs, clichés, redundant words and phrases?
9. Are my facts accurate? Have I used quotations and dialogue when appropriate? Cited my sources correctly?
10. Does each sentence communicate exactly what I want to say?
11. Have I used transitional words and phrases to help my readers follow the organization and fluency of my ideas?
12. Have I demonstrated control over spelling and capitalization?
13. Have I used punctuation that helps communicate my meaning and message to my readers?
14. What part of my writing still needs improvement?
15. What will my readers remember about my piece after they have finished reading it?

Note: The writing lessons *The Writer's Voice* will provide tools that will help you continue to learn to revise and edit.

Student Voices

The Teacher Says to Write

She says to write naturally
like I speak, or something.
      I don't know how to do that.
      Write like I speak!?!
      WHAT!?!
I could write a paper about…
Uhhh….
being or stage, or something like that
'cause I'm in plays and stuff.
Yeah, I could do that.
But writing naturally?
Uh-Uh.
Man, if I tried that, it would like...suck.
She says no adjectives or adverbs;
Use comparisons.
No adjectives or adverbs!?!
I can't write like that!
I'd end up with word gumbo…
a mosh pit instead of a metaphor,
a low-fat dessert
stripped of good stuff,
a spamburger instead of a hamburger,
the fruit in the fridge people ignore
when they reach for the Rocky Road.
Man, if I tried to do that, I'd have
the Publisher's Clearing House
of All Assignments—
destined for the trash.
      ~Sally Clark (1996:7)

Visible, Invisible

The cursor blinks
in a confined rampage
polluting the blank screen.
Words illustrate
the meaning closed
by the brain's initial thoughts.
Blinking-on-the-cursor
will continue to blink-off-
keeping the time
with the sound of the keys.
Such a cursor
dares to continue manipulating
the keys to speak
the word that are no more
than the brain's initial thoughts.
      ~Mallory Gladstein (2004:75)

Your Turn:
In your Writer's Notebook, show how you feel about writing for teachers or "graders" of standardized tests. What frustrates you? Inspires you? Motivates you? What subjects do you like to write about? What subjects do you try to avoid? How do you feel about punctuation, spelling and grammar rules? What do you think before you start a composition? What do you usually think when you have finally finished? If you feel brave, try to write a poem.

LESSON 3.
GRAMMAR AND MECHANICS: THE "VOICE" OF PROOFREADING

Parts of Speech?
Punctuation? Spelling?
Sentence Fragments,
Comma splices? Run-ons?
Pronoun-Antecedent
Agreement?
Verbs, Verbs, Verbs!

EDITING

Proofreading

"When a thought takes one's breath away, a lesson on grammar seems an impertinence."
—Thomas Higginson, Preface to
Emily Dickinson's Poems, 1890.

What, *Really,* Are Parts of Speech?

Most students started learning about the Parts of Speech in first grade, but for many reasons, they never seemed to grasp their importance. However, imagine trying to build a house without the right nails. Now, try to imagine building a correct sentence without the correct parts of speech. Below, you will find a jingle that might help you remember these important tools of the language trade. **Just for fun, try reading it with a "rap" beat.**

Parts of Speech "Rap" Poem

1. Nouns name people, places, ideas, things,
   like **Smith, New York, love** and **wings.**

2. Pronouns are used in place of nouns:
   I think, **she** sings, **they** work, **he** frowns.

3. Adjectives add something to nouns,
   Like **old** New York and **little** towns.
   And don't forget that **many, few,**
   numbers and **colors** are adjectives too.

4. Verbs come next—the words that tell
   of action, being and state as well:
   work, become, exist and **curb**—
   each of these is called a verb.

5. Adverbs add something to the meaning
   of adjectives, like **brightly** gleaming. *
   To verbs, they also add a thought,
   as when we say, "was **nearly** caught.'
   And **lastly**, an adverb has the chore
   of making other adverbs tell us more
   than one alone could hope to tell,
   like "she sang that **very** well."

6. Prepositions show relation,
   as **with** affection, **in** our nation.

7. Conjunctions, as their name implies,
   are joining words—they are the ties
   that bind together day **and** night,
   calm **but** cold, dull **or** bright.

8. Interjections are words that show sudden emotion as
   Alas! Hah! Oh!

Thus briefly does this jingle state, the parts of speech which total eight.
~**Anonymous** [1]

How Do Parts of Speech Make Meaning?

Musicians make music with just seven notes; writers have just eight parts of speech to make meaning in prose and poetry. Use the following examples, or models, to arrange parts of speech into short "pattern" poems. As you write, pay close attention to the way the words look on the page and the sound, or rhythm, of the words when you read them aloud.

Model—Modern Haiku:
Line 1: 1 article (a, an, the) + 1 noun + 1 adjective + 1 conjunction + 1 adjective
Line 2: 1 verb + 1 conjunction + 1 verb + 1 adverb + 1 noun that relates to the first noun

> The wrinkle, ancient and shadowy,
> Carves and defines   immediately a face.
> **~Lynne Dozier**

Your Turn:
Write a complete sentence about an object in your locker, backpack or desk, using the pattern in the example above. Place it on the page in your Writer's Notebook so it looks like a poem. Then, rewrite it without the adjectives and adverb. Which version do you like better? Which version sounds more mature? More thoughtful?

Model—Bio Poem:

Line 1: Person's name
 Line 2: 2 adjectives which describe the person, connected by coordinate conjunctions (for, and,   nor, but, or, yet, so—the "fanboys").
Lines 3, 4, and 5: A phrase beginning with past or present tense forms   of verbs that show specific events or activities in the person's life.
Line 6: A wrap up phrase synonymous with the first line.

Model—Bio Poem:

> Abraham Lincoln—
> honest and just—
> fought a bitter war,
> led a broken nation,
> lives on through history,
> A Man for the Ages.
> **~Lynne Dozier**

> Mark Twain--
> Sarcastic and satiric
> Poked fun at politics
> Created a slave hero
> Wrote the first "true" American novel.
> A target of book censors.
> **~Lynne Dozier**

Your Turn:
Use the information about a friend, classmate or member of your writer's group that you gathered in an interview (Lesson 1). Then, create a word portrait—a Bio Poem—that includes specific details about the person. When you finish, give it to your teammate to save in his/her Writer's Notebook. Use the pattern for a Bio Poem above as a guideline.

How Does Punctuation Affect Meaning?

When speaking aloud, we punctuate our words constantly with body language. Our listeners hear commas, dashes, question marks, exclamation points, quotations marks as we shout, whisper, pause, wave our arms, roll our eyes, wrinkle our brows. In a piece of writing, punctuation plays the role of body language and helps readers hear us the way we want to be heard.

Punctuation rules should not scare us. As guidelines, they help us use our own common sense; they help us remember that we cannot expect readers to work to decipher the attitude and tone we are trying to express. However, punctuation marks cannot save a poorly written sentence. The better the sentence, the easier it is to punctuate.

In this section, you can find the most important punctuation marks, rules and suggestions for using them to achieve an effect and improve clarity:

Comma [,]

1. **Use a comma after an introductory clause or phrase:**
   After touring the Coliseum, we went to the hotel for a shower and a nap.
2. **Use a comma to separate elements in a series:**
   I visited the Sistine Chapel, St. Peter's Basilica, and a café on the corner of Vatican Square.
3. **Use a common to separate independent clauses joined by <u>for, and, nor, but, or, yet, so</u>:**
   I will return for another visit to Italy, but I want to visit Canada first.
4. **Use a comma to set off a group of words that may not be essential to the sentence:**
   Art, created by Old Masters, can tell many stories about history.

Semicolon [;]

A more sophisticated mark of punctuation than the comma, the semicolon separates 2 main clauses, but keeps those thoughts tightly linked.
I love to eat pasta; he loves eating Italian ice cream.

Dash [—]

The dash creates a dramatic pause to prepare for an expression needing strong emphasis:
I'll love you forever—if you'll take me with you on trips around the world.

Ellipsis […]

The ellipsis indicates an unfinished thought, or trailing into silence.
"I was just wondering…" John said.

Parentheses [( )]

Parentheses help writers pause to drop in some chatty information not vital to the story or essay:
Despite Tom's adventurous spirit ("I love climbing steps to church bell towers," he bragged), he knew nothing about choosing good restaurants.

Parentheses also indicate the page numbers when a writer cites information, quotations and ideas from other sources.
"Punctuation rules should not scare us" (Lynne Dozier, 28).

Colon [:]

A colon is a tip-off to prepare for what comes next: a list, a long quotation, or more explanation. The message of a colon is:
  "Pay attention: more words are coming at you."

Quotation Marks [".. .....'']

These marks indicate the direct words or thoughts of a speaker or character:
  Tom said, "I can't swim."
  "I wish I could swim," Tom thought.
Notice the comma comes outside the quotation in the first example and inside the quotation in the second example. Not logical? Never mind. Do it that way anyhow.

Quotation marks also indicate titles of short stories, articles, poetry and TV shows: "Dangerous Game," "Hallmark Stories," "Song of Myself," and "C.S.I."

Apostrophe [']

The big headache happens with possessive nouns.

If the noun is singular, add ' before the 's:
  I hated Betty's tango.
If the noun is plural, add an ' after the s:
  Those are the girls' coats.
We also use apostrophes to join two words in a contraction. If you write *it's,* you are saying *it is.*
  Once in a while, it's (it is) easy to confuse the uses of an apostrophe.

Italics, and Underlining

These marks indicate titles of books, films, dramas, newspapers and magazines. Use italics when typing and underline titles if handwritten:
  A Student Guide, Romeo and Juliet, Newsweek, and Houston Chronicle.

Hyphen (-)

We often get confused about using hyphens. Generally, stick to these examples and you'll be safe:
Fractions: two-thirds, one-fourth
Words that begin with anti-, non- and neo-: anti-aircraft, non-payment, neo-conservative
Separate words with a hyphen between syllables when the whole word won't fit on two lines.

All the Rest [.] [?] [!]

We all know about ending a sentence with a period or a question mark. Do it. Sure, we can also end with an exclamation point, but do we have to? Usually it makes the writer sound silly and breathless. Filling the paper with!!!!! won't make up for excitement the words have not provided.

Your Turn:
In your Writer's Notebook, practice punctuating the group of words below in different ways. Notice that every time you change the marks of punctuation, you also affect meaning. Do not change the order of words—only the punctuation. When you finish, share the sentences with your classmates by reading them aloud. Examples:
  1. Jack Smith called, "Betty Jones is here."
  2. "Jack," Smith called. "Betty Jones is here."
Be sure to read your sentences aloud to hear the tone of voice and differences in meaning.

Does Good Grammar Count?

Yes, good grammar counts! Your writing is the "face" you present to readers who might not know you. Errors in grammar make a poor impression on readers. You should always search your own writing for errors and ask others for help as well. Even emails deserve attention; you should never forget that your email messages could go to anyone with the click of button. In this section, you will find the six most common grammatical errors and examples that show how to correct them so your compositions always present the most positive image:

#1. Overuse of the Passive Voice The bridge <u>was built</u> by soldiers trained in that skill. **Correction:** Soldiers trained in that skill <u>built the bridge</u>.	**#2. Shifts in Verb Tense** Smoke <u>billows</u> from the house as people <u>ran</u> in all directions. **Correction:** Smoke <u>billowed</u> from the house as people <u>ran</u> in all directions.
#3. Pronoun/antecedent Reference All the <u>boys</u> interested in trying out for the football team gave <u>his</u> name to the coach. **Correction:** All the <u>boys</u> interested in trying out for the football team gave <u>their names</u> to the coach.	**#4. Dangling Participle** <u>After sitting</u> in the garage for weeks, my brother found some rotten tomatoes. **Correction:** My brother found some rotten <u>tomatoes sitting in</u> the garage for weeks.
#5. Use of Non-Parallel Structures Some college graduates attend law school because they hope to get high-paying jobs, <u>not being ready to work</u>, or because they are not sure what else to do. **Correction:** Some college graduates attend law school because they hope to get high-paying jobs, do not feel <u>ready to work</u>, or because they do not know what else to do.	**#6. Comma Splice & Run-on Sentences** Some states have banned smoking in public <u>places, soon</u> others will follow. (CS) Some states have banned smoking in public <u>places soon</u> others will follow. (R-O) **Correction:** Some states have banned smoking in public places; soon others will follow. *or* Some states have banned smoking in public places, and soon others will follow.

Your Turn:
Review the pieces you have written in your Writer's Notebook. Find sentences that contain these "Most Common Errors," and fix them. If you are not sure if they are incorrect, read them aloud to see if they sound "right." If you are still unsure, take them to someone whose opinion you respect—a teacher, a parent—or the pretty girl or handsome boy sitting next to you who seems to make good grades in English classes.

How Can I Avoid Writing Sentence Fragments?

The use of some "key" words may alert you to the possibility that you have written a sentence fragment, an incomplete thought that lacks either a subject or a verb. As you proofread, check sentences that begin with:

1. **"ing" Words:**
      Ginger earns money. **Babysitting for the Palermos.** (SF)
       Correction: Ginger earns money babysitting for the Palermos.

2. **Glue Words (as, although, because, if, until, when, whenever):**
      Because it was cold outside. My car would not start. (SF)
      Correction: Because it was cold outside, my car would not start.

3. **WH words (who, whose, which, that, what):**
      We sat near a man. **Who howled with laughter.** (SF)
      Correction: We sat near a man who howled with laughter.

S-A-C: Sentence Analysis Chart

You can check the accuracy, completeness and variety of your sentences by creating a Sentence Analysis Chart. For this chart, I used sentences from the essay, "France—the People" in Lesson 6: Description.

First Four Words	Verbs	Adjectives	Number of Words in Sentence
From behind the fence	sat, talked	black, red, clean-shaven	34
The ironwork balcony on…	surrounded	shuttered	20
The street below	didn't hold	sweltering, humid	31
But the son said	began to play	_____	10

Your Turn:
Take the first sentences of four different paragraphs you have written in your Writer's Notebook. Copy the first four words of each, and then list the verbs and adjectives. Finally, count the number of words in each sentence. Use the sample above to guide you. Have you avoided sentence fragments? Used different sentence beginnings? Kept verbs in one tense? Used "golden" adjectives? Avoided extra words? Composed sentences with a variety of lengths?

How Can I Combine Choppy Sentences?

Readers not only see the words on the page, but they also hear them. If all sentences in a piece of writing follow the same structures and patterns, reading them becomes monotonous to readers. A certain kind of rhythm happens if sentences in prose and lines in poetry have varying lengths, patterns and constructions. Read the examples below aloud and listen to the "choppiness" of the short sentences and the rhythm and flow of the longer sentences.

Weak/Choppy Sentences:
1. Writers should think of writing as conversation. 2. The conversation is "one-way." 3. The conversation is between a writer and an audience. 4. The audience is invisible. 5. The audience cannot question the writer. 6. The audience cannot hear the writer's tone of voice.

Stronger "Combined" Sentence:
Writers should think of writing as "one-way" conversation between a writer and an invisible audience who cannot question the writer or hear the writer's tone of voice.

One way to create interesting, effective sentences is to combine short, choppy sentences. You can combine them with the use of **phrases (**_participial, gerund, infinitive)_, **coordinating conjunctions** (_for, and, nor, or, but, yet, so)_, or **subordinating conjunctions (**_who, which, that, whose, whoever, after, because, until, whenever, although, unless_). You should also eliminate repeated words.

> **Your Turn:**
> Combine each of the following groups of simple sentences into one longer, more rhythmic sentence by using the suggestions above. Feel free to rearrange words and phrases in more logical order and make sure you eliminate repeated words.

1. The links between ideas must be clear. The links are among words. The links are among sentences. Transitional words and phrases are links.

2. A paragraph must be well organized. Each paragraph has a function. The organization is internal. Paragraphs in an essay must be sequenced. The sequence is logical.

3. Writers must imagine the readers. Readers try to understand. The readers have only words to guide them. Readers must infer attitude, tone and purpose of the writer.

4. A writer's task is to help readers. The readers make "connections." The "connections" are among words. The "connections" are among sentences. The "connections" are among paragraphs. The "connections" are among ideas.

5. Communication is the writer's goal. The goal is primary. Writing must make sense to readers.

> **Your Turn Again:**
> In a follow-up paragraph, using the model you just created, discuss a specific suggestion for helping writers become more sensitive to the needs of their readers. Save the paragraph in your Writer's Notebook. Fold down the page's corner so you can find it easily.

Does Spelling Count Two?

Spelling counts too! Nothing leaves a worse impression on a reader than careless proofreading and lack of concern for proper spelling. However, the English language has so many exceptions that it is hard to learn and master all the rules. For a complete explanation of ways to learn to spell better, read the essay in Lesson 13, "Teaching Johnny to Spell."

In the meantime, use the poem, "A Little Poem About Spelling," to remind you that the best way to correct spelling is to proofread carefully.

A Little Poem about Spelling

Eye halve a spell ling chequer
It came with a pea sea
 plane lee marques four my revue
Miss steaks eye kin knot sea

Eye strike a quay and type a word
And weight four it two say
Weather eye am wrong oar write
It shows me strait a weigh

As soon as a mist ache is maid
It nose be four two long
And eye can put the error rite
Its rare lea ever wrong

Eye have run this poem threw it
I am shore yore pleased two no
Its letter perfect awl the weigh
My chequer tolled me sew.
--Jerrod H. Zar [2]

Note: An unsophisticated spell checker will find little or no fault with this poem because it spell checks words in isolation. A more sophisticated spell checker will consider the context in which a word occurs. Either way, a writer has the final responsibility to choose the best words and then spell them correctly.

Your Turn:
Choose a draft from your Writer's Notebook. Prepare a second draft by using a word processor. When you have finished typing it, use the "spell check" tool to complete another proofreading.

As you edit and proofread, make sure that you are aware that the "spell checker" does not check homophones—words that sound alike, but have different meanings and spellings. Some commonly misspelled homophones are:

- They're, there, and their
- Which, witch
- Here, hear
- Your, you're
- Sale, sail
- Affect, effect
- Threw, through
- Loose, lose
- Principal, principle
- Past, passed
- Accept, except
- Weather, whether
- Too, two and to
- Than, then
- Where, wear

Note: Avoid colloquial spellings like "bcuz," "wassup," and codes used in text messaging, "blogs" and social networking sites when writing pieces for teachers, parents, and more formal audiences. Again, remember your audience!

How Do I Use a Grammar/Style Checker?

A "grammar/style checker" on your computer can serve as a personal editor because it "reads" your writing and indicates areas where you can improve clarity, correctness and conciseness. While it will not turn a writer into a Hemingway overnight, this technology tool can help identify and correct these possible problems:

1. long sentences and paragraphs
2. passive voice verbs
3. incorrect punctuation
4. overly complex words
5. wordiness
6. redundancy and repeated words
7. possible misuse of homophones ("effect" for "affect," "there" for "their")
8. grammar problems (shift in verb tenses, non-parallel constructions, and incorrect pronouns, for example)
9.   words with negative connotations

Set your computer to track revisions:

- Go to "tools" or "review"
- Click "Spelling & Grammar"
- Click "Options"
- Check all boxes
    - √spelling & grammar as you type
    - √spelling in context
    - √grammar & spelling
    - √readability statistics
    - √grammar only and grammar & style

Then, highlight the text or select "all" to check the spelling, grammar and style.

When you finish, a box like the one on the left will appear which shows the "readability" statistics, grade level and reading ease for your piece of writing.

Readability Statistics

Counts	
Words	147
Characters	743
Paragraphs	9
Sentences	10

Averages	
Sentences per Paragraph	1.2
Words per Sentence	14.3
Characters per Word	4.9

Readability	
Passive Sentences	0%
Flesch Reading Ease	60.9
Flesch-Kincaid Grade Level	8.3

OK

How Can "Tracking" Improve Revisions?

Effective writers makes use of as many techniques as possible to help clarify meaning, engage readers and achieve their purpose. Technology has provided tools that, if used consistently and carefully, can help make revision, editing and proofreading more efficient. The steps below will help you document this step of your writing process by "tracking" your changes.

1. On the far left side of the new toolbar is an icon that will allow you to make changes and insert comments. Type your changes. As you edit, revise and correct the text, your changes will be highlighted in red. A white box with an arrow pointing to the change will indicate if you have deleted words, phrases, sentences, punctuation, and indicate the type of action you took to revise.

2. Continue your editing and revising throughout the written draft. Save the current document in a file folder identifying the type of assignment and draft number. (Ex. College Essay, Draft.). You can also ask friends to help by adding their comments to your draft. Just ask them to click on "new comment" on the tool bar.

3. Then print the document with all of your changes marked in red. This will show your teacher that you have considered editorial comments.

4. Review the comments and changes you made. When you are ready, click on the icon that says, "Accept changes." Then print the document and save under "College Essay, Draft 2."

5. Repeat the same process of tracking, highlighting, saving and printing your changes until you are sure you have revised, edited and proofread as thoroughly as possible. Save it under the file name of title or type of assignment, e.g. "Final College Essay."

6. Prepare to turn in all drafts with the final copy you intend to submit for the teacher's evaluation. Each draft, if you have revised carefully, will have fewer and fewer tracked and highlighted changes. In addition, when you completed the final copy, you can delete all comments, changes and corrections.

7. To change the "Reading Ease," and "Grade Level" of your writing to reach a specific and targeted audience, adjust the length of sentences and number of paragraphs.

Your Turn:

Select one of your drafts from your Writer's Notebook. Rewrite it making any changes you think might improve it and make it more interesting for your readers. As you rewrite, "track" changes according to the directions.

When you believe you have finished revising and editing, measure your composition's readability with the Grammar/Style Checker. Try to increase the grade level by combining sentences and using the Thesaurus to find synonyms with more syllables for some words.

What If Lincoln Had Used a Computer?

Abraham Lincoln delivered the Gettysburg address on November 19, 1863, at the dedication of the Soldier's National Cemetery. He delivered this speech, one of the most important in American history, four and a half months after the Union Army defeated the Army of the Confederacy. In a carefully crafted address, just over two minutes long, Lincoln restated principles of human equality in the Declaration of Independence, proclaimed the Civil War as a struggle to preserve the Union, and sought to ensure the survival of America's representative democracy.

The five known manuscripts of the Gettysburg Address differ in a number of details and exact wording. Did President Lincoln really draft a version on the back of an envelope? Did he add words extemporaneously as he looked over the rows of graves? Did the reporters who heard him take accurate

notes? We do not know all the answers, however, we do know that if Lincoln delivered this speech today, his words would circle the globe through electronic recordings and social media, and his speech might look very different from the one he delivered more than a hundred years ago. For a moment, let us imagine what the first paragraph of the Gettysburg Address might have looked like if Lincoln, or a speechwriter, had used a grammar/style checker to edit his ideas:

Original Version, 1863

Four score and seven years ago, our fathers brought forth on this continent, a new nation, conceived in Liberty, and dedicated to the proposition that all men are created equal. Now we are engaged in a great civil war, tests whether that nation, or any nation so conceived and so dedicated, can long endure. Thus, we are met on a great battlefield of that war. We have come to dedicate a portion of that field, as a final resting place for those who here gave their lives that that nation might live. It is altogether fitting and proper that we should do this. (Reading level—10.9)

Revised Version, 2012 (revised according to today's standards and style)

Eighty-seven years ago, our founders formed a new nation, born in Liberty, and dedicated to the idea that all people are created equal. Now a great civil war tests the survival of that nation. We meet today on a great battlefield of that war. We will dedicate a portion of that field as a final resting place for those who gave their lives so that this nation might live. (Reading level—7.2)

> **Your Turn:**
> When using a grammar/style checker, what is lost? What is gained? How would you describe the style of Lincoln's original version? How would you describe the style of the revised version? How do you know the original version is more than a 100 years old? Choose a draft in your Writer's Notebook and use a Grammar/Style checker to help you revise it according to today's standards.

What Else Should I Know About Grammar?

Types of Nouns:

- **Abstract noun**: names an idea or concept. (**Beauty** is in the eye of the beholder.)
- **Concrete noun**: names a physical object (The **brick** landed on his **head**.)
- **Proper noun:** Gives a specific, capitalized name of a person, place or thing. (**John,** proud to be born in **Texas,** considers it the best place in the **United States**.)
- **Appositive:** renames or explains the noun that precedes it. (My father, the **grouch**, smiled on special occasions.)
- **Gerund:** A noun formed by adding –ing to a verb. (My son loved **swimming.**)
- **Infinitive**: A noun formed by adding "to" to a verb. (**To cut** calories is the best way to lose weight.)

Types of Pronouns:

- **Demonstrative pronouns**: words that point out nouns (**these, that, those, this**)
- **Interrogative pronouns**: words that indicate questions (**who, what, where, when, how, why**)
- **Personal pronouns:** indicate gender and person to whom the pronoun refers (**I, me, my, we, our, you, your, he, she, it, they, him, her**)
- **Antecedent:** the word to which the pronoun refers. (Because **Jack** overslept, **he** didn't eat breakfast.)

Types of Verbs: In addition to showing action, person and number, verbs show mood, voice and time/tense.

- **Indicative mood:** used to indicate facts, questions and opinions and directly. (It didn't rain at our house today. Did it rain at yours? I love rainy days.)
- **Imperative mood:** Used to issue commands. (**Bring** me the pencil.)
- **Active Voice:** The subject performs the action. (John **swept** the floor.)
- **Passive Voice:** The subject receives the action. (The floor **was swept** by John.)
- **Verb Tenses**: indicate time action takes place.

	Simple	Perfect	Progressive
Past	played	had played	had been playing
Present	play	have played	have been playing
Future	will play	will have played	will have been playing

Other Sentence Concerns:

- **Comma Splice:** two sentences joined together with a comma
- **Run-On:** two sentences joined together without any punctuation.
- **Sentence Fragment:** an incomplete thought, lacking a subject or verb.
- **Parallelism:** a similarity of structures in a series of related words, phrases, or clauses.

What Are Editing Symbols?

Editors and writers use symbols to indicate areas they want to target for editing and proofreading. If these symbols show up frequently during editing sessions, you   can consult *The Elements of Style* by E. B. White and William Strunk or the Purdue University writing lab (www.english.purdue.edu) for extra help.

Grammar Usage/Mechanics:

√	**Misspelling**
¶	**Paragraph. Begin a new one here.**
≠	**Grammar at fault. You need help writing parallel structures.**
∅	**Comma error or apostrophe error. Either needed. Or not needed.**
P/p	**Participial phrase at the beginning of a sentence must refer to the grammatical subject. "Failing to understand this, your prose will read awkwardly," means your prose fails to understand—not you.**
i/o	**Split infinitives tend <u>to always</u> <u>read</u> awkwardly. Try to correct them.**
VTS	**A pointless change of tense which leaves the reader confused about time and order of events.**
SF	**Not a sentence. Technique okay, if effective. Otherwise not. Here not.**
R-O	**Run on sentences. Two or more sentences joined without punctuation or conjunctions.**
CS	**Comma splice. Use of a comma to join sentences instead of a semicolon or conjunction.**

Style:

B. S.	Be specific. Definitely vague. Or you have used a generalization or an abstraction where you need a concrete detail, fact, or example.
AV	Use the active voice. "She was hit by the ball," is not as hard hitting as "The ball hit the girl."
———	Delete. Superfluous. Unnecessary. Redundant. Repetitive.
^	Insert. You've left some important words.
?	Either you are confusing or the reader is confused or both.
AWK	Awkward. This sentence is related to the auk a thick-bodied short-neck bird without grace. Read aloud, recast and restyle.
R	Repetition used for unintended or undesirable effect.
∂	Cliché. Trite, overworked, overused expression.
OW	Overwritten, overstated, overworked. You're straining, trying to hard.
Pret	Pompous, pretentious, self-indulgent—you are enjoying yourself so much you have forgotten about your readers.
"I"	Author intrusion. You are preaching, judging, interpreting too much. SHOW readers and trust them to understand and draw conclusions.
POV	You have violated the point of view, bounced from one mind to another, one speaker to another, without preparing your readers.

LESSON 4.
ESSAY or "I-SAY":
THE "VOICE" OF A MIND
AT WORK

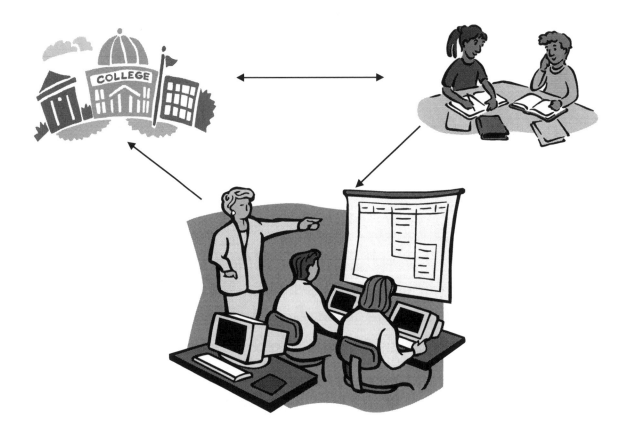

"**The drama of the essay is the way the public life intersects with my personal and private life. It's in that intersection that I find the energy of the essay.**"
—Richard Rodriguez.
The Hunger of Memory

What is an Essay?

Many students associate writing essays with standardized testing where they read the prompt, "Write an essay about a time when..." However, the essay form has a long history and should inspire, stimulate, interest and even entertain both the writer and the reader. The essay format provides opportunities for writers to speak directly to readers. Essay writers can write on any topic they have in mind with whatever attitude they feel, and use many different strategies and techniques that best communicate their ideas and opinions.

Review the "Table of Contents" in an anthology of essays, or those listed in your English or Advanced Placement textbook. Then, read several short essays that either you or your teacher has chosen. Use the questions below to help you explore the essay form and determine your own definition of "an essay."

1. Do you think essays are less creative, exciting and original than short stories, novels, poems and plays? If so, why? Why not?

2. In what ways does the essay accommodate a great variety of subjects, messages, styles and tones? Some critics have called the essay form "literature's soapbox." Is this an accurate description? Why?

3. An essay may take one idea and develop it, exploring all of its ramifications, or it may present several ideas which come together at the end to reveal a basic insight. What seems to be the advantages and disadvantages of these two different approaches?

4. An essay may be formal, detached, and carefully structured, or informal, conversational, and personal. Do you think both kinds of essays are equally difficult to write? Which kind do you prefer to write? Which do your prefer to read?

5. An essay may be quiet, calm, and measured, or intense, emotional and impassioned. Are you moved and influenced more by one approach than the other? Does extreme emotionalism impair the lucidity and effectiveness of an essayist's argument for you? Or does it lend fire, conviction, and credibility to the writer's words?

6. What kind of personality do you imagine it takes to be an essayist? Why would an essayist need keen powers of observation and perception, plus a reflective mind? Why do you think most essayists choose to express their findings, opinions, and insights directly, rather than through fictional characters?

The essay form allows writers to explore many different topics, use many methods, and techniques to achieve many different purposes.

Essay: "Flying with Words"[1]

I learned to read by sitting on my Dad's lap and watching him point out letters and words in the *St. Louis Star Times* newspaper. Soon, I could read headlines that contained words that began with the same letter, "Heroes Hurt Hitler," "Champions Clash in California," "President Praises Patriots." Encouraged by a father whose passions for conversations and writing letters lasted until his death, I began a love affair with language.

From the first day of school, I knew I could read better than other kids could. Once, in kindergarten, I read the word, "gallop," in a story in a Dick and Jane basal "reader." The teacher, sitting next to the Big Book, a pointer lying across her lap, looked surprised. She furrowed her eyebrows, leaned forward in her chair, looked at me and said, "How did you know that word? We have not studied the hard 'g' sound yet, and I have not taught that sound yet. Has someone read this story to you before? You memorized it, didn't you?"

Behind me, other kids giggled. I said, "No, ma'am. I just know "gallop" because I sounded it out. Besides, it fits the rest of the story. Jane is riding a stick horse. Horses gallop." "Well," she said, "I still have to teach the other kids, so why don't you finish the story by yourself? Over there in that corner?" I pushed my chair to the place where she pointed, and finished the book. With each turn of

> **I pushed my chair to the place where she pointed, and finished the book.**

the page, I hoped Dick and Jane would do something more exciting than, "See Spot run." The cartoons in the newspapers I read at home had lots of action and adventure: Dick Tracy caught the bad guys, Wonder Woman flew around buildings, and Blondie yelled at Dagwood. That day, I sat alone in the corner, and while the other kids struggled with words and waited for the teacher to help them, I watched the birds outside the window leave their nests to swoop and soar—their wings silhouetted against the sky.

Today, I still read books with "hard words" that often deal with "hard ideas." They sit in a pile on the table next to the couch where I curl up in the evenings, ready to explore their pages. Over my shoulder, I hear my Dad's voice reminding me, "You should read all the books you can, but you only need to read three for an education: *The Bible* for philosophy, Shakespeare for psychology and *The Decline and Fall of the Roman Empire* for history. Some nights, instead of reading other people's words, I sit at my desk, or at the kitchen table, writing my own sentences and watching them scroll across a computer screen.

Through the early experiences sitting on his lap with a newspaper or book between us, through his letters, and his conversations, my father left me a legacy—a love of language. Now, it's my turn to contribute this gift to my children, grandchildren and students at my school. When children own many words, and understand their power, they can fly.

> **Your Turn:**
> Write an essay that shows your readers the importance of words and language in your life. Before you write, look carefully at the essay. How is the "I" present—a voice shaping the text and influencing the reader? What point does the essay, "Flying with Words," make about the power of words and language? How do you know?

Student Voices

The essay, "Flying With Words," and the poem below, "Wednesday Afternoon," provide pictures of fathers, as seen through the eyes of daughters. Besides the way they look on the page, how does the essay version differ from the poetic version?

Wednesday Afternoon

My father's three hub-capped minivan
creaks up the driveway
to our beagle's barks and whimpers.
He fights his aged knees
that survived stolen bases and dirty tackles,
while pools of sweat swim laps
through his forty-something wrinkles.

Dad stumbles through the door
with his second button in the third hole,
mumbles "hey" en route to the shower,
tosses the stack of credit card bills
and ads on the kitchen table,
and smiles his "I just did something wrong" smile
because mom hates when the mail's not by the door.

Daddy trots from his room with damp hair
that glistens with silver that neither of us admits
hops into his recliner which our dog has claimed,
flips to reruns where he attempts to explain
the difference between Hawkeye and Trapper,
and suggests we eat out tonight
though he knows Mom's meat loaf is in the oven.
                    ~Becki Kielaszek (2004:74)

Your Turn:
Think of a person who has impacted your life, and write 500 words in an essay that shows how that person influenced your life. As you write the essay, include techniques that "show not tell"—quotations, actions and descriptive detail. Even though you write an essay, read it aloud and see if it sounds "poetic."

Do Essays Have Different Purposes and Forms?

Essays have many forms, methods, modes, types, domains of writing—whatever you want to call them. Writers use five basic methods: narration (relating events), description (creating pictures), exposition (providing information) persuasion (stating and proving opinions) and creative/literary writing (entertaining). In most cases, writers use these methods in natural combinations. For example, narration frequently includes descriptive paragraphs; research papers and critical analyses may include all forms and methods to develop the thesis, or main ideas and prove a point.

For assignments, teachers often break essays and compositions into different categories depending on the specific and primary purpose of each of them.

Narration	Description	Exposition	Persuasion	Creative/Literary
College Admission Essays	Reports on specific places, events, objects	Business letters	Arguments, Debates, Proposals	Novels
Résumés	Character sketches and profiles	Newsletters, catalogues, guidebooks, pamphlets	Editorials, Commentaries, Newscasts	Drama
Journals, Diaries	Recommendation letters	Newspaper, magazine articles	Speeches	Poetry
Personal Letters, Emails		"How to" instructions & manuals	Advertisements, posters	Short Stories
Anecdotes		Summaries and reports	Reviews & Criticism	
Autobiographies, Biographies			Travel brochures	

Your Turn:
For this writing practice, choose a common object like chocolate, an activity like baseball, or an event like Mardi Gras and try to combine 2-3 methods to tell a story, create pictures, explain, or argue for or against the object, activity or event.

How Do I Plan and Write an Essay?

The opportunities presented by the essay form allow writers to speak out directly on any subject they have in mind, in any tone of voice, and to use whatever tools and techniques they believe will communicate their ideas. Above all, when you write an essay, **choose a topic** you're really interested in and already know something about, but remember to stick with the major point you want to make, and don't try to show how much you know about it in a limited space.

Narrow your topic so your information will fit easily into the size of the essay you intend to write. "Cancer has received much media attention because of the rapid increase of persons diagnosed with the disease; it is a disease that has many causes and many treatments" might require a book to discuss. "Pollutants have affected the rates of cancer in Houston" might take a few pages. The following steps in writing an essay should also help you:

Steps in Writing an Essay

1. Choose a topic—What subjects do I really care about?
2. Plan/Brainstorm—What do I know, or think I know, about the topic?
3. Write a thesis—The purpose of this is essay is to [prove/explain/describe/argue…]
4. Gather Information—What else do I need to know about my topic?
5. Form an Outline/ "Map"—How will I arrange and organize my ideas?
6. Write the Body of the Essay—How does my evidence support my thesis?
7. Write an Introduction—How do I "hook" my readers? What is my thesis? Have I provided enough background information so my readers can understand my point of view?
8. Write a Conclusion—Have I "looked back" by summarizing, restating my thesis? Do I "look forward' by leaving my readers with a memorable statement?

Your Turn:

Choose one element from each column below and draft an essay that meets the requirements for audience and purpose. For example, you might want to write a humorous essay about rules and regulations for a teacher to follow.

Subject	Purpose	Audience
A Favorite Sport	Inform/teach	Teacher/Coach
Women's Rights	Entertain	Elderly neighbor
A Political Candidate	Argue/Dispute	Fifth grade cousin
Rules/Regulations	Evaluate/Criticize	Parent/Step Parent
Prunes/Broccoli	Describe/Portray	Employer, Boss
A book or film	Analyze/Explain	Parent/Step Parent

How Do I Write a Thesis Sentence?

A **Thesis Sentence** states the opinion or main idea you want to communicate or defend AND your intention and purpose for writing an essay. It provides you—and your reader —with a clear "rudder" for maintaining your focus, direction and balance. With a strong thesis, your readers will know what to expect and you can avoid the muddy waters of indecisive and disorganized writing.

Use this "sentence stem" to help form a thesis:

The purpose of this essay is to (show, explain, describe, argue, analyze, evaluate) that [**this part of the stem will actually form a thesis sentence to use in an essay.**]

Example: The purpose of this book is to (show that) [**when student writers have opportunities for instruction and practice, they can learn to write effectively.**]

Note: Eliminate the words, "The purpose of this essay is to" when you write your final thesis. sentence.

A thesis should:

1. Avoid subordinate ideas that often trap inexperienced writers.

   Weak: In spite of the danger, that many guilty parties may go unpunished by law because the resulting publicity make a fair trial impossible, the Senate is justified in holding public hearings on wrong doings in government.

   Strong: The Senate has justification for holding public hearings on wrongdoings in government departments.

2. Suggest your intention and your attitude toward the topic of the essay. Immature writers often feel they must hit their readers over the head by using phrases like "My purpose in this essay is…" or "It is my opinion that…"

   Weak: My purpose in this paper is to support the view that a college education provides lifelong benefits.
   Strong: A college education can provide lifelong benefits.

3. Use specific, concrete language and avoid figurative, emotional, vague and inexact language.
   Weak: Documentary television dramas are like figures in a wax museum.
   Strong: Documentary television often misleads audiences into accepting a distorted view of history.

Your Turn:
Find the thesis sentences writers used in essays you read in class that state the author's intent and purpose. Copy them in your Writer's Notebook as examples of strong thesis sentences. Then, write your own thesis sentences stating your opinion about each of these topics: environment, family, heroes, work, teaching and learning, science and technology, arts and leisure. Save them for an essay you plan to write later.

How Do I Write an Antithesis Sentence?

An **antithesis is** a sentence that contains a syntactical parallel that stands in opposition and offers a direct contrast to the idea stated in the thesis. Children use antithesis all the time as a way to "bargain," stall or "buy time":

> "I'll go to bed, <u>but</u> first read me a story."
> "I'll eat my green beans <u>although</u> I'd rather have a Popsicle."

Writers use antithesis when they want to discuss contrasting ideas or opinions.

> "Writers of best sellers, especially nonfiction, often confirm their readers' prejudices, endorse their opinions, ratify their feelings and satisfy their wishes.; however, interpretive writers of classics, interpret and observe life, question and then challenge the beliefs of readers.

Note: Transitional words and phrases ("Lesson 7: Description—the 'Voice' of Imagination," 86) help connect a thesis with an antithesis and help show the contrast between ideas.

Elements of a Strong Thesis

Topic + <u>action verb</u> + [controlling idea.]

Loyalty towards a country's values often <u>inspires</u> [heroic self-sacrifice.]
The Federal government should <u>provide</u> [funds for solar power.]

Elements of a Strong Antithesis

Topic + <u>action verb</u> + [controlling idea] + *transition* + (contrasting idea)

Loyalty towards a country's values often <u>inspires</u> [heroic self-sacrifice], *however,* (sometimes it can lead to a distorted view of patriotism.)
The Federal government should <u>provide</u> [funds for solar power] *although* (doing that might cause a raise in taxes.)

<u>**Note:**</u> We call words like "should, often, sometimes," and "might" **"qualifiers"** and using them shows that the writer understands that readers or listeners might disagree with the position they have taken.

<u>**Your Turn:**</u>
Choose three of the thesis sentences you wrote in the previous "Your Turn" exercise, and turn them into antithesis sentences using the models above as examples. Save them for an essay you plan to write later.

What Are Rhetorical Strategies?

Scholars have identified at least eleven Rhetorical Strategies, or methods, that writers use to develop and provide evidence that supports the main idea of an essay: **Definition, Example/Illustration, Classification, Cause/Effect, Compare/Contrast, Description, Anecdote/Narration, Testimony/Quotation, Analogy/Metaphor, Argument/Persuasion** and **Process.**

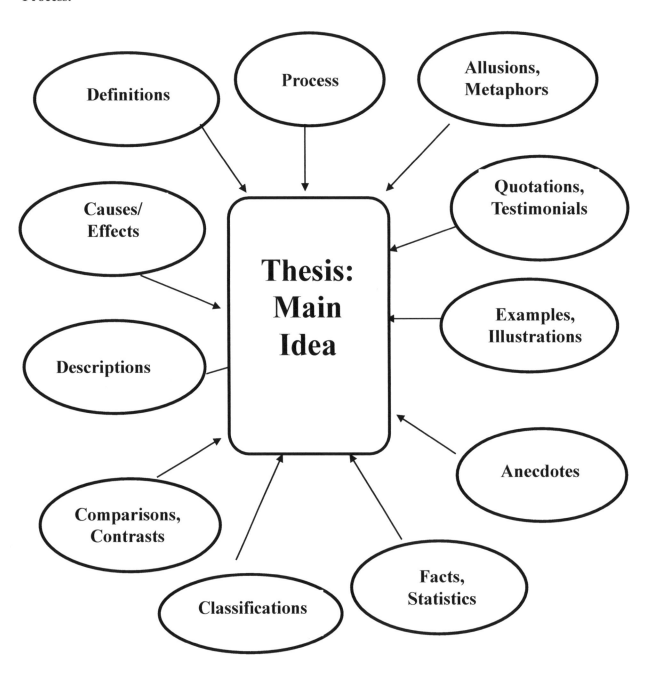

How Do Writers Use Rhetorical Strategies to Develop Essays?

A paragraph is a group of sentences that share a common topic, idea or purpose. Writers change paragraphs when they change topics, ideas, places, speakers, or sometimes as a visual aid to readers. When you combine several paragraphs to provide support for a thesis, or main idea, you write an essay. An essay generally needs to accomplish three goals:

1. Develop and explain your purpose, stated in a thesis— "Tell me what you're going to tell me."
2. Convey information— "Then, tell me."
3. Summarize main ideas— "Now, tell me what you told me."

Your Turn:
Use each of the following rhetorical strategies to write an essay about Spring Break. Each paragraph should use a different strategy.

1. Definition: (Spring Break means…)

2. Exemplification/Illustration: (During Spring Break, people can "for

    instance,…" "for example…")

3. Classification: (Different ways to spend Spring Break include…)

4. Cause-Effect: (Spring Break often causes...it can affect….)

5. Compare/Contrast: (When compared to Christmas Break, Spring Break…)

6. Description: (On Spring Break, we can hear, smell, taste, touch and see…)

7. Anecdote/Narration: (Once during Spring Break…)

8. Testimony/Quotation: (My parents once told me, "Spring Break…")

9. Analogy/Metaphor: (Spring Break reminds me of …)

10. Argument/Persuasion: (Spring Break should/should not…)

11. Process: (How to enjoy Spring Break…)

Your Turn:
Review the essay, "Flying With Words" in this section, highlight and then, identify in the margin, places where the writer has used one of the rhetorical strategies. Then, take a position on this question: Is the essay a valuable form of literature? Why? Or why not? Use a variety of strategies to develop your position.

How Do Leads "Hook" Readers?

Writers have the first two sentences, approximately twenty seconds, to "hook" readers and "reel" them into essay, story, poem, drama or speech. Failure to capture a reader's attention quickly means you will have to work twice as hard to keep them reading after the first paragraph. Use the following examples to help you write strong "leads," or opening sentences:

1. Concrete Detail about a Place:

> People jammed into the small room so that they filled every   last bit of space, and still others tried to look through the windows on each side of the door.

2. Information From the Past:

> In the fifth grade, I could put spin on a curve ball, spike a football and make perfect baskets from the end of the driveway —even though I was a girl.

3. Startling Dialogue or Quotation

> "Thief!" a man shouted. "I'll never bring my car to this shop again for an oil change, and your 'specials' aren't very special."

4. Straight Fact:

> I skipped the sixth grade, so I never learned how to do fractions.

5. Contradiction or Contrasts:

> I looked for God in church. I found Him at the Grand Canyon.

6. Concrete Detail about a Person:

> Last week, a friend of mine, a generous and charitable person, complained   that a woman with food stamps slowed down the   checker at the grocery store.

7. Historical or Background Information:

> I had forgotten all about a student's attempted suicide until my friend told me how depressed her daughter had become when she didn't make the cheerleading squad.

8. A Combination of Leads:

> She sat straight in her kindergarten chair, her feet crossed at the ankles. "The pencil is too big for my fingers," she said to the teacher towering above her.

Your Turn:

Copy the first sentences, or "leads," of several essays you have read in class into your Writer's Notebook. Identify each type of "lead" sentence according to the models above and save them as examples to use in your own essays.

What Kinds of Leads "Turn Off" Readers?

Often, writers begin a composition by writing the first sentences that come into their heads. They give little thought to how their words might affect readers' interest in, and enthusiasm for, reading their essays and compositions. Below, you will find opening sentences that show a writer's lack of thought in composing a "lead," or "hook." In parentheses and italics, you can read the thoughts of a reader who lost interest after the first line.

1. The Apology:

Although I don't know much about candidates for president, I thought I'd write a paper about them because I know my teacher likes politics.
("I'm sorry, but I don't want to waste time reading about candidates, especially since you say you do not know anything about them.")

2. The Complaint:

I waited until the last minute to write this paper because I really don't care much about the election, and I don't think it's very important.
("If that's the case, I'll just skip reading this one.")

3. The Platitude, Cliché, or Some Other Trite Expression:

Some political candidates are good and some political candidates are bad.
("Some student compositions are good, but this one will be bad.")

4. A Reference to the Title:

 The title of my paper, "Candidates for President" indicates I will write about candidates who are running for president of the United States this year.
("After announcing the topic in the opening sentence, this student probably won't have much else to say that's interesting or important."

5. The Rhetorical Question, Quotation, Definition:

Have you ever voted for President? One time, a candidate said, "….."
Webster's Dictionary defines a candidate as...
("These kids must think they're still in high school writing for a state standardized test. Can't they think of anything interesting to say? So, what else is new?")

Your Turn:
Look back at the first sentences of several of the compositions you have written so far. Identify each type of "lead" according to the models provided on these two pages. Have you "hooked" your readers, or have you "turned them off?" Rewrite them so they now "hook" your readers.

How Do I Write Conclusions?

Look Backward

1. <u>Return to the Introduction</u> (the italicized words refer to a comparison made in an introduction to an essay about job hunting):

Despite all these suggestions, *finding a summer job may still be as difficult as locating an inexpensive apartment near campus.* But at least we can be confident that we have gone about it efficiently and looked into all the possibilities. The rest is up to luck.

2. <u>Restate the Idea Stated in the Thesis:</u>

Looking for a summer job need not be a haphazard process. Job seekers who conduct a systematic, efficient search should produce results.

Look Forward

3. <u>Forecast, or Predict the Future:</u>

Despite these suggestions, job hunters may not find summer work. The growing demand for these positions and the diminishing supplies of them mean that many young people will not find employment. The result could mean students go to summer school which could increase enrollments. The end product might include many early graduates who still might not be able to find jobs. And that makes the future look even bleaker.

4. <u>Call for Action:</u>

The important part to remember is to get started looking for a summer job today. Job hunters can write letters to federal agencies, check into local and state government possibilities, get a copy of the Summer Employment Directory, and follow the suggestions about seeking work in small businesses. They who hesitate may be lost this summer.

5. <u>Discuss Implications:</u>

The implications of these suggestions should be apparent. Students will have a difficult time finding summer jobs this summer. We may wait for Lady Luck to smile on us or we can roll up our sleeves and start searching for ourselves. We can follow these suggestions or find our own way—or we can go to summer school.

6. <u>Point Out the Importance of ideas and information discussed in the essay:</u>

Perhaps the most important thing to remember about these specific suggestions is that students should carefully research an undertaking like finding a summer job. Some people go through life haphazardly, meeting problems with hastily conceived, last-minute answers. Other people anticipate problems and study how to meet and solve them. To do so usually reaps rewards.

What Else Should I Know About Conclusions?

When writing conclusions for your compositions, and reviewing examples from authors, consider the suggestions below. Review these guidelines to use when you write your own essays.

1. Do not offer an apology, afterthought or sound an extraneous note. The conclusion should be like a parting handshake—firm and brief. Both present a final, but favorable, impression on readers.

2. Not one of the previous examples start with the overworked words, "in summary," or "in conclusion." Discard these feeble mechanical signals.

3. Try to conclude with a catchy statement, attempted in *example 4*, for instance.

4. In several of the examples, short sentences—or fragments—end the paragraphs, and They "snap" the essay to a close. Sometimes an uncommon sentence like the last sentence in example 6, which begins with an infinitive, makes an point. Even

5. punctuation—like the dash in example 6—can help achieve a sense of finality.

6. Consider making your last sentence the shortest sentence in the paragraph. Give your **readers** something to think about!

7. If you're still struggling with how to write a conclusion, step back, reread it and ask yourself, "And so?" or "So what?" Your answer might end or conclude your composition.

Avoid Ordinary, Trite, Common Endings and Resolution of Conflicts:
1. They lived happily ever after.
2. He, she, it, they died.
3. He, she, they woke up. It was all a dream/nightmare.
4. He, she, they rode off into the sunset.

Create Uncommon, Inventive, Creative Endings and Resolutions:
1. Epiphany—a moment of profound insight.
2. Full circle—allusion to image, detail, and idea in opening sentences.
3. Non-resolution, open-ended—the next chapter, paragraph might be....

Your Turn:
Copy the last sentences of several essays into your Writer's Notebooks. Decide whether each looks backward or forward and indicate that in the margins. Save these examples as guides for concluding sentences in essays you plan to write later.

How Do I Create Titles?

Reasons for Titles:

1. Draw readers into a work.
2. Provide information.
3. Guide the interpretation.
4. Make the work more interesting.
5. Help others identify the work.
6. Provide a means for artists and writers to honor their work.

Purpose of Titles:

1. Name the subject or topic.
2. Describe the content.
3. Underline or reinforce theme.
4. Focus on one element.
5. Challenge or mystify the audience.
6. Dedicate the work to someone.
7. Suggest mood or tone of work.

Techniques for Creating Titles:

1. Consider a title as an introduction to the work.
2. Keep titles short; use subtitles if necessary.
3. Search the work itself for titles.
4. Use literary, poetic techniques:
   - Alliteration—*Fear of the Future, Dead Before Death*
   - Rhetorical Question—"Ain't I a Woman?"
   - Puns & Word Play—"Nine in Stitches Saves Time"
   - Command—"Don't Cry for Me, Argentina"
   - Personification—"When the Rock Spoke to the Flower"
   - Allusion—*Listening for Aphrodite*
   - Controversy—"Culture and Anarchy"
   - Strangeness, Juxtaposition—"Purple Rain"
5. Consider Collaborating—artists ask writers for titles; writers use art for titles of books.
6. Use concrete nouns and action verbs. Avoid adjectives and adverbs.
7. "Untitled" is still a title, but it provides little help to readers.
8. Remember: titles cannot be copyrighted.

Your Turn:
Search an anthology of short stories or essays, write down your favorite titles and explain their connection to the literature. Write down the titles of your favorite books and explain the significance of the title to the main ideas, conflicts, characters, or setting in the book. Make sure you punctuate the titles correctly—quotation marks around stories, essays and poetry. Underline or italicize books or dramas.

Academic Essays vs. Personal Essays

Writing situations also affect the way writers choose words for their essays. Abraham Lincoln surely thought about the parents of soldiers who lost their lives at Gettysburg, and his speech needed to touch their hearts. However, if you write an essay for your teacher about the significance of his speech, you will face other pressures and circumstances. Generally, differences between academic and personal essays include:

ACADEMIC ESSAYS	PERSONAL ESSAYS
• Written "on demand" in timed situations;	♦ Written using several stages of the "writing process;"
• Prepared for general academic audiences (teachers, professors, AP/SAT evaluators);	♦ Prepared for specific audiences (peers, parents, readers of newspapers, magazines, anthologies);
• Evaluated as a "draft";	♦ Evaluated as a "publishable" product;
• Achieves the specific purpose of showing an understanding of material and a "mind at work";	♦ Achieves a variety of purposes (entertains, inspires, persuades, motivates, enlightens);
• Maintains a formal, academic, professional and objective tone;	♦ May contain informal, personal, satiric, humorous, sad, joyous, angry, caustic, critical, tones;
• Shows analytical, interpretative, logical and evaluative critical thinking skills;	♦ Shows creative, imaginative and innovative thinking skills;
• Developed with rhetorical strategies necessary for expository and persuasive modes and purposes;	♦ Developed with dialogue, actions and descriptive language geared towards purpose and audiences' needs;
• Utilizes structured paragraphs (Topic sentences, Evidence and Commentary-TEC);	♦ Utilizes paragraph lengths based on audiences' readability and interests;
• Uses formal essay structure (introduction with thesis and background information, body paragraphs and conclusion);	♦ Uses chronological, spatial, order of importance, cause-effect, compare-contrast organizational structure;
• Uses a 3rd person detached, objective point of view and avoids the pronoun, "you."	♦ May use 1st person, 3rd person limited, or omniscient point of view.

Why Are Admissions Essays Important?

Colleges look for individuals who will graduate in a timely manner, find a place in a competitive job market, and in time, give back to the university through donations and support of foundations and athletics. College Admissions officers believe that reading a student's admissions essay will help them hear the "voice" of a candidate for admission—and through the process, an applicant becomes more than a SAT score or class rank number.

Students can use the college essay to help shine a light on those abilities, character traits and contributions that make them unique and important. A college essay, more than any other aspect of the admissions process, "sells" a candidate for admission.

A few years ago, Danielle Romain, took an idea from a poem, "Traveling Man," published in *Aquilae Stilus* (1996), and wrote an essay, which she submitted, to Harvard University. One Saturday morning, she received a phone call from the admissions director at Harvard who said, "Danielle, do you have a winter coat? Well, you better buy one. You will need it here at Harvard. I have never read such an exciting applications essay. Start packing your bags." A few years later, a Harvard degree in hand, Danielle started her career on Wall Street where she lives and works today.

Justin Storms, a graduate of the University of Texas and Columbia University Law School, woke up the admissions officers at UT with the title of his admissions essay, "A Study in the Stupidity of College Essays" (*Aquilae Stilus,* 1996: 18-19). His humorous approach, which compared entering the UT Honors program to entering Hell, after a short visit to Essay Purgatory, guaranteed his quick acceptance. Justin currently practices law in New York. Both Danielle and Justin attended universities on scholarships.

Characteristics of Effective College Essays

1. Don't tell your life story. Instead, focus on one important incident or aspect of your life—something that will make readers want to learn more about you.

2. Be honest! Don't try to tell the admissions officers what you think they want to hear. Be yourself and write about something important to you. If you care about your topic, so will your readers. Don't try to hide the "real you."

3. Be funny—but be careful. A touch of humor, handled well, can enhance an essay, but if you are not usually funny, don't try it now!

4. Be courteous. Make the admission officer's job easier by following guidelines for length. Use easy-to-read fonts, no smaller than 10 points. If you handwrite your essay, write legibly.

5. Proofread. Proofread. Proofread. Fresh eyes can help find grammatical, syntactical and mechanical errors, so ask a friend or teacher for help.

Note on Plagiarism: Purchasing an essay from the Internet tempts students anxious to get into a college. However, college admissions officers have read many thousands of student essays, and can recognize professional efforts quickly. A few words typed into many available software tools can also quickly find "cheaters" and students tempted to plagiarize. Plagiarism of any kind usually results in automatic expulsion from colleges and universities.

How Do I Write a "Wow!" Admissions Essay?

1. Choose your topic well. Everybody has a "hallmark" story to tell so find yours. Avoid typical stories about divorce, your experiences as a volunteer or breaking up with your boyfriend or girlfriend—unless you're sure your story is different from the 30,000 other essays submitted on the same topics. Don't use the opportunity to brag about yourself. Sometimes, writing about failure shows more about your success than writing about an award you received.
2. Observe rules of good writing which you will explore in your English classes and in this book. If you can't remember all of them, then just think: "SHOW DON'T TELL!"
3. Add specific details, avoid clichés and speak in a true and honest voice. Read it aloud to a friend, your dog or a tree in the backyard. Change every word that does not t sound like the "real" YOU speaking. If you do not use the word, "amongst" when talking with friends, then do not use it in an essay for college, for example.
4. Keep it short. Edit so that your essay word count falls within the application essay suggestions word count and the space provided.
5. Remember, the admissions essay has to separate one bright student from another bright student. In a competitive university, almost all the students will be in the Top 10% of their graduating classes and have excellent SAT/ACT scores. Many will have "valedictorian" on their resumes. So, dare to go beyond the obvious and "think outside the box."
6. Have Fun! After all, where else do you get to do all the talking?

Sample Prompts for College Admissions Essays

1. **Northwestern University**: "Recall an occasion when you took a risk that you now know was the right thing to do."

2. **Rice University:** "What would your friends be surprised to find out about you?" "What life experiences or cultural background can you offer Rice?"

3. **Stanford**: "Discuss a photograph or conversation that was meaningful to you."

4. **Massachusetts Institute of Technology (MIT):** "Make up a question that is personally relevant to you, state it clearly, and answer it. Feel free to use your imagination, recognizing that those who read it will not mind being entertained."

5. **Harvard:** "Indicate a person who has had a significant influence on you, and explain that significance."

6. **Yale:** "Write an essay that responds to the following quotation: 'Stereotyped beliefs have the power to become a self-fulfilling prophecy,' by Elizabeth Arire in *Men and Women in Interaction: Reconsidering the Differences.*

7. **Notre Dame:** "Describe a 'hero' in any event, time period or other circumstances."

8. **University of Texas**: "Choose an issue of importance to you—the issue could be personal, school related, local, political, or international in scope—and write an essay in which you explain the significance of that issue to yourself, your family, your community, or your generation."

Student Voices
"Gastronomically Speaking—One Sunday Afternoon in Argentina" ~Shanthi Nataraj [2]

"Look...the intestines are more fun to eat if you tie them in a knot." My host's brother, Matias, picked up the long white tube on his plate, knotted it and said, "When Veronica and I were kids, we used to pretend we were eating shoelaces, instead of intestines."

I wrestled my own slippery tube to my mouth. I had lived in three countries, but Argentina proved to be the strangest, gastronomically speaking. When I applied to be an exchange student to Argentina, I studied its culture, so the Argentinians' near-obsessive love of soccer and their habit of kissing everyone on the cheek hadn't surprised me. None of my research, however, had prepared me for my first *asado,* a Sunday ritual similar to a barbecue.

I use the word "ritual" because it brings to mind the pagan ceremonies of animal sacrifice, which is exactly what the *asado* seemed to be when I wandered into the backyard to watch its preparation. My host's father, who we called, "Papa," stood beside a rectangular hole, resting on a grate, and burned a stack of newspapers. As the ashes fell through the grate, Papa swept them to the right side of the hole. The meat, resting on another grate above the right side, slowly cooked from the heat of the ashes.

"Good morning," Papa greeted me. I blinked several times. "There must be an entire cow on that grill," I said. Papa just laughed, and even today, I'm convinced we ate a whole cow. My stomach argued, later that day, that I alone must have eaten an entire herd. Seven of us gathered around a rectangular mahogany table in the bright, dining room that first Sunday in Argentina. Just as I was chewing on the last inch of my "shoelace" appetizer, Papa paraded into the room with two sizzling platters filled with what looked like ashes. "Here, Shanthi, try some," he prompted, forking a large black mass onto my plate. My sixteen-year-old hostess, Veronica, reached over and offered me cheese. "It's much better when you sprinkle on some Parmesan," she encouraged. I sprinkled some yellow dots on the lump.

"Great," I thought. "Now, I have to cut into something that looks like a cheetah with its colors reversed." I sliced the charred lump down the middle and smiled at my own hesitation. Inside lay a juicy eggplant without a hint of smoking ruins of a cow. Across the table, her older brothers brandished their steak knives as they insulted each other's soccer teams. Alejandro, their brother-in-law, tired of being teased for drinking too much of the "barbequers wine," rooted for a third team.

"These, dear," Papa told me, "are the kidneys." He pointed to several small, black heart-shaped pieces. "Would you like it rare or well done?" asked Papa. Veronica and Matias leaned over and whispered, "It's better rare."

I'd never eaten rare meat before, but then again, I'd never eaten kidneys or intestines either. They all tasted like chicken.

> **Your Turn:**
> Choose one of the college prompts on the other page and write your own admissions essay. Do not forget that you are writing for an admissions counselor who reads many essays and has little time or appreciation for boring, trite compositions. Avoid the obvious. Stay within the word limit or space.

LESSON 5. NARRATION: THE "VOICE" OF STORY TELLING

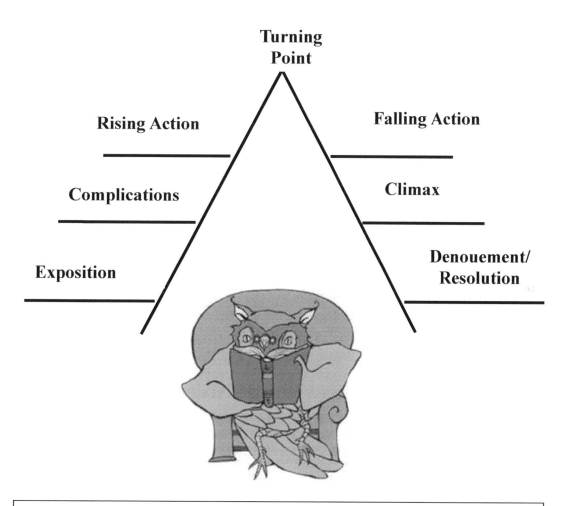

Turning Point

Rising Action

Falling Action

Complications

Climax

Exposition

Denouement/ Resolution

"It was a dark and stormy night. Suddenly a scream pieced the air...Good writing takes enormous concentration."

---"Peanuts" (1988)

What Is Narration?

Long before people could write, they gathered in groups to draw pictures, tell stories and sing songs—the oldest and most basic forms of communication. Some stories include surprise endings and strong psychological, or internal, conflicts while others have vivid characters and intense settings. Some stories make readers and listeners laugh, others make them cry, and others make them question human motivations and relationships. Effective storytellers, however, share the techniques of effective writing—**action verbs, concrete details and conversation**—when they create vivid pictures, moods and layers of meaning when they recount stories about people, settings and events.

Sometimes, however, narratives do more than entertain. For instance, the medical profession studies parent narratives, or case studies, to understand a patient's point of view before deciding on a specific course of treatment. Law enforcement officers write down stories from victims, witnesses and suspects in order to piece together an event accurately. Journalists use first hand narratives of experiences and eyewitness accounts for their reports and news articles. Cartoonists use narratives to present conflicts and editorial points of view, and many college admissions officers use narrative essays to choose students.

A popular song of another generation asks, "Why was I born? Why am I living?" these nagging questions point to the need for human beings to tie the fragments of our lives together—to give meaning to our lives by focusing on the actions, goals and ideas we value. This need may be more acute for Americans because we come from so many different parts of the world and generations often find themselves cut off from the customs, beliefs and the patterns of life shared by our ancestors. Telling our stories help connect our lives and experiences to those of other people and other generations.

Sometimes writers paint gloomy and pessimistic pictures of their lives, yet even the grimmest portraits can bring knowledge and self-awareness that leads to change and understanding. Many contemporary writers explore changes in society and conflicts within families. In the writing of today's America, the lines between fiction and nonfiction are blurred, and cultural diversity has become a characteristic. When we read memoirs, letters and autobiographies, we can often discover the connections between writers' experiences and our own.

Writers share their memories, experiences, and journeys with their readers.

Narrative Essay: "Hallmark Stories"

"Grandma, can we go to the book story?" Megan, our four-year-old granddaughter asked at the end of our shopping trip. Our neighborhood bookstore, or "story," had become our favorite place to visit. She helped me open the big, wooden doors, and we walked to the children's section where she directed me to sit in a chair while she brought me book after book to read to her. Finally, she chose one to carry to the counter to buy, and as we left. She said, "Grandma, the book 'story' is my favorite place to visit."

Often, Megan and her cousins sat on their grandfather's lap while he read to them. They chose their favorite books from a basket near his over-sized leather chair and took them to him to read over and over. They turned the books right side up if they were upside down, and they pointed at bunnies and monkeys and green squares and red triangles. They pushed the buttons on the waterproof books they played with in the bathtub, waved their hands to the music they created and squealed with amusement at how clever they were. They wiggled and giggled and yawned and ate cookies, the crumbs falling into the creases of their nightshirts.

Reading stories together remind us that grandchildren are God's way of showing us that our children paid attention. Sharing family stories, or our "hallmark stories,"[1] with them while they sit at the kitchen table, in our

> **Reading stories together remind us that grandchildren are God's way of showing us that our children paid attention.**

laps, or on the patio, reveals dimensions of ourselves, breaks us open to them; their reactions to our stories shows us who we are as humans.

When I sat on my father's lap as a child, he told me stories about Jefferson Davis, "a distant cousin," he claimed, and about both of my great grandfathers who fought in the Civil War. I grew up knowing that one, a poor "dirt farmer," hated slavery and went to war to fight with his friends. A private, he fought in the Battle of Shiloh, and walked all the way back to his home in Georgia with a bullet in his shoulder. My father remembered feeling it move under the skin when, as a child, he would touch it.

My other grandfather, a cavalry officer and the owner of a large farm in Webster County, Georgia, believed he fought for states' rights, property rights and the rights of individuals to govern their own lives. He watched Atlanta burn and then walked home down Georgia's red, clay roads to rebuild his life. He offered freedom to his slaves, but some of them remained on his farm until he died.

Thomas Davis and Daniel Drew, my great-grandfathers, never spoke to each other; their political differences caused by the Civil War severed their connections permanently even though their children, Annie and Jesse, married and gave birth to nine sons, including my father, Dan Drew, who always loved telling stories to anyone who would listen, but especially to his children and grandchildren.

The night of their fiftieth wedding anniversary, my father-in-law's stories showed the grim face of the Depression to his son and grandchildren. For the first time, we learned that when he was thirteen, his parents became ill with tuberculosis. Unable to care for their seven children, they sent them to live in an orphanage, a common occurrence during that time of severe economic hardship in families. Separated from each other, the three brothers slept on cots in one room and the four sisters on cots in another room. With little to eat, they lived in bare and cold conditions that harsh winter.

After a few months, my father-in-law, his brothers and sisters returned to their parents' home, but the Depression still gripped their lives. The night of their anniversary, he told us, "Often during the night, I went with my dad to steal coal for the furnace from the trains that ran by our "flat," or apartment. We dug potatoes from garbage cans on side streets." As the oldest son, he left school after the sixth grade to help feed his family so they could survive the Depression.

Jim Dozier, who died at age 86, served in the Army Air Force in London during World War II, worked all his life in a dressmaking factory, married, raised a son who became the first college graduate in their family, and purchased his first home when he was forty-five. He always paid his bills in cash, pretended he could read a newspaper, and filled his plate first when he sat at the head of the table. He disliked talking about the Depression because, "I don't want to embarrass my son or have anyone feel sorry for me."

In both our families, we learned little "herstory." When asked about their childhoods, our mothers said, "Not much happened. I grew up, got married and had children." Raised by serious, diligent German and Polish immigrant fathers, and married to hardworking, and psychologically complex husbands, my mother and mother-in-law learned to ask little for themselves. Through their actions, rather than their stories, they taught my husband and me to respect education as a means to achieve independence and control our futures.

However, my "herstory" includes a hallmark, or "trademark," story about a time when I confronted censorship in the form of the town librarian. Mrs. Osborne, an owlish woman, watched me, over the tops of her wire-rimmed glasses, walk through the aisles of the library and choose books.

> **"You can't check these out. They aren't suitable for a girl your age to read."**

Often, when I took my selections to her, she would say, "You can't check these out. They are not suitable for a girl your age to read. Find a book in the children's section." After buying several books that Mrs. Osborne refused to check out to me, my father finally said, "I'm not buying any more books. Let's go to the library." We did, and he told Mrs. Osborne, "You will let my daughter check out any book from any shelf she wants. I'll judge whether they're 'suitable' or not." She scowled when, as a teenager, I brought *Gone With The Wind, War and Peace* and *Uncle Tom's Cabin* to her desk for checkout. I share that story with my students to remind them that book censorship threatens the power of ideas.

I also love to tell a story about second chances. Before I attended college, my writing experiences consisted of drafting poems, keeping a journal, and writing book reports for high school classmates who paid me fifty cents apiece for them. In my first college English class, an Honors course, Dr. Bierk, my professor, assigned a research paper as our first assignment. I chose the topic, "F. Scott Fitzgerald: Spokesman for a Lost Generation," because I loved reading *The Great Gatsby*, and, like many college freshmen, thought it might be an easy topic. I waited until a week before the paper was due to begin my research and write the paper. I typed it on an old Smith Corona typewriter and hoped the professor would not count off for typing errors.

When Dr. Bierk returned it a week later, he had drawn a D- -- - across the title page in a semi-circle. I read the words he had written inside the loop, "This is the sloppiest piece of writing I have ever read in my entire teaching career." I did what any seventeen-year-old college girl might do: after class, I went to his office and cried. I offered the excuse that at my high school in Hayti, Missouri, we had never written any research papers. From the other side of his desk where he sat in a chair that swiveled so he could turn his back on students and look out the window, he told me, "I understand. Your high school teacher, Bruce Cole, was my roommate in college, so here's what you can do: if you can rewrite the thesis and summarize what you learned from your research on the final exam, I will drop the grade. In the meantime, buy a style manual and learn to write."

At the campus bookstore, I bought and studied *The Elements of Style* by Strunk & White, Dr. Bierk dropped the D - - - -, and I received a "B" for the semester. A second chance from a teacher who had allowed me to rewrite a poorly planned, sloppily researched and carelessly revised assignment nudged me along the writing path towards a career as an English teacher. Years later, on a brief visit to the new Humanities building at Southeast Missouri State University, I saw Dr. Bierk—both of us much older—leaning across a desk in the main office and talking with students. Even though I wanted to thank him for helping me, I did not want to interrupt his conversation which I imagined was as important to the students then as mine had been thirty five years earlier, so I came home and wrote him a letter—one of many thank you notes, he, no doubt, had received throughout his career.

Besides stories about family, reading, and writing, my "herstory" will also include tales about hiking in the Grand Canyon, playing "A" level tennis, riding in a hot air balloon in Wyoming, fishing for salmon in Alaska, eating in a Hemingway's favorite café on Rue du Montparnasse, crying at Shakespeare's grave in Stratford-on-Avon, breaking a finger at Mardi Gras in New Orleans, seeing "Chicago" performed on Broadway, attending an awards ceremony in the White House Rose Garden, snorkeling in the Caribbean, sightseeing in Russia, walking through the Roman catacombs, and eating a picnic lunch at Thoreau's Walden Pond.

I am still collecting "hallmark" stories and still enjoy sharing them. In my classroom, all I have to do is stop in the middle of a lesson and say, "And that reminds me of a story." All heads turn towards me waiting to see what will come next. As I recall the adventures, experiences and people who have touched and influenced my life, I realize that my journey will take many more paths and many more doors will open. About journeys, Walt Whitman wrote, "Failing to fetch me at first keep encouraged/Missing me one place search another, I stop somewhere waiting for you." Like Whitman, I will probably have another story to share when you find me.

Your Turn:
A "hallmark" story involves an event that signifies a point which changed you, taught you an important life lesson, impacted your learning and helped you reach a new level of maturity. That event becomes your trademark story that could have only happened to you at that particular time. For this assignment, choose an event from your life and write a letter in which you share that experience with your future grandchild. As you write, think about how your grandchild might feel about you and how the story you share might influence them in some way.

What Are Elements of Narration?

REPORTER'S FORMULA	FICTION	NONFICTION
Who does the narrative involve?	Characters	People
Where does the narrative take place? When does it take place?	Setting (time, season, mood, weather, atmosphere)	Place (time, season, mood, weather, atmosphere)
What happens? What is the turning point? Climax? Resolution?	Plot	Series of events
How do events affect and/or change the characters? How are they motivated?	Conflict	Problem
Why are events, experiences important, significant, meaningful or purposeful for both the reader and the writer?	Theme (insight about human nature and experiences)	Thesis (an idea that defines writer's purpose and guides readers)

A Story Board Can "Map" Sequence of Events in Narration

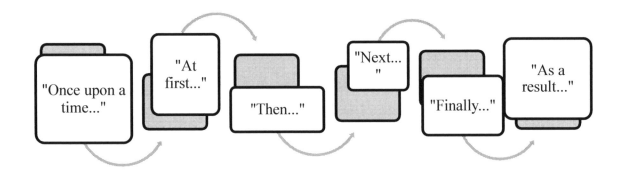

"Once upon a time..." "At first..." "Then..." "Next..." "Finally..." "As a result..."

Your Turn:
Choose a favorite fairy tale, originally written to teach young children moral lessons, and draw pictures that "map" out the sequence of events, or plot, in the tale. Don't worry about your artwork. Just get out your crayons and have fun.

How Can I Combine Elements Into a Story?

All stories, whether "true" in nonfiction, or "made-up" in fiction, contain the same elements. Many true narratives appear stranger than fiction; many fiction stories seem totally believable. The way that authors combine the elements makes them memorable to readers.

Character	Setting	Conflict	Object	Theme/Big Idea
Donkey	An athletic field	Aliens invade a city (Individual vs. Society/individual)	A gold key	Trusting others makes life more meaningful.
Musician	A forest	Transportation breaks down. (Individual vs. Technology)	A jar of jelly	Stay true to our dreams.
Knight	A mountain top	An animal approaches (Individual vs. Nature)	A diary	Laughter is the best medicine.
Ghost	A classroom	A character loses a job (individual vs. Fate)	A pebble	Courage will overcome obstacles.
Sales Clerk	A castle in Europe	A friend shoplifts CD's (individual vs. Self)	A hammer	Sometimes wishes come true.
Airline Pilot	A Shopping Mall	An image appears in a mirror (Individual vs. Supernatural)	A cup	Taking a risk brings maturity.

Your Turn:
With a partner, or team, choose one item from each of the categories and write a brief story. Then create a "storyboard," or "map" to make sure you have organized the story elements into logical, sequential order. Plan to share by reading it aloud with classmates, or friends, in a Read-Around.

Note: an "object" is a plot device whose sole purpose is to help move the events of the plot towards the resolution, or ending.

How Are Plots, Topics and Themes Different?

Fire and Flame

The leaves fell,
spiraling downward,
the hand of the wind
guiding their descent.
The small children
rushed and danced
and played in the colors,
burying themselves in
piles
like animals in their burrows.
Sometimes all you could see
was a shoe or
a red piece of flannel
from a light fall jacket.
The children gathered the leaves
by handfuls or
armfuls or
as many as they could carry
to take home and show Mother.

Mother loved these simple gifts,
but she never let inside.
"The leaves must stay in the yard,"
she always told the children.
So the children took the leaves
and ran in the yard and
opened their hands and
opened their arms and
freed the leaves to dance
once more in the wind,
twisting and
turning and
spiraling toward the earth
in erratic patterns,
coloring the air and
earth with fire and flame.
                    ~**Kristen Treadwell, (1995:97)**

Plot	Topic/Subject	Theme
A summary, written in paragraph form, of the events that occur in a poem, story or novel. To find the plot, ask, "What happens?"	Topics in prose and poetry listed in words and phrases. To find the topic, ask, "What is it about?"	The "big idea" the author tries to convey about the subject stated in a complete sentence. To find the theme, ask, "What is it **_really_** about?"
Example: In "Fire and Flame," children playing in piles of fall leaves, try to give them to their mother who, even though she loves the fall leaves, does not want them inside the house. They return them to the yard where they continue tossing them in the air as they play.	**Example:** 1. Children's games 2. Colors in the Fall 3. Mothers and children 4. Changing seasons	**Example:** Children, nature's most perfect creations, learn through play, song and dance which sometimes appears "messy" to adults.

How Do Abstract Nouns Identify Themes?

Writers **imply** themes—the "big idea" in a story—the general statement about life in general, the author suggests or states. When readers **infer** or determine the idea behind—and between the lines—written on the page, they reach a new awareness and understanding. Since an abstract noun names an idea, you can use one, or a combination of the following abstract nouns when trying to determine the theme, or "big idea" in fiction and poetry.

Abstract Nouns

Ambition	Faith/loss of faith	Patriotism
Appearance vs. Reality	Falsity/Pretense	Past/Future
Custom/Tradition	Family/Home	Parenthood
Betrayal	Free will/Will power	Patriotism
Bureaucracy	Games/contests/Sports	Poverty
Chance/Luck/Fate	Generations	Prejudices/Stereotypes
Children/Birth	Greed	Prophecy
Creativity	Guilt	Racism
Coming of Age	Old Age	Repentance
Courage/Cowardice	Heart vs. Reason	Rebellion
Cruelty/Violence	Heaven/Paradise/Utopia	Renewal
Defeat/Failure	Heroes and Villains	Revenge/Retribution
Despair/Discontent	Initiation/Rite of Passage	Ritual/Ceremony
Disillusionment	Individualism vs. Conformity	Sexism/Feminism
Domination/Suppression	Illusion vs. Reality	Scapegoat/Victim
Dreams/Fantasies	Journeys	Slavery/Bondage
Duty/Loyalty	Law/Justice	Supernatural
Environment	Language and Culture	Time/Eternity
Education/School	Loss and Grief	Tricks/Behavior
Escape/Exile	Materialism vs. Spiritualism	War/Peace

Your Turn:

Find a short piece of narration—a poem or an anecdote—and create a chart like the one on the previous page that analyzes its plot, topic/subject and theme. Remember, you are looking for "What happens?" "What is it about?" "What is it really about—the 'big idea'?"

How Do I Write a "Theme Statement?"

Most effective writers analyze the efforts of other, more accomplished writers. As you read, learn to study the ways writers choose words, create sentences and use techniques of language to communicate a writer's theme, the "big idea," the main purpose and message. Below are some sample sentences stating possible themes in famous pieces of literature:

Catcher in the Rye by J.D. Salinger
The illusion that we can condemn what we see as imperfect is as naïve as the belief we can flee an imperfect world. Part of maturing means we embrace a world we believe is flawed.

Huckleberry Finn by Mark Twain
Our journeys and experiences often force us to confront lies, prejudice and falsity in society.

Hamlet, Prince of Denmark by William Shakespeare
As we mature, the ability to question what we have learned to hate or condemn becomes necessary if we are to gain wisdom.

Use these models to help you write a strong theme statement:
Draft: The purpose of the short story, "The Most Dangerous Game" by Richard Connell is to [question the **nature of violence** when the hunter becomes the hunted.]

Revision: In the short story, "The Most Dangerous Game" Richard Connell questions the **nature of violence** when the hunter becomes the hunted.

Note: Remember, that the best stories and novels may have many themes. Your goal is to choose one, and then offer evidence that explains and supports your opinion.

Use these suggestions to analyze theme:
1. Reduce the piece of writing to one abstract noun.
2. Expand the noun into a phrase that connects to the composition.
3. Write a sentence that states the theme, or "big idea." Avoid clichés.
4. Cite at least three quotations in the text that can support and prove your analysis of the author's theme.

Your Turn:
Choose a favorite fairy tale, fable or nursery rhyme, and write a thematic statement using the suggestions and models provided in this lesson. What does the "big idea"—the main message and purpose seem to be? Avoid clichés.

How Do I Choose A Point of View?

Writers choose a narrator, or point of view, deliberately. In an essay, the author looks at a subject, or topic, from an angle or position. In a story, or poem, the author chooses the character to relate the events that occur. In each case, the author's point of view determines the level and amount of information readers receive and understand about events, characters, places—or ideas. Generally, a writer can choose either participant or non-participant points of view, and the choice of point of view can change a piece of writing and its effect on readers. Below, you can read characteristics and samples each point of view:

I. **Participant Point of View—First Person:**
    1. Allows the reader to understand only what the "I" understands;
    2. Understands and grasps the inner thoughts of only one person or character;
    3. Summarizes events and then retreats to think about their importance;
    4. Contributes to dramatic irony—the difference between what the narrator knows and what the reader understands;
    5. Provides an "eyewitness" account.

Model:

"I broke my retainer again today. I was taking off my green shorts, it fell out of my pocket, and I stepped on it. Luckily, it broke cleanly so I glued it together. Then I remembered I had left it in my pocket when I had taken it out. I wish someone would invent something that would assure your retainer would always return safely to your mouth."
          ~Tricia Ellet, "My Diary," (1995:38)

II. Non-participant Point of View—Omniscient

1. Observes, Godlike, all the actions and describes all the thoughts and feelings of all the characters and participants;
2. Can shift focus from a close view to a larger perspective;
3. Comments on events and characters, explaining and interpreting their significance and motivations to the reader.

Model:

"She knew from the moment the two of them walked in the door that she wouldn't be refilling their cups. They were only drinking coffee, and coffee was a free refill. He sat across from her at the booth and watched the waitress glide by, distractedly asking her for some more coffee, please. He didn't really think he would get any coffee, nor did he really want any more."
          ~Justin Storms, "Café" (1995:28)

III. Non-participant Point of View—Third Person Limited

1. Creates the authenticity and realism of life;
2. Allows readers to watch people and events through the eyes and mind of a single person;
3. Understands everything about a particular character;
4. Unifies a story more than other points of view;
5. Implies a sense of distance from other characters.

Model:

"For several months he had lived in this forgotten cave along the subway tracks. The floor of the cave was traced with abandoned trash and rat droppings and the walls, which enclosed him, used to be pale yellow, but now they were black with the dirt of time. The ceiling was home to a family of roaches that liked to be upside down and Joel admired them for that."

~David Ortiz, "Miserable World" (1995:112)

In the poem below, who is telling the story? Which point of view did the poet choose to describe the people in the scene? What is the narrator's attitude towards "them?" How do you know?

American Credit

Strutting a neon lit avenue
they display their merchandise
on a pot hole plagued road.

They huddle together
to avoid the biting wind
and wait for some sordid wretch
in search of cheap illegal labor
to exploit their situation.

They swarm any vehicle,
not even inquiring
as to what the work will be
or what they'll get paid;
knowing they'll be left
if they stop to ask.

Just three rules:
No checks
No credit cards
Solamente dinero…
Amigo.

—Harbeer Sandhu (1993:52)

Your Turn:
Choose a topic and then write about it from different points of view. For instance, how would a soldier describe a battle in war? A general in his headquarters observing events through binoculars?

How would a student in danger of failing a state-mandated test discuss its importance? A legislator or school administrator?

How would a senior citizen describe a sunset in the hill country? A teenager who needs to follow a curfew and make it home before dark?

How would a homeless man describe his place on a corner? A policeman? A driver of a sports car? Notice, how you choose different words and details for different audiences.

How Do I Write Conversation and Thoughts?

Readers love to read what characters and people are thinking and saying in a narrative essay or short story. However, even the most imaginative writers cannot communicate effectively if they do not punctuate dialogue correctly. When writing dialogue, it helps to follow these basic suggestions:

1. Enclose direct words and thoughts—everything actually being said, or thought, in quotation marks. For example:

   "John," Mary **whispered**, "you are very handsome."

   "John is very handsome," Mary **thought.**

2. Begin a new paragraph whenever a different person begins to speak. Once readers understand which characters are talking, or thinking, you may eliminate "dialogue tags" like "said," "thought," "replied," "answered." For example:

   "John, have you ever seen the Astros play from a box seat? Well, my boss gave me two tickets, and I hate to drive downtown by myself."
   "Sure. I'd love to go. One time, my brother and I went with some friends from college, and we watched the game from behind first base. But, I bet the view would be better from the seats you have."

Note: Always remember to indent and make a new paragraph when you change speakers.

Your Turn:

What characters say, and the reaction they provoke in other characters help to define their personalities for readers. One way to do this is to develop a picture of your characters through conversation. Now, practice writing dialogue that creates pictures, write conversations for the characters involved in one of the following situations below:

- A girl meeting her father at the door when she's two hours late from her date.
- A boy meeting a father after he took a girl home two hours late from a date.
- A boss firing an employee who needs the job, but has not performed well.
- A mother telling her ninety-year-old mother that she will have to go to a nursing home.
- A teenager asking a rock star or famous athlete for an autograph.
- A salesman selling a teenager his/her first car.
- A husband/wife telling their children they will be getting a divorce.

How Can I Use Slang and Dialect?

Today, we often speak a mixture of slang, colloquialisms and everyday "chitchat." This kind of informal language helps show the character and personality of the character, or person, speaking. Take some time to listen to everyday conversation around you—especially, the phrases and pauses that occur without thinking when talking with others. Sometimes, this kind of language can make reading harder if used too much. The one true test of dialogue is that it sounds like real people talking.

Spain

Before the sun melts
Behind the green-shaded hills,
Un *barco grandee* sails across the world,
Bringing *los pasajeros* to an easy halt.
The boat horn screams
And *el* conductor announces,
"Madrid capital *de Espana*. Enjoy."
Six bulls run down main street
Ready to fight at the *Plaza de Torros*.
Here is the field where loyal *afficianadoes*
Join to watch *futbol,* and *ruido*
Of the *mercadoes, personas, estadios, y los trenes.*
Remember to watch el sol
die behind the mountains.
> **—Angela Freeman (1996:12)**

Deranged

Are you staying after school today?
Yeah.
Why?
I have to type.
For what?
Aquilae Stilus.
Again?
Why?
'Cuz I have to.
Why?
I dunno.
Is it fun?
What do you think?
Do you type your own stuff?
No.
You type <u>other</u> people's stuff?
Uh huh.
How long do you type?
Couple of hours.
WHY?
I DON'T KNOW!!!
Is it worth it?
I'm not sure yet.
You're stupid.
Okay. I am..
Are you staying tomorrow?
Uh huh.
Do you have a life?
WHY DO YOU DO IT?
"Cuz I'm mad. I'm stark raving mad.
Is it worth it?
Yeah.
> **—Loubel Cruz, (1995:46)**

> **Your Turn:**
> Review one of the "Your Turn" exercises in your Writer's Notebook and revise it by adding dialect, words and phrases, that help to identify a person or culture. Make sure that you provide enough context clues so that your readers can "guesstimate" the meaning of the words you have used and the identity of the people talking.

What Other Techniques Help Tell Stories?

Your Turn:
Use your own knowledge and experiences with literature to find   definitions and create examples of the terms most frequently associated with stories, novels, films and dramas. When you "get stuck," you can use the Internet to find definitions and examples, or just run your finger over the word on your digital device to find a definition. Record the terms, definitions and examples in your Writer's Notebook.

Eight Basic Plot Lines (Maybe)
- Voyage & Return
- The Quest
- Group/Individual in Environment
- Boy meets Girl
- Revenge for either real or imagined injustice
- Fish out of Water
- Rags to Riches
- "Fish out of Water"

Literary Genres
- Sci-fi/fantasy
- Rite-of - Passage
- Mystery/horror
- Humor
- Romance
- Adventure
- Fable/Fairy Tale
- Historical Fiction

Literary Devices in Fiction and Nonfiction

- Flashback
- Foreshadowing
- Symbolism
- Plot (exposition, rising action, turning point, climax, denouement)
- Setting
- Protagonist/Antagonist
- Allegory
- Foil
- Comic relief
- Parable
- Characterization
- Complication
- Irony
- Point of view
- Apocalyptic
- Archetype
- "in media res"

LESSON 6.
DESCRIPTION:
THE "VOICE" OF OBSERVATION

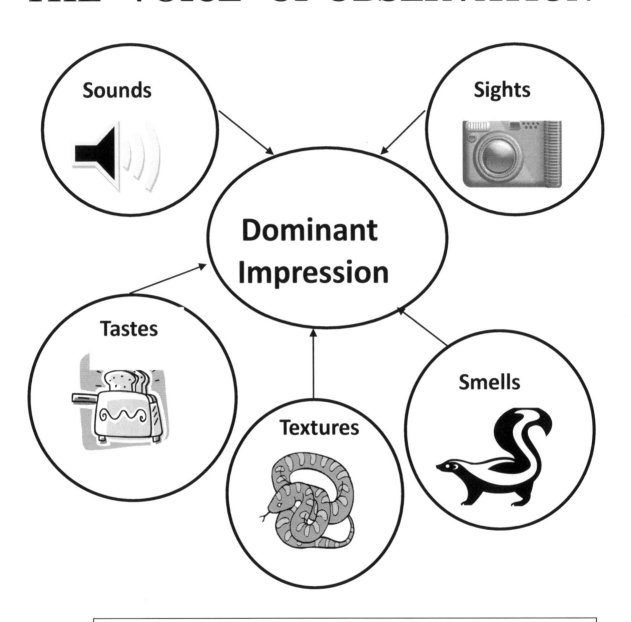

"Let these describe the indescribable."
—Lord George Gordon Byron (1788-1824)

What Is Description?

Just for a minute, imagine your world without colors—grass without green, sky without blue, sun without yellow. Imagine a world that has only one musical note, and where everything feels like corduroy, tastes like salt and smells like lavender. Our senses of taste, touch, hearing, sight and touch guide us down unknown paths, help us choose food, warn us of danger, and help us understand human emotions. Our senses are so important that when we lose one through blindness or deafness, our other senses work overtime to compensate for those losses.

Writing description demands that writers use their senses to be in close touch with the world around them. They must observe people, places and objects carefully and then record them realistically and vividly. Skilled and mature writers use these powers of observation to recreate the same scenes they may have experienced or imagined, and the people they may have known or created. Writers hold readers' attentions by helping them see what the authors have seen, hear what they have heard, taste what they have tasted, smell what they have smelled, and touch what they have touched.

In order to learn from our surroundings and appreciate our world, we should have knowledge of facts, details and events, and in order to appreciate our worlds, we need to engage our senses. It also helps if writers are sensitive to their readers and write so that they can identify with the people and places the writers describe. If writers can put themselves in someone else's place, physically and psychologically, they can become more aware of other people's emotions, attitudes and ideas.

The elements of description—concrete details, imagery and figures of speech—recreate those pictures in the "mind's eye" of the reader and can improve almost any essay, story and poem. Professional writers use the language of description to sell us products, bring life to essays, stories and articles, enrich our communications and influence our thinking. Writing good descriptions tests our powers of observation and helps us become more aware of our worlds and our experiences.

Once student writers master the techniques used to tell stories through narrative techniques and create word pictures through description, they can combine them with other methods and other forms of essays: comparison/contrast, cause and effect, definition, classification and most importantly, narration, exposition and argumentation.

Writers use observation and imagination to create pictures in readers' minds.

One Place: Two Descriptions

Hayti, Missouri 2003 [1]

Hayti, Missouri, a town in the southeast corner of Missouri, an area known as the "bootheel," is located between St. Louis and Memphis, Tennessee, on Interstate highway 55. Hayti has a population of approximately 3,000 people. Farming is the main occupation. The Burlington Northern railroad serves the community and makes seven freight stops a day. The nearest public airport is Mid-Continent. Its runway is 3,200 feet long with a sod surface, is not lighted, and it has no storage. Maintenance is available, but fuel is not.

The Greyhound bus line also serves transportation needs with stops between St. Louis and Memphis. The City of Hayti has 52 acres available for new businesses within the confines of the industrial park. Companies currently located in the park are Loxcreen, an aluminum extruder company, and United Parcel Service. Thirty-six businesses including Clevenger Drug Store, Whitener Monuments and Barkovitz's department store comprise the Chamber of Commerce.

Hayti's public elementary, junior high and high schools are located next to each other at the north end of the town between the park and the cemetery. In 2003, Hayti graduated 55 seniors; 25% of them had children under 3 years old. Currently, the high school is undergoing a 2.3 million dollar renovation project.

Mayor Herb DeWeese and other city officials oversee the business of the community from City Hall, a two-story building, located on the town square in the center of the business district.

The Town Square 1959 [2]

Boys and girls, hair braided in cornrows and pigtails sat on curbs behind the truck stop, ate day-old bologna sandwiches and drank RC colas. On Saturdays, they clutched dimes to buy Turkish taffy from the jars at the front of the store where I worked.

Behind the boarding house, train whistles echoed across the streets that rippled with the heat that burned our bare feet gritty with dirt as we ran across them on a summer day. Old men, in denim blue overalls, sat at a long table at the railway boarding house, waiting, forks in the air, for my friend's grandmother to serve lunch, their main meal of the day. They never spoke a word to each other as we watched them through the open porch window, their heads nodding and jerking with each bite of roast beef and mashed potatoes.

On the other side of town, men, women and children, heads covered with red bandanas, burlap sacks folded across their laps, rode trucks to the cotton fields, where they stooped in the summer sun. Their hands, cut and scarred, picked cotton from its prickly shells. A hundred pounds a day earned enough to buy food for a meal that night.

Shadow figures swayed behind green-tinted windows at the pool hall that I walked past on the way to the Library. They sat on red leather stools, and clinked coins in the jukebox. At noon, jazz and blues mingled with the Methodist's Church chimes that signaled a workday half-finished.

After school, we sipped marshmallow Cokes at the drug store counter; on Saturday nights, we waltzed in pairs at the Skate-around and on Sunday morning, we wore starched white shirts and dresses to our churches.

Your Turn:
Underline the statistical data and other facts used in this description. Use this model to help you write an objective description in your Writer's Notebook.

Your Turn:
Highlight phrases that appeal to readers' senses of sight, smell, hearing, taste and touch. Use this model to help you write a subjective description.

How Are Objective and Subjective Descriptions Different?

Objective description assumes that writers can accurately and factually describe people, places, animals, objects and scenes as they truly are, regardless of the personal perceptions, associations and impressions in the mind of an individual writer. The **factual and objective** description proclaims: **This is the way it is.**

Subjective description assumes writers are entitled to personal reactions, responses, impressions, feelings about subjects they see, hear, smell, taste, or touch. In the process of describing, writers often reveal as much about themselves as their subjects. The **personal, subjective** description proclaims: **This is the way it appears to me—the writer.**

	Objective	Subjective
Purpose	To present information	To present, or make, an impression
Approach	Factual , unbiased, neutral	Personal, interpretive , biased
Appeal	To reader's understanding	To reader's emotions
Tone	Matter-of-fact, detached	Sentimental, provocative, emotional
Development	Complete, exact details	Selective, some facts and details
Language	Simple, clear, factual	Rich, suggestive , evocative, literary
Point of View	3rd person limited or omniscient	1st person
Uses	Industry, government, business, professions	Plays, poems, personal narratives, and memoirs

Your Turn:
Choose a place that has special meaning for you, and write two different descriptions: an objective, factual and unbiased view and an emotional, subjective and interpretive view. See the models on page 76 to help you.

How Do Words Appeal to Readers' Senses?

As a writer, if you want to make your essays and compositions "come alive," you will choose words that help your readers see what see what you see, smell what you smell, taste what you taste, hear what you hear and touch what you touch. To get a "feel" for writing description, choose **one** phrase from each group below and write a sentence that appeals to a reader's senses. As you write, try to create similes using "like" or "as." "Show Don't Tell." Avoid the obvious and remember that food usually appeals to all of the senses—a reason it is so hard to stay on a diet.

Sights:
1. Eating potato chips
2. A jet landing
3. Traffic on a highway

Smells:
1. bar-b-q
2. A gym locker
3. a dentist's office

Tastes:
1. Peanut butter
2. A hot pepper
3. Ice cream

Sounds:
1. A rainy afternoon
2. A tornado or hurricane
3. The cafeteria at lunch

Textures:
1. Walking barefoot on a surface of your choice
2. Smoothing wrinkles in corduroy, silk, or cotton shirt
3. Making a mud pie.

Student Voices: Legends

Early morning light
breaks over the horizon
of slumbering stars.
Remnants of a fire
crackle to ashes,
snores echo
through canyon walls.
Two horses stomp,
chasing dream cows
and Indian raiders.
An owl swoops
from its nocturnal perch.
A rustle, awake
time to get up
to find food
and cover tracks,
to saddle horses
and set off once more
into that undiscovered day
beyond the sunrise.
    —Dave Lankford (1995: 21)

Your Turn:
Find a favorite photograph of a place you visited, or a house where you lived, a family event you remember. Then, write a description that "recreates" a moment in time that occurred just when the camera snapped the photo. Include many details that help the reader experience that moment just as you did. Do not use the first person pronouns, "I," "me," or "my," so your readers focus on the scene rather than on you.

How Does Imagination Create Description?

As you practice, it helps developing writers to put themselves in someone else's place to become more aware of that person's attitudes and emotions. If writers try to imagine what it might be like to be an object—a pencil or a telephone, for instance—they can find new ideas about ways to communicate clearly. We call making an idea or object appear lifelike by providing details associated with human characteristics **personification**.

Study the models in this section to see how this paragraph personifies both a chain saw and a pine tree. Pay close attention to the writer's use of specific nouns and action verbs.   What does the author want to show in each of the descriptions? Who seems to be speaking in each of the selections? How do you know?

A Chain Saw

The chain saw snarls, bucks and bites through white pine and spits out chunks of wood. The tree sways, trembles and the saw bites deeper. After its final cut, the pine tree groans, begins to teeter. The saw rips deeper and tears at the pine's core. The tree sways again, hesitates and a shudder passes down its length. After the saw shuts down, the pine's groan becomes crackling, mortal—imperceptible at first. But gravity's pull forces the tree to fall through its neighboring trees; it shatters limbs—theirs and its own. The noise crescendos as the pine tree crashes to earth.

~ **Lynne Dozier**

Underline the action verbs. Circle the concrete nouns used in this paragraph.

Student Voices: Hey, Kid!

Hey, Kid!
Don't you dare
drive me fast
squeal my tires
splash through mud
kill small animals
chip my paint
dent my bumper
stain my seats
blow my speakers
or I'll break down on you
the last place
you'll EVER want to walk.
~**Bryan Clifton (1993:52)**

Underline the action verbs. Circle the concrete nouns used in this poem.

Your Turn:

Describe a process you are familiar with—a fire destroying a home, a motorcycle climbing a hill, water rushing through a canyon, a garbage disposal chewing up food, a car going through an automatic car wash.

Your Turn Again:

Write a few sentences in which you imagine you are an object or animal.   What is life like for you? What makes you happy? Sad? What are your hopes and aspirations? How do others treat you? How do you affect other objects or animals?

Write one description as a paragraph and the other one as a poem. Read them several times aloud to decide how you want to use punctuation.

Descriptive Essay: Berlin—A Place[3]

Imagine Washington, D.C as a barren plain: Pennsylvania Avenue covered with rubble and ruins, the White House a burned out shell, the Washington Monument, half its height, the obelisk torn and jagged. Imagine steps leading to the Capitol as the only entrance left standing and the Smithsonian Institute, broken and gutted, the history of a nation scattered over miles of empty streets.

If you can imagine the damage to those buildings, then you can picture Berlin, Germany at the end of World War II. Berlin once held sixty synagogues where 176,000 Jewish citizens worshipped; today, only 15,000 Jewish men, women and children attend five synagogues. That statistic testifies to the real devastation Hitler caused for Berlin during the "Nazification" of social institutions and the spread of Hitler's racist, intolerant, tyrannical political and economic leadership.

After Allied bombs destroyed over 90% of the original structures, the architects and engineers redesigned and rebuilt Berlin. Today, tourists can ride a hot air balloon over the bunker where Hitler, and his mistress, Eva Braun, committed suicide. Grass and weeds grow wild where the Gestapo headquarters and its torture chambers once stood, marked by a sign, "Topography of Terrors," written in English. In some buildings, square patches of concrete fill the holes left by Allied bullets and bombs dropped on Berlin in 1945. The front end of a United States C-45 airplane protrudes from the wall of the German National Museum of Science—a symbol of the Berlin Airlift, which delivered food and medical supplies to Berlin's starving and sick population when the war ended.

A concrete and marble bookshelf in front of Potsdam University marks the place where college students, at the urging of Hitler Youth dressed in brown-shirted uniforms, burned 20,000 books in the early days of the Third Reich. Now, in Berlin, hotels on Kant, Budapesta and Kingelhoffer streets with names like The Palace, The Forum, and the Inter-Continental, compete for tourists with Holiday Inn, Hilton and The Westin. Shops offer Cartier diamonds, Rolex watches, and Versace scarves. Foot Locker, the Gap and Office Depot offer products to people who work and live in the area. The bombed out shell of the Kaiser Wilhelm Memorial Church, stands as a reminder of the great war that destroyed this city in 1945. The church's bell tower, called "hollow tooth" by Berliners, chimes every hour.

Today, men and women, most born after World War II, hold key positions in the German government and military. In school, students learn little about Hitler or World War II in their textbooks, and like American teenagers, listen to "rap," play video games and watch movies. Berlin has covered its memories—and its nightmares— with tree-lined sidewalks, concrete parking lots, and four lane intersections. It has built over its history with glass, chrome, brass and marble. This current generation of German leaders and citizens, eager to sell cars, televisions, crystal vases and kitchen knives, has grown older and wiser and seems comfortable declaring a clean slate. They show a willingness to move into a future that has forgotten—or at least hidden—its past.

> **Your Turn**:
> Make a list of all the historical and factual places, people and events mentioned in this description of modern day Berlin. Use the Internet to find out more information about each of them.

How Do I Describe a Place?

Usually, descriptive paragraphs are written using spatial order; left to right; top to bottom, inside to outside, outside to inside. The use of transitional words and phrases can help the reader to follow the order. A paragraph frame like the one below can also help you learn to organize description. Italics indicate transitional words. To practice with a paragraph "frame," that includes transitional words,   write a short description of a classroom, your bedroom, or another room you know well using the model below:

At the front of the room _____ .*On*

one wall _____ . *On the opposite wall*

_____ . _____ occupy

most   of the room. The floor is _____ .

_____ are visible *from the door. In one corner*

_____ . *In the other* _____

The whole room feels as if _____ .

Your Turn.

During the next 24 hours, find a time to visit a place where you can observe activity which has many sounds—a mall, a park, the lunchroom, your backyard. When you choose a place where the sounds are interesting, rhythmic, musical, or harsh, record what you hear in a list. Then, use the following paragraph "frame" to help you use the sounds to help write a paragraph about the scene.

I am sitting (on, in, at) _____ . I hear _____ and _____ and _____ . They sound like _____ . They remind me of a time _____ when _____ _____ . The sounds make me feel as if _____ . When I hear them, I always think about _____ .

When you finish, share your paragraph with your writing group. Ask them to draw pictures (yes, you can use crayons) that illustrate the place described in the paragraph. Then, vote on the description which best creates pictures in readers' minds. Next, select a member of your team to read the winning paper aloud to the rest of the class.

Descriptive Essay: France —The People[4]

From behind the sunglasses' black lens, I am an anonymous voyeur—just another woman sitting on a bench in front of a hundred year old maple tree—eating a tomato and mozzarella sandwich from its paper wrapping. Ironwork balconies and shuttered windows, with blue, red and green clothespins hanging empty on clotheslines, surround the Plaza of the Hotel De Ville.

However, the balcony windows do not hold my attention for long. A street musician, dressed in a black T-shirt, black sport coat and black beret (yes, French men really do wear berets), begins to play the theme from *Les Miserables* on his flute. His notes compete with the sounds of a saxophone coming from around the corner. I lean back against the tree, enjoying the concert, the sun and the hum of voices from the people eating lunch and drinking wine in the cafes.

Then, from the other side of the square, a man, grey and balding, red-faced and bent, takes a seat on the edge of the fountain in the center of the square. He unstraps a duffel bag, extracts a guitar and amplifier and connects them together. He takes off his dirty, denim jacket, bends over, wiggles his behind at the onlookers and dances a few steps to a beat only he can hear. He then begins to warm up, playing chords, which to my untrained ear, sound like the jazz guitar sounds of Pat Metheny, Ottoman Liebert or Stevie Ray Vaughan in melancholy moments.

The next minute, the flutist rushes from between the tables where he had been passing his beret and collecting coins. He curses and waves his arms at the old man playing the guitar. His threatening voice   disturbs the old man who hurriedly shoves everything—guitar, amplifier, denim jacket—back into the bag and stumbles off through the rows of tables and chairs. He staggers into a café on the shady side of the square without looking back at the place in the square where he had just played his music.

For another hour, I watch a variety of street musicians come and go, in the center of the square—as if each had an assigned time on the lunchtime entertainment program. First, a father and teenage son who play 50's Roy Orbison and Jerry Lee Lewis rock and roll, some blues a la Eric Clapton and B.B. King appear. The father does a little Jimi Hendrix move, his guitar above his head, behind his back and between his legs while the son collects money in a leather pouch.

Another guitarist, wearing baggy, African print pants, enters the scene, almost as if on cue. A gold trumpet hangs on a chain around his neck— a bright object shining against his black shirt. He leans his bicycle against the maple tree, props his guitar next to me on the bench, and walks across the square to a store on the corner. I reach over, pat the coolness of the guitar and reassure myself that the whole scene is real—and not part of a script in a bad French movie with hard-to-read subtitles.

The audience returns to their food, wine and conversation. They ignore the sound of my pen moving across the yellow page as I record the details I have just observed. In fact, they even ignore the musician with the gold trumpet who has returned, drink in hand, to play Cole Porter 40's era American show tunes in the sun dappled square.

Your Turn:

Use the following chart to identify and list the descriptive words and phrases used in the descriptive essay, "France—The People."

Sights	Sounds	Smells	Tastes	Textures

How Do I Describe People?

Appearance can, but does not necessarily, reveal the temperament and personality of a character. The main techniques writers use to describe a person's personality, character traits and temperament include:

1. The author tells the reader directly (John had a mean streak.)
2. The author shows the reader through the character's words ("I have a desire to destroy things," John said.)
3. The character reveals his thoughts directly to the reader ("I would enjoy breaking those wine glasses," John thought.)
4. The character acts (John smashed his fist through the car's windshield.)
5. Other characters tell readers how they feel about a character in question ("I wouldn't go out with John alone," Mary said. "Sometimes, he can be violent.")

Look for   techniques of effective description of a person in the poem below:

Snapping Negatives —An Indian Naming Poem [5]

Her name tells
of her biggest passion and greatest flaw.
Despite her gift to paint with light
for all the villagers to witness,
she fumbles in darkness with thoughts.
She spent her nights stripping
the barbs from feathers,
rather than seeing beauty in broken forms.
Her life was occupied
by a pessimistic spirit in her bones.
She hunted for release
until the answer came
in the barbs beneath her feet.
The snap of a shutter relieved
the burden of her mind.
She slept through the thunder
on even the blackest nights.
Too young in her journey to grasp
The silver clouds,
she focused on the negatives.
                    ~Kirby Gladstein (2010:62)

Your Turn:
Create a short description that reveals a character's temperament and personality. Use at least 2 of the methods mentioned above. You might try describing one of these characters: a young   political rebel; a selfish girl/boy; an impatient parent/teacher; a generous/kind neighbor; a disagreeable and hard-to-please boss. The person you describe can be yourself (although that's hard to do) or a person you invent who is much like you. Try to place it on the page so it looks like a poem.

How Do I Create A Dominant Impression?

An important part of writing effective description involves creating a dominant impression—a mood or atmosphere for your readers. In the descriptive paragraphs you have written, you may have wanted your readers to feel safety, happiness, sadness, suspense or some other emotion, and you created this mood through the use of sensory details and vivid, specific words and language. When writing description, you should also vary your sentence structures and avoid using the same subject-verb pattern in all sentences.

If you want to learn to play a guitar well, you would listen to, and then try to, imitate the particular style of a great guitarist. You can also improve as a writer by studying techniques used by great authors. Study the sentences below, and then create your own sentences based on the patterns like I did. As you practice, look for the main nouns, verbs, and phrases.

1. "He fell back, / exhausted, / his ankle pounding."
                    --Ralph Ellison, "Flying Home"
   John lurched forward, / frustrated, / his hair flying.
                    —Lynne Dozier
2. "Long before the sun/ struck the face of Lookout Mountain, /
      curls of smoke rose/ from the earth houses/at his feet."
                    --Mari Sandoz, "The Birdman"
   **Shortly after the boy /broke the window of the neighbor's house, /
   squeals from sirens/ echoed around the corner/into the street.**
                    —Lynne Dozier
3. "The fields were green / and there were small green shoots / on the vines; / the trees along
      the road had small leaves,/ and a breeze came from the sea."
                    —Ernest Hemingway, *A Farewell to Arms*
   **The roads were bare/ and there were jagged, broken barbs on the fence; the
   birds in the sky had large black wings,/ and the wind blew from the west.**
                    —Lynne Dozier

What mood does each sentence create in the reader?

Your Turn:

Below are four groups of concrete, specific nouns. Choose one of the groups and create a paragraph that describes a place you might find the objects. Be sure you include words that capture the sights, sounds, smells, tastes and textures of the place. Then, create a person and place them in the scene. Try to tell a brief story—an anecdote.

1. Window, mirror, frame, mist, moonlight
2. Shadow, streetlight, puddle, gutter, paper
4. Field, sun, tennis shoe, blade of grass, dirt
5. Shop, saw, wood, dust, thumb

Read your composition to a teammate. Edit all adverbs and adjectives—unless they're "golden." Change all your "be" verbs to action verbs. Rewrite, restructure and rearrange the sentences to provide a variety of patterns and lengths. Save the piece in your Writer's Notebook.

How Can I Describe Ideas?

Hearing a writer's voice, creating images in your mind, reading with your heart and soul, as well as your intellect, can enrich your life, broaden your   experiences and take you to places where dreams—and nightmares—become a reality. Authors can take readers to a witch trial, the future, a riverboat, the Wild West, the roaring Twenties, or a war zone. They can help readers understand hypocrisy, greed, fear, poverty, discrimination and totalitarianism.

Readers often have to work to meet writers halfway on the journey, but understanding some of the generalizations about the way authors think and the ideas they communicate, can help guide the trip. Generally, writers:

♦ Devalue materialism;
♦ Value spirituality over formal religion;
♦ Demonstrate passion for the "carpe diem," or "live for today" theme;
♦ Express thoughts counter to their cultural training;
♦ Become social historians and/or critics;
♦ Value individual rights over the rights of society;
♦ Attack pride;
♦ Look critically at war;
♦ Believe families provide the most dramatic kinds of conflicts.

For an example of a description of an idea, read the poem below that describes "life."

A Secret
 Like every good secret,
lying under the lawnmower in the garage,
behind a favorite book with folded pages,
resting on the tip of your pencil.
Life waits impatiently for someone
to discover its tributaries,
to sift through it,
to pull out the juicy parts
and make up beginnings and ends.
      ~Gavin Daniels (1995:42)

<u>**Your Turn:**</u>
Choose one of the following assignments and follow the directions.
1. Describe a landscape as seen by an old women/old man whose disgusting and detestable old husband/wife has died. Do not mention the husband/wife or death.
2. Describe a lake as seen by a young man/girl who believes he/she has just met the girl/boy of his dreams. Do not mention the girl/boy or the lake.
3. Describe a landscape as seen by a bird. Do not mention the bird.
4. Describe a building as seen by a man/woman whose son has been killed in   war. Do not mention the war, death, or the father/mother.
5. Describe a beach, viewed by a person who has just lost a home in a tropical storm. Do not mention sand or wind.

How Can Transitions Help My Readers?

You must never assume that your readers know what you know. You might be able to leap from one idea to another, but your readers need transitions, or "stepping stones" to help them make connections between paragraphs in expected, accessible and visible places.

Transitions	Use	Examples
besides, what's more, furthermore, in addition, for example, for instance, in other words	To add another thought To add an example or illustration	Two postcards are often more effective than one letter. **Besides,** they are cheaper. He has lost confidence in his game. **For example,** yesterday he got nervous at the end of the match.
in fact, as a matter of fact, therefore, consequently,	To add emphasis to an idea To highlight idea that follows	Last week I was ill; **in fact,** I had to stay in bed until Friday. The president vetoed the bill. **Consequently,** it never became a law.
of course, to be sure, though, still, however, on the other hand, nevertheless, rather	To show an exception To offer an opposing idea	He said he would study all day. I doubt that he did, **though.** I enjoy music; **however,** I don't understand rap and hip hop.
next, finally, meanwhile, later, afterwards, nearby, eventually, above, beyond, in short, in summary, in conclusion	To arrange ideas according to time, space or order of importance To sum up several main points	**First,** drink some juice. **Next,** have a bowl of soup. **Then,** eat the sandwich, and finally have some coffee. Scientists say that we should eat food that contains the proteins, fats, and vitamins we need. **In short,** they recommend a balanced diet.

Your Turn:
Combine drafts of both subjective and objective descriptions into one longer essay. Make sure you use transitions to help your readers make connection between paragraphs.

LESSON 7.
EXPOSITION: THE "VOICE" OF INFORMATION

When I provide evidence to support my opinions and ideas, I sound like an authority—believable and trustworthy.

"**Tell me what you're going to tell me. Then tell me. Then tell me what you told me.**"
—Professor to college students

"**Multiple choice tests show what you *don't* know. Essay tests show what you *do* know.**"
—English Teacher to high school students

What Is Exposition?

The term, "exposition," means, in a general sense, "setting forth." As a method of writing, it is one of the most practical, demanding and useful skills that a person can master.

Expository writing differs from narration, description and persuasion in the response it elicits from readers. After reading narration, readers usually think, "I enjoyed that..." After reading description, they respond, "We saw, heard, smelled, touched and tasted that..." After persuasion, they think, "We're convinced that..." However, after reading exposition, readers should say, "We understand that..." or "We learned that…"

Exposition is the writing of the working world, and the writing that enables the world to work. In college, you will write essays, critiques, case histories, lab reports, abstracts, summaries and research reports asking you to explain what you thought, discovered and learned. After college, whether you work as a lawyer, engineer, manager, doctor or teacher, you will have to write reports, memos, letters, proposals, and summaries explaining what you did, found, accomplished, concluded or recommended. Many of you will never earn a living as writers, but most of you will have to write to earn a living.

Exposition is the method used in research, and it entails thinking logically about a subject, evaluating facts for relevance and truth, organizing materials in support of a purpose. Too often, the reports and presentations we write for classes, standardized tests and businesses are dull, dry and boring. But there is no rule that says they have to be lifeless, unexciting and mind numbing. Expository writing must contain facts and details, examples and illustrations, but effective writers will present their evidence from an interesting angle, discarding irrelevant, obvious and tedious information. Strong and effective expository writing cultivates a lively style, informative as well as entertaining and readable.

Today, the transaction between writers and readers—instant and immediate—demands careful thought attention to detail, and control of diction and syntax. More than ever, in a technological world and media saturated society, we need to communicate in a confident, convincing and concise manner.

Writers communicate information, insights and knowledge to their readers.

Expository Paragraphs: Explaining Values[1]

Love

While washing dishes, I stood at the kitchen window and watched him walk around the edge of the pool, carefully surveying the growth of each flower and shrub in the landscape. Occasionally, he bent over to prune a weary, dead bloom. "He looks old and tired," I thought. "Worrying about his Mom and Dad's health is taking a toll on him. When he has something on his mind, he takes more time watering and caring for his flowers and ferns." Once, when I asked him why he was spending so much time in the yard, he said, "Plants don't talk."

"I have neglected him this summer," I thought. I dried my hands, took a pitcher of water from the refrigerator, filled a tall glass with ice cubes and water and walked outside. I handed him the glass and said, "The kids will go back to Austin today. Tomorrow morning, I'll grind some beans for coffee and fix some French toast. After breakfast, we can go to the hardware store, and then buy a new rod and reel, if you want. And then you can take a nap in the afternoon. How does that sound?"

Solitude.

Upstairs, my husband and I built an office in our youngest son's empty bedroom. We boxed up his swimming trophies, collection of hats, books and model cars. In the empty room, we put two built-in desks and bookcases, a recliner, family photographs, plaques, golf and fishing memorabilia. Now, in place of boys' bunk beds, we have his 'n hers computers. We redecorated our youngest daughter's room for our granddaughters: painted flowers on the wall behind a make-believe picket fence, built shelves for my childhood doll collection, replaced "rock star" posters with paintings of little girls holding flowers. We bought a doll's house, a trundle bed and a children's table and chairs.

In our oldest son's room, we replaced a twin bed with a couch, took out a wall to make a game room, painted the room cranberry red, and put up a wallpaper border with trains. We repaired a 50 year old Lionel train and installed it permanently on a 5' x 7' board—hills, tunnels, train whistles and all. We turned our oldest daughter's room into a guest room, complete with ruffles, lots of pillows, a bedside table with a lamp, a magazine rack and a small desk. We restored a chest that belonged to me as a child, and filled a basket with soaps and shampoos. A vase of silk flowers sits on the chest.

Last week, tired of writing grants, making presentations, and teaching classes, I spent a day without answering the phone, turning on the television or checking my email. During that quiet time, I read magazines, cooked a casserole, baked a cake, folded laundry, and looked out the windows at our backyard—an oasis during the summer and a source of calm all year long. For twenty-five years, the noise of our children filled our home. Today, I cherish my time alone, and the quiet privacy of my own thoughts.

Your Turn:
Choose an important value in your life like hope, trust, patience, or faith and write a few paragraphs that "Show" that value and its importance in your daily routines. As your write provide descriptive details, facts, examples, direct words and thoughts as evidence to support your ideas and opinions.

How Can I Develop Informative Paragraphs?

A paragraph is a group of sentences that share a common topic or purpose. Writers change paragraphs when they change topics, ideas, places, speakers, or sometimes as a visual aid to readers. When you combine several paragraphs to provide support for the thesis, or main idea, you write an essay. For more information about the essay form, review "Lesson 4: The Essay—or 'I-Say.'"

An expository essay generally has three parts:
1. An explanation of purpose, main idea— "Tell me what you're going to tell me."
2. The information you want to communicate— "Then, tell me."
3. A summary — "Now, tell me what you told me."

There is, of course, no set length for an expository essay, but readers should always recognize these essential parts—an introduction, body and conclusion. The main goal of an expository composition is to communicate correct, factual information in a clear, concise and confident—yet interesting—style that we'll discuss in more detail later.

Your Turn:
In your Writer's Notebook, practice communicating information by writing paragraphs that respond to the instructions in the following exercises:

1. **Process** —Imagine a novelist from out of town is staying overnight at a hotel near your home. The following day he will visit your school to talk with students. Write instructions for the process of getting from a hotel to your house and from your house to your school.

2. **Explain** "how to" put in contact lenses, house-train a dog, impress a girl or a guy on a first date, get along with your mother/father, or combine work and leisure.

3. **Define** the following by using examples, comparisons or actions:
   A. A friend is…
   B. Happiness is...
   C. A calculator is…
   D. A "bully" is…

4. **Using Classification and/or Comparison/Contrast:**
   Explain the differences between summer and winter;
   Discuss the ways football and soccer are alike;
   Explain the beauty of a sunset vs. the beauty of a sunrise;
   Discuss the ways rock music and classical music are different;
   Explain the ways these forms of music are alike;
   Discuss different kinds of English teachers—the good, the bad and the ugly!

Why Are Topic Sentences Important?

Writers state the main idea, or topic, of most paragraphs in the **topic sentence,** usually the most important sentence in a paragraph. Sometimes, a   paragraph has an **implied main idea** and the writer provides information that invites readers to infer the function and purpose of the paragraph. When you write well-organized paragraphs, they will usually make a well-organized essay.

Elements of Effective Topic Sentences
Topic + Action Verb + [controlling idea]

Loyalty towards a country's values often inspires [heroic self-sacrifice.
The Federal government should provide [funds for solar power.]

Creating strong topic sentences can help you write paragraphs that communicate clearly, concisely and convincingly the ideas you want to communicate in a paragraph. Like a thesis, they serve as a "rudder" to keep your paragraphs on track.   In this section, you can find several different suggestions and examples of ways to create effective topic sentences that will help you develop and communicate your   idea or opinion.

1. **Generalization:** All boys are good in math. All girls are good in English.
2. **Summary:** In conclusion, we know that at least two things cause addiction.
3. **Comparison:** Mark is shorter than Randy.
4. **Contrast:** Jane is quiet, but Susan is noisy.
5. **Cause-effect:** If you put your 100% cotton shirt in the dryer, it will shrink.
6. **Opinion:** I think that she is the best teacher.
7. **Definition:** A peninsula is a piece of land surrounded by water on three sides.
8. **Process:** First, mix the butter and eggs; then, add the dry ingredients; next, beat until well blended.
9. **Problem-solution:** Andrew was skinny and then he began to lift weights.
10. **Example:** The lunch line offered a selection of meats, vegetables, salads, fruits, breads, desserts, and beverages.
11. **Transition***: While* he was sleeping, I slipped out of the room.

Your Turn:
Choose a topic you want to discuss and write a topic sentence that identifies your topic and your controlling idea. Then, write sentences following the prescription below. Each number refers to one of the ten   sentence techniques. For example:
Formula: 3-7-5-6 (comparison, definition, cause-effect and opinion):
John is a nastier than a snake. By nasty, I mean rude and inconsiderate. His rudeness has made him unpopular; I don't think anyone likes him.

Now try these formulas: 4-10-3-2   and 8-6-9-1 or make up your own combination.

How Does "Mapping" Information Help?

When architects design buildings, they use a floor plan to guide the process. A floor plan for a skyscraper would look different from a floor plan of a home or school because the purpose of the building and the people who might use it have different requirements. Just like an architect, a writer should think about structure, or floor plan, of an essay, which can change because of the audience and purpose. In this section, you can find examples of graphic organizers [2] that can help you, determine the best structure for the paragraph or essay you intend to write:

Compare/Contrast
A=Differences
B=Similarities

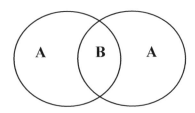

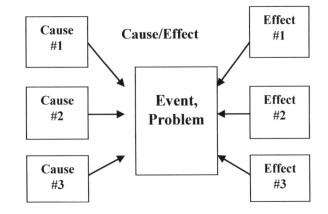

Cause/Effect

Definition

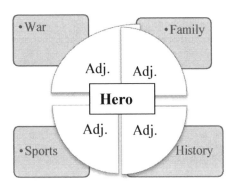

Classification

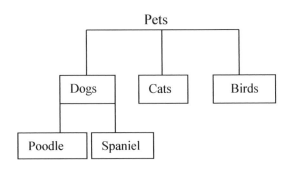

Process—"How to"

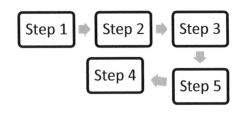

Example, Illustration

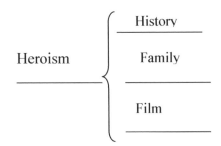

How Can Outlining Information Help?

Using a formal outline can also help you organize your information logically and completely before you start writing. However, sometimes, it helps to use "reverse outlining" to check your organization AFTER you have written an essay. Either way, an outline should identify the most important and least important points in a piece of writing and follow the same pattern and structure. You can use your computer to find outlines for a variety of documents that might look like this example:

Thesis: In Ruby Payne's research with poor and minority students, discussed in her book, *A Framework for Understanding and Communicating with Students and Adults from Poverty,* [3] she found that a majority of students living in poverty did not have access to language's formal register, the register used in most academic situations. The five language registers Dr. Payne discusses are:

I. Frozen language (language that does not change)
  A. Prayers, legal and historical documents
  B. Used by clergy, lawyers

II. Formal Register (language focused on form)
  A. Impersonal, formal presentations
  B. Used by teachers, professors in academic settings

III. Consultative register (conversational language)
  A. Language used in two-way conversations
  B. Used by adults at work and with strangers

IV. Casual Register (general, contains ellipses, slang and profanity)
  A. Language contained in letters and conversations
  B. Used by friends and peers

V. Intimate Register (excludes public information)
  A. Includes jargon, code words,
  B. Message conveyed by tone and melody
  C. Used by spouses, lovers, twins

Conclusion: A person can go from one register to the next register without any conflicts. However, when a person moves from one register to another register, and skips a level or more, this is considered antisocial behavior (Payne, 71).

Your Turn:
Prepare an outline for an article you have read in a magazine or newspaper or on the Internet. Then, prepare to write an essay for class on a topic you have chosen. Use either a "map" or an "outline" to help organize your information before you write.

What is "Bloom's Taxonomy?"

Dr. Benjamin Bloom, along with a team of educators and psychologists, created a taxonomy, or classification, that categorizes levels of thinking that commonly occurs in educational and academic settings. The questions range from easily recalled information to more complex thought processes. "Bloom's Taxonomy" [4] provides a useful structure for categorizing test questions, since teachers and professors design questions and curriculum within particular levels. If you can determine the levels of questions that appear on your exams, you will have tools that will help you study using the most appropriate strategies. The chart below shows these categories and provides examples of action verbs that identify thinking skills.

Evaluation: Making Judgments
Conclude, critique, reframe,
challenge, defend, judge, decide,
appraise, justify,

Synthesis: Putting It Together
compose, combine, express, plan, revise,
generate, propose, create, collaborate,
modify

Analysis: Taking It Apart
Dissect, outline, compare/contrast, debate, inventory,
calculate, diagram, cause-effect, prove

Application: Using Information and Knowledge
illustrate, dramatize, construct, model, prepare, construct,
solve, practice, use

Comprehension: Understanding Meaning
describe, summarize, explain, discuss, translate, classify,
generalize, conclude, paraphrase, predict

Knowledge: Recalling and Recognizing Information
define, list, label, match, memorize, repeat, record, arrange

Your Turn:
Find a test you have taken, or download a practice SAT/ACT/AP test, and beside each question, identify its level according to Bloom's Taxonomy. Look for key verbs to help you.

How Does Exposition Show "Thinking?"

Instructors give essay tests to determine if students can make connections between ideas and apply course information to new situations. The main reason students do not perform well on these kinds of assessments is that they do not understand the task and fail to answer the question completely. These key verbs may help:

Key Verb	Writing Task	Sample Prompts
Analyze	Take something apart to show how it works	Analyze the ways the author uses figurative language to achieve his purpose.
Argue, challenge, defend	Take a stand on an issue and provide evidence to support your position	Argue whether a writer's opinion or idea is valid.
Compare/Contrast	Discuss similarities/differences	Compare and contrast the purposes of Thoreau's "Civil Disobedience" and Martin Luther King's "Letter from the Birmingham Jail."
Define	Provide specific details that make a term, or word, unique	Define the term "romanticism" as it relates to E.A. Poe's poem, "The Raven."
Discuss	Provide examples/illustrations	Discuss how T.S. Eliot uses imagery to express disillusionment with American society in the 30's.
Describe	Create a picture in words	Describe a view from the window of the perspective of two different people.
Evaluate	Show the significance, importance or value of an opinion, ideas, or proposal.	Evaluate the effect of Queen Elizabeth's speech on her audience in 1620.
Summarize	Provide a brief overview of events or important ideas	Summarize the plot of Maya Angelou's *Heart of a Woman*.

Your Turn:
Read a short story or essay and create your own examples of essay questions modeled after the suggestions. Then, write a response to at least one of the questions you created.

What Types of Questions Can I Expect On SAT/AP/ACT Tests?

In general, essay "prompts" and multiple-choice questions fall into just a few categories. When you become familiar with these types of questions, you can understand what information you need to respond to the question and feel more comfortable with the test format so you can work more quickly and efficiently.

1. **Questions about Language:** Most of the questions on standardized tests assess your ability to understand how language works in a passage. They ask you to analyze syntax (word order), diction (word choice), point of view, figures of speech and imagery. However, the ability to recognize these techniques is not enough: you must understand how and why the use of language produces an effect in readers.

2. **Questions about the Author's Meaning and Purpose:** These questions appear frequently and measure your ability to interpret what ideas the authors intend to communicate and what they want to achieve by writing the passage. As with questions about language, these questions are closely tied with the author's choices of diction, images, details, language and syntax (DIDLS).

3. **Questions about Tone, Point of View and Mood:** These questions test your understanding of the author's attitude towards the topic and the tone of the voice used to communicate the main ideas and achieve a mood. To prepare for these questions, you should try to paraphrase and make notes in the margins. You can find suggestions for paraphrasing in "Lesson 12: Analysis."

4. **Questions about Organization and Structure:** For these questions, you need to understand if a passage follows a comparison/contrast structure, if it gives a definition followed by examples, descriptive statements that lead to a generalization, or a series of anecdotes that support an opinion. You also need to understand how one paragraph relates to another paragraph and how a single sentence works within a paragraph.

5. **Questions about Writing Methods, Strategies and Techniques:** These questions ask you to recognize and evaluate the differences between narration, description, argument exposition and creative/imaginative writing. The test makers might also ask you about figures of speech and the use of imagery. You need to understand why a particular method, or technique is effective for communicating an author's ideas, tone or point of view.

> **Your Turn:**
> With your teacher's help, review a practice, or sample,   AP or SAT standardized test. As you read the questions, identify each type according to the list above. Remember, the list does not include all questions. You might encounter some that do not seem to fit into a category, but understanding the main types of questions should increase your familiarity with these kinds of tests and improve your ability to respond.

What Are SAT/AP "Prompts?"

Sometimes, especially on standardized tests, like SAT or Advanced Placement tests,   you will not have a choice of topic. You will be given a "prompt" that might consist of a short passage to read or a thoughtful quotation, questions to help guide your ideas, and then instructions for you to follow. For instance, consider the quotation, questions and instruction included in the prompt below:

Sample SAT "Prompt"

(Quotation):
"That which we obtain too easily, we esteem too lightly. It is dearness only which gives everything its value."

---Thomas Paine

(Questions and Instructions):
Do we value only what we struggle for? Are things that come easily less valuable than things we have to work for? Plan your response, and then write an essay to explain your views on this issue. Be sure to support your position with specific points and examples. (You may use personal examples or examples from your reading, observations, or, knowledge of subjects such as history, literature, science.)

At other times, you might choose your own topic. In either case, you should determine your purpose, write a sentence that states the idea you intend to discuss, gather information, outline or diagram your main points, draft an introduction, body and conclusion and make sure you spend some time revising, editing and proofreading.

Tips" for writing essays for standardized test exams:

1. Read the prompt carefully so you understand the writing task and what you are expected to do. Pay attention to the verbs used in the prompt (see Bloom's Taxonomy).

2. Avoid just summarizing. The instructor/grader has read and studied the passage/quotation used in the prompt. You do not need to 'retell' it.

3. Spend about 5 minutes planning and brainstorming the important points and   information you want to discuss. Use Outlining or "Mapping" to help you.

4. Write a thesis that includes the most important word (s) from prompt, but do not just restate the prompt.

5. Use the clue words— "I think…" "The text says/My proof is…" "And so…" to provide proof/evidence/commentary using the T-E-C formula (*The Writer's Voice*, 99) as a guideline. You should erase those "clue" words before you proofread.

6. Use 3rd person…Do not use "you." Restrain "I."

7. Use "for instance" or "for example" as transitions to help your readers move from point to point and follow your logic.

How Do I Write Essays For Tests?

School assessment—checking your understanding of learning objectives—comes in many forms: lab reports, group discussions, oral/visual presentations, teacher-made tests or standardized state and national tests, many of which will ask you to show your understanding in an essay format. These periodic assessments—whether tests or projects— help both you and your teachers identify strengths and weaknesses, and can, when used correctly, maximize educational achievement.

Teachers, SAT/AP/ACT test administrators and college professors, as part of their training and experiences, understand the need for fairness. They learn quickly to:

1. Read each essay quickly and to assign a score immediately.
3. Read mainly for what the writer has done well.
4. Avoid using length as criteria for evaluation.
5. Keep in mind that any essay even a marginal, or brief, response should be
    judged according to the criteria in the general grading rubric.
6. Remember that each essay is a first draft written under pressure in about 40
    minutes by a young, perhaps struggling writer.

You can understand the importance of writing legible and well-organized essays by placing yourself in the roles of your readers who are often irritated as they pore over page after page, often barely able to decipher hasty scrawls and to follow rambling explanations.

> **Your Turn:**
> Choose a topic, an audience, purpose and strategy from each column   below and write an essay for a teacher that develops the main idea, or thesis, that you intend to communicate. As you write, revise and edit, consider these questions: What details would you include? Leave out? What level of language would you use? Formal or informal? What techniques would best sustain the interest of the audience?

Topic	Audience	Purpose	Strategy/Technique
A sport	A visitor to U.S.	Inform/teach	Facts, details, statistics.
School lunches	Your principal	Entertain/delight	Description,
Political Position	Congressman	Argue/Dispute	Examples, quotations, illustration
A book or film	Parent	Evaluate/Criticize	Cause-effect/ Classification
Memorable Event	College Admissions Officer	Reflect/Contemplate	Anecdote/Metaphor

How Do I Develop Paragraphs for Exams?

The types of essay questions used by teachers, instructors and professors in college classes generally assess students' abilities to show an understanding of information presented in either lectures, assigned readings, or classroom discussions. When writing an "academic" essay, you should remember to incorporate "little bits of quotations" as support for your comments, opinions and ideas.

This formula for Topic, Evidence and Commentary (**T-E-C**) might help you provide "textual" evidence and commentary when responding to something you have read:

> **Boldface: Topic/Assertion (I think...)**
> *Italics: Evidence/Examples (My proof is...the text says...)*
> <u>Underline: Commentary/Interpretation/Analysis (And so—my conclusions..)</u>

Sample Paragraph Showing "T-E-C"

<u>**Prompt:**</u> Discuss the most important message of the article, "Wounding the Spirit: Discrimination and Traditional American Indian Belief Systems" by Carol Locust.

   In her article about the American Indian belief systems, Carol Locust's thesis proposes that American Indians have experienced discrimination because of their traditional beliefs, especially when those beliefs conflict with those of the dominant culture's of the educational system. Her purpose in the article is to influence changes in an educational system *that "was not designed to honor diverse racial and cultural groups" (25)*. **As she explains the** *"sacred and holy" (26) belief systems of the Indian tribes, influenced by their tribal affiliations and memberships, outside religion, and length of time off the reservation (27)***, readers understand that the inability of the education system to understand these values promotes discrimination.** <u>Her pleas that</u> *"As Indian people we ask that educational systems recognize our right to religious freedom and our right, as Sovereign Nations, to live in harmony as we were taught," (43*<u>), has ramification, not only for the education of Amerindians, but for the education of other minority cultures.</u>

<u>**Note:**</u> Commentary in the above example indicates your opinion, response, or reaction to the specific topic you discuss in an essay. Commentary is a difficult skill to master because all the opinions and interpretations must come from you. Essays require thinking and many students are not used to doing much thinking. Life, however, does not ask us to fill in the blanks, and college, work and our experiences rarely offer opportunities to choose one right answer. You should not be afraid to express and write your own opinions. Once you have gained confidence, the process of analyzing, interpreting and evaluating the information we read, hear, see, experience and learn will become easier.

> <u>**Your Turn:**</u>
> Review some of the essay answers from a test you have taken either for practice or for a grade. Then, use your markers or colored pencils to color code the parts of a strong answer. Did you have opinions? Do you prove each of them? Embed little bits of quotations? Conclude with an "and so" sentence that shows why your information and ideas are significant?

The 8 Minute SAT-ire Prep Course
Nguyen Phan (1994: 67-68)

These pages are intended to aid you on the SAT test. They are a comprehensive study guide compiled after long periods of research consisting of the author's making all this up. Here is an abbreviated grouping of the sorts of questions you will encounter on the test.

Math Question:

1. Bob is traveling away from Point X at noon on Train A at 45 mph. Joe is traveling away from X on Train B at 60 mph. How long will it take Joe to realize that since he did not score well on his SAT, he will forever be working at a dead-end job for a supervisor wearing horn-rimmed glasses named Earl?

   A. 60 minutes

   B. 3:30 but 4:30 Central and Mountain time

   C. π

   D. Bob will not realize this because he has the IQ of a gorilla who's eaten too much MSG.

Test of Standard Written English:

Choose the underlined word that is misspelled.

The commission <u>investigating</u> the accident at the <u>laboratory</u> was less interested in why the
                         A   B

the experiment was <u>concocted</u> than in whether it was <u>conducted</u> properly. No <u>eror.</u>
                    C   D   E

Reading Comprehension:

Answer the questions for each passage based on what is stated or implied.

A peculiar composite of values surfaces upon first reading historians and then poets afterwards. In fictitious exposition, nobleness, honor and the like are of the upmost importance; in reviewing history, they are completely insignificant. These values are omnipresent in poetry; they are all but absent from history. What one must do is to think poetically and prosaically at the same time.

The author in this passage is trying to

   A. Derive his impression of literary culture.

   B. Impress his derivation of cultural literalness.

   C. Culture his literal impression of derivation.

   D. Become President Abraham Lincoln.

*AN IMPORTANT HINT:

In making the SAT, the committee is very generous. They dole out 400 points to those who can completely fill out the information for the SAT score. In filling out your SAT, you must write your name in pencil. Most names start with capital letters (unless you're eecummings), but being the benevolent souls they are, the committee has opted to let you print your name on the scantron in capitals and/or small lower-case letters. Bubbling in circles is a skill developed throughout the academic career of a student. Teachers prepare children for this important skill starting as early as kindergarten. Remember this? "Shade inside the lines, boys and girls. Joey! Take that crayon out of your nose right now!"

Vocabulary:

The key to vocabulary is to not be intimidated by polysyllabic words. Deciphering words on the SAT using Latin roots is your best bet. For instance, suppose you do not know the word *polysyllabic*. You could break the word up like so:

poly=Polly=Parrot=bird
syll=Silly
abic=bic= a type of razor

So, a phrase using the word, polysyllabic, has to do with "silly birds using razors."

Preparations Before the Test

1. Spend the evening relaxing.
2. Eat a good breakfast, but avoid foods that may cause gastrointestinal discomfort as you will be sitting in one place for a long time.
3. Put the cat out.
4. Floss.

Telling Your Friends About Your SAT Score

In dealing with Ivy League bound peers it is important to approach the topic of SAT scores with subtlety. The following table will provide you with a plan of action when confronted about your score:

1250-1600	Say you did not do as well as you could have and never mention your score voluntarily. Make your peers think, "Man, I hate him!" when you emphasize how poorly you thought you did.
1000-1249	Tell them you only took the test once and that was after a long night of watching movies on TMC.
400-999	Avoid your friends. Get new ones. Don't come out in the daylight.
0-399	You're probably having trouble reading this section, so don't worry about it.

If you want further instruction on ways to make your SAT score jump by at least a 2 digit number, you can do so for a limited time only at the low price of $19.95. Make all checks payable to The Journalism Department, room 115. Void in certain states. California residents add 8% sales tax.

LESSON 8.
ARGUMENTATION
THE "VOICE" OF OPINION

"Where there is much desire to learn, there
of necessity will be much arguing, much writing,
many opinions; for opinions in good men is but
knowledge in the making."
—John Milton (1608-74)

What Is Argumentation?

Argumentation is a form of communication that a writer uses to influence or change the attitude or behavior through their use of language, structure and ideas that appeal to their readers' intellects (logos), their emotions (pathos), and/or their sense of right and wrong (ethos).

We use argument every day in conversations as simple as trying to convince a friend to go to a movie we want to see, or as challenging as trying to convincing a stranger to sign a petition, convince the electric company that they have overcharged us on the last bill, or persuading parents that they should extend a curfew. When trying to convince someone to change their way of thinking, or act in a different way, we may employ gentle coaxing or make pointed demands.

Mastering the art of argumentation offers both rewards and satisfaction. In college classes, professors will ask you to confront issues that require you to write reports, essays and exams that "take a stand" and present effective arguments. After college, no matter what profession you enter, or career you choose, you will spend much of your time trying to sell people some product, service or idea. Persuasion—part argument and part enticement—and built on both logic and emotional preference, often involves examining an issue with distinctly opposing sides that readers and listeners can evaluate and debate.

An effective argument requires not only strong, well-constructed reasons, but also the skillful presentations of facts and evidence. Writers of effective persuasion and argumentation shape and design their convictions and opinions about a topic to appeal to a particular group of readers. Your audience might have strongly felt opinions or they might not care one way or the other. Unlike some advertisers, television, radio "talking heads" and politicians, responsible writers and speakers do not try to storm people's minds or shout them down. They can persuade by gentler means—and share their views with readers open-minded enough to consider them.

As future leaders, you have a responsibility to think about problems and offer solutions to social, economic and cultural problems that confront the United State locally, either nationally, or globally. Persuading others to consider your ideas requires not only strong, well-constructed arguments, but also a thoughtful presentation of facts and evidence that support your ideas and the position you take on an issue or problem.

Writers cause events to happen and opinions to change.

Argument: Character Education

College Essay Prompt—Agree or disagree with the following statement:
"A Character Education program is necessary in most schools today."[1]

More than a hundred years ago, Herbert Spencer wrote, "Education has for its object the formation of character." In the last few years, the emphasis on accountability, basic skills, and high stakes testing have compelled educators to look at students primarily in terms of numbers and percentages.

In spite of the research of educators and psychologists like Piaget and Montessori, who stress the cognitive processes of childhood development, teachers sometimes neglect the emotional growth of youngsters in favor of an educational environment devoid of feelings and sterile in its approach to learning. Sadly, some teachers, particularly in secondary schools, see students as having brains like pitchers. They believe all they have to do is pour in information, tip students over and watch the facts pour out. This teaching method does not require processing, change or connection for either the student or the teacher.

Today, more than ever, we need education to develop students' characters in American schools, but educators and legislators cannot agree as to what this program should include because they are unable to agree on a definition of "character." If they ever find a consensus, state legislators might implement a curriculum in the form of workbooks, worksheets, and programmed instruction including practice tests that could "benchmark" results. Standardized achievement tests, administered yearly, would determine the program's effectiveness.

> **An appreciation of the arts helps young people perceive the world's problems, and gives them the resources to help them cope.**

Teachers would receive a list of character education objectives and a copy of Texas Instructional Character and Knowledge Skills (TICKS) curriculum guidelines. One day a week, on TICKS day, students would practice developing character and making value judgments. At the end of the school year, newspapers would print the results of the TICKS test and the Texas Education Agency (TEA) would recognize schools that had "Exemplary" characters. Some school administrators might receive bonuses for creating characters in their schools. This kind of recognition would increase property values of homes in a school's attendance zone, encourage teachers to leave their jobs in schools where students failed to achieve good character and flock to schools where students have excellent moral character. A further analysis of results would prove that some racial groups lack moral values and character development. School districts could then label these students "character challenged" and place them in special TICKS classes where they could spend more time filling out character building worksheets.

Since we hope this will not occur, we trust educators to have the maturity, presence and wisdom to minister and serve the affective needs of students in their classrooms. Effective teachers act as coaches, facilitators, mentors and consultants, encouraging students to participate as part of a learning community, make decisions, and develop skills necessary to work as part of a team. Through community service, volunteer work, peer teaching, and celebration of ethnic/cultural holidays, students can gain appreciation of other students and find opportunities to test their ideas against the ideas of others.

Almost two thousand years ago, Ovid, the Roman philosopher and author of *Metamorphoses*, wrote, "A faithful study of the liberal arts humanizes character and permits it not to be cruel." Music, art, literature, and drama provide poetry, stories, ideas, metaphors and images that promote critical, interpretive and critical thinking. An appreciation of the arts helps young people perceive the world's problems, and gives them the resources to help them cope.

The moral dilemmas presented by writers like Thoreau, Frederick Douglas and Martin Luther King, artists like Andrew Wyeth, Edward Hopper and Picasso, composers like Aaron Copeland, Mozart and Scott Joplin can help students learn to participate in the world around them and develop moral autonomy. When music, art and poetry are part of the daily curriculum, schoolwork can seem like play for   students whose need for beauty, peace and harmony is often sacrificed in favor of competition and upward mobility.

When challenged by classrooms rich with music, art and poetry, both students and teachers can participate in character education. Love, and other acts of teaching, includes helping young people find their own unique and individual voices. I believe the best way to define a persons' character is to seek out the particular mental or moral attitude in which, when it came upon them, they felt more deeply and intensely alive and active. At such moments there is a voice inside which speaks and says, "This is the real me."

Pledge Allegiance
Every morning
I pledge allegiance to my bowl of cheerios
sip a cup of coffee
and look at the morning headlines.
103 people killed in two devastating plane
       rex
       Hawley, a Vietnam vet entered a
convenience store late last night
       killing
thousands of american youth,
 gang warfare spreads throughout
       the
       country,
 brett simons found dead
with a needle in his arms
       agreement with iran
       broken
into about 3 a.m. this morning,
 the home of the smiths went up in
       flames
from the power plant explosion at
       dawn
glendale, convicted of child abuse
and charged with the crime
       is on the rise.
I sip my coffee and send my son
 to private school with his captain america lunchbox
and his brand new tennis shoes.
        ~Justin Cone (1995:91)

Your Turn:
What headlines appear in today's news? What do you find disturbing? How do you deal with them? How can our leaders solve the problem of violence in the United States and war in the world? Write a poem or essay about problems in your community that most upset you.

What Topics Can I Argue?

When choosing a topic, you should avoid rehashing old arguments, topics that do clearly have two sides and problems that have no solutions. You should also remember that the best arguments link to a "big idea"—an important issue that affects a wide audience. Your task is to bring a fresh, interesting and insightful point of view to a problem or issue that confronts many people in today's society in hope they will agree with you.

The Internet contains lists of topics similar to those used on SAT/ACT and AP tests. Some are stated as declarative sentences and some are stated as questions. Review some of them below:

Topics or "Prompts" for Writing Arguments:

1. The war on terror has contributed to the growing abuse of human rights.
2. High school graduates should take a year off before entering college.
3. All citizens should be required by law to vote.
4. Americans should have more holidays and longer vacations.
5. People have become overly dependent on technology.
6. Censorship is sometimes justified.
7. Privacy is not the most important right.
8. The continuing decline of CD sales along with the rapid growth of music downloads signals a new era of innovation in popular music.
9. The solution to the impending crisis in Social Security is the immediate elimination of this anachronistic government program.
10. The primary mission of colleges and universities is to prepare students for the workforce.
11. Financial incentives should be offered to high school students who perform well on standardized tests.
12. Should college athletes be exempt from regular admissions policies?
13. To encourage healthy eating, should higher taxes be imposed on soft drinks and junk food?
14. Should all citizens over the age of 65 be required to pass a driving education course before they can renew a license to drive?
15. Do schools put too much emphasis on learning basic skills?
16. Should schools help students understand moral values and social issues?
17. Do newspapers, magazines, movies, television and the Internet determine what is important to most people?

Your Turn:
Mark two or three topics that you think you might like to argue for/against in an argumentative essay. As you work through the exercises in this section, start planning and thinking about how you will develop and write your own argument.

How Do I Outline An Argument?

To choose a topic for an argument, you should consider your personal experiences, insights and position, but your personal views, no matter how strong they are, need reasons, proof and factual evidence to be convincing.

You also need to confront opposition to your opinion. To make the process of writing an argument easier, imagine you are a lawyer whose duty is to defend an innocent person. No matter how passionately you believe in the defendant's innocence, unless you can prove your case to the jury by presenting sound evidence, your client will go to jail. Stepping into the shoes of a lawyer, as you write, will help you build a strong and convincing argument.

To help present your opinion and evidence that supports it, you should carefully structure your argument. Below, you will find a possible outline for sections of an argument that discusses a problem and a possible solution:

I. Introduction: (one paragraph that engages readers and establishes your credibility)
    A. Create an attention-getting "lead";
    B. Summarize the controversy, explain relevance of problem to readers and why it needs a solution;
    C. Present Thesis/Antithesis—a clear statement of your position.

II. Body of the Argument (several paragraphs):
    A. Claim # 1: Strong reason and evidence that supports it;
    B. Claim #2: Second reason and evidence that supports it;
    C. Claim #3: Third and most important reason and evidence that supports it

III. Address Opposing Viewpoints (a couple of paragraphs which make you appear rational):
    A. First Opposing View and evidence that refutes it;
    B. Second Opposing View and evidence that refutes it;
    C. Evoke an emotional response from your reader.

IV. Present a Solution or Compromise
    A. Suggest a compromise or provide a possible solution;
    B. Document the validity of the solution with evidence from reading and knowledge.

V. Conclude with "punch"— (See "Lesson 4: The Essay— 'I-Say'")
    A. Look Backward: Summarize your main reasons and ideas;
    B. Look Forward: Challenge readers to change their minds, or act in some way.

Your Turn:
Review the essay, "Character Education." Mark the sections that correspond to the suggested out line with the proper numbers and letters. (I, A, II, B). Read and review "The Declaration of Independence" and check to see if it follows the outline above. As you write your own argument later, you can modify this outline according to the nature of the topic, your readers and you purpose. Remember your own "voice" is important. Thomas Jefferson is not Martin Luther King who is not Jonathan Swift who is not Abraham Lincoln.

How Can I "Map" My Argument?

Sometimes, it helps to use a graphic organizer to help you "see" your organization. A strong organization pattern helps you to know what to write and helps your readers or listeners know what to expect.

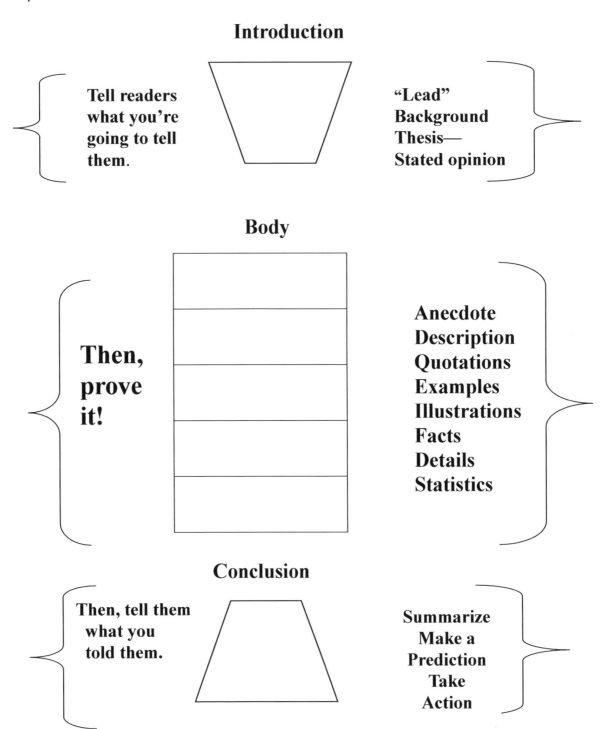

Introduction

Tell readers what you're going to tell them.

"Lead"
Background
Thesis—
Stated opinion

Body

Then, prove it!

Anecdote
Description
Quotations
Examples
Illustrations
Facts
Details
Statistics

Conclusion

Then, tell them what you told them.

Summarize
Make a
Prediction
Take
Action

How Does the "Rhetorical Triangle" Help Support My Opinions?

An argument, to be effective, must reach out to readers and listeners. Generally, your readers will fall into four categories:

- Readers who already agree with your ideas and just need reinforcement;
- Readers, inclined to agree with you, but who want more evidence and proof;
- Readers, neutral on an issue, who need more explanation before they decide;
- Readers, skeptical about an issue, who want to hear both sides explained in complete detail.

As a writer, you should choose **words** that appeal to readers on **emotional** and **logical** levels, but you must also use **ethical** means to convince them that a course is true, an action is valid, or an idea has merit.

The Rhetorical Triangle [2]

Many years ago, Greek philosophers identified three categories of argumentative appeals, resources, strategies and devices writers use to connect with, and persuade readers; smart writers know when and how to use each of them in order to accomplish their purposes. They are:

1. **A rational appeal (logos)** asks readers to use their intellects and their powers of reasoning. It relies on established conventions of logic and evidence.
2. **An emotional appeal (pathos)** asks readers to respond out of their beliefs, values, or feelings. It inspires, affirms, frightens, angers.
3. **An ethical appeal (ethos)** asks readers to look favorably on the writer. It stresses the writer's intelligence, competence, fairness, morality and other qualities desirable in a trustworthy debater, teacher or authority.

For strong examples of the use of rhetorical appeals, read Martin Luther King's "I Have a Dream" [3] speech below:

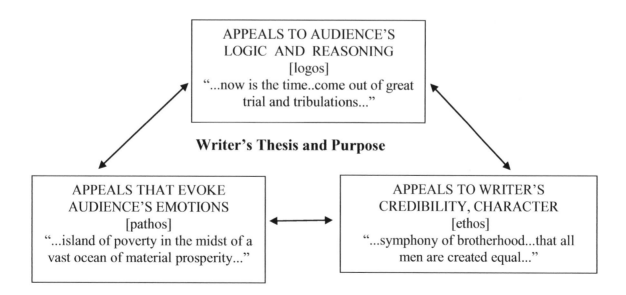

APPEALS TO AUDIENCE'S
LOGIC AND REASONING
[logos]
"...now is the time..come out of great
trial and tribulations..."

Writer's Thesis and Purpose

APPEALS THAT EVOKE
AUDIENCE'S EMOTIONS
[pathos]
"...island of poverty in the midst of a
vast ocean of material prosperity..."

APPEALS TO WRITER'S
CREDIBILITY, CHARACTER
[ethos]
"...symphony of brotherhood...that all
men are created equal..."

How Do I Take a Stand?
Form A Rhetorical Position?

When the Founding Fathers encouraged and led representatives from the thirteen colonies to declare their independence from King George of England, they knew the Declaration of Independence needed to affect not only the actions of the King, but also the hearts and minds of the citizens of a country not yet united as a government.

Their choice of words, every sentence and phrase, example, and fact they presented as evidence   had to move people on both sides of the Atlantic Ocean to accept and applaud a new land that would "hold these truths to be self-evident, that all men are created equal, that they are endowed by their Creator with certain unalienable Rights, that among these are Life, Liberty and the pursuit of Happiness."

Below you can find some possible ways to present your position, and structure your evidence so others accept your ideas:

1. State a thesis and then refute it.

2. Suggest possibilities and dismiss all but one.

3. Pose a problem and then solve it.

4. Form a hypothesis and test its implications.

5. Express an opinion and then contradict it with facts.

6. Narrate several unrelated episodes and then link them in a surprising way.

7. Use chronological narration and then shift to reflection.

8. Report in an appreciative and descriptive manner.

9. Recollect memories dispassionately and objectively.

10. Compare and contrast events, actions or ideas with other events, actions, or ideas.

Plbtbtbtbt

All arguments between people
eventually digress back
to childhood gestures.
stick out your tongue,
and/or go "plbtbtbt!"
or "nanny-nanny-boo-boo,"
or just scream
and run away.
Only difference is that nowadays
you don't come back
two minutes later
and play tag.
~**Robert Gacutan (1995:138)**

Your Turn:

Find a copy of the Declaration of Independence that shows revisions and changes at :http://www.ushistory.org/declaration/document/rough.htm Why do the Founding Fathers change certain words? Delete some phrases? Change the order of the list of grievances? What changes did the writers make in the introduction and the conclusion? Why do you suppose they made these changes? Which of the above methods did they use to take a stand against King George and Great Britain?

How Can I Learn To Think Logically?

The discourse pattern, or logical arrangement and progression of ideas of an argument or oral presentation for informational purposes, will vary depending on the culture and native language of the writer/speaker. For example, languages like Spanish, French and Italian, ideas develop ideas through inductive reasoning and may include digressions. To an English speaker, these speakers may seem unfocused, long-winded and flowery. On the other hand, to a Spanish or French speaker, English might seem cold, arrogant and confrontational because of its "straight to the point" discourse pattern.

Speakers and readers of English expect a thought pattern organized in sequence and linear in its development. For example, a standard paragraph in English generally begins with a general statement of its content (a topic sentence) and then carefully develops the statement and connects the ideas to a thesis. The flow of ideas occurs in a straight line from the opening sentence to the last sentence. According to Dr. Montano-Harmon, logic and reasoning is not universal; the arrangement of ideas is culture bound. [4]

Sound and effective arguments involve logical, organized, well-supported ideas and examples, forming a hypothesis or major premise, supporting it with evidence and drawing a conclusion. The chart in this section may help you understand these principles of thinking logically.

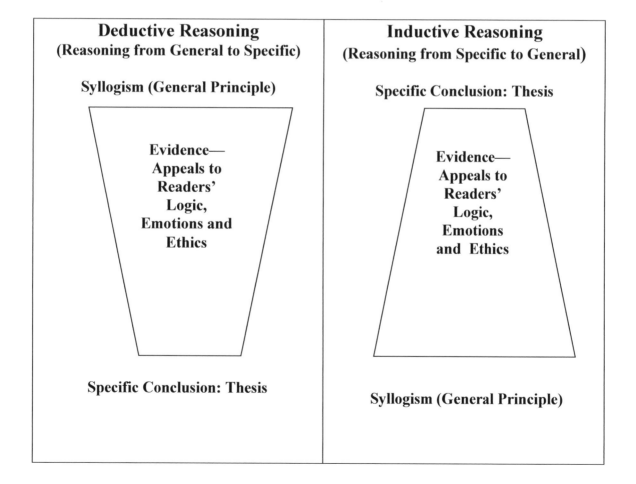

Deductive Reasoning
(Reasoning from General to Specific)

Syllogism (General Principle)

Evidence—
Appeals to
Readers'
Logic,
Emotions and
Ethics

Specific Conclusion: Thesis

Inductive Reasoning
(Reasoning from Specific to General)

Specific Conclusion: Thesis

Evidence—
Appeals to
Readers'
Logic,
Emotions
and Ethics

Syllogism (General Principle)

Hypothesis (an "educated" guess stated as a question)	Now You Try It: Hypothesis
Question: Should race, culture, or family background influence admissions to universities? **Evidence:** 1. *Only 2% of UT students are Hispanic even though Hispanics make up 28% of the population in Texas. 2. Minority students bring a diversity of ideas to college learning experiences. 3. The Texas Top 10% admission rule has not increased minority enrollment **Conclusion/Thesis:** Affirmative action is necessary to increase minority enrollments in public universities. *Statistics not validated	**Your Question:** **Your Evidence:** **Your Conclusion/Thesis:**

Syllogism (A general principle stated as a declarative sentence)	Now You Try It: Syllogism
Major Premise/Assertion: Admissions to universities should not be influenced by race, culture or family backgrounds, but on the academic abilities of each candidate. **Minor Premise:** Tom Smith, a U.S. Senator's son, was admitted to Yale University because of his family's social and economic background even though he had less than average grades and SAT score. **Conclusion/Thesis:** Therefore, Yale University should not have admitted Tom Smith to Yale University.	**Your Major Premise/Assertion:** **Your Minor Premise:** **Your Conclusion/Thesis:**

> **Your Turn Again:**
> Review the argumentative essay you've drafted and review it to see if you have written it logically. Did you use Deductive or Inductive Reasoning to conclude your essay?

What Factors Influence Opinions?

Corporations and political parties spend millions of dollars trying to convince people to buy their products or vote for their candidates. However, they are not the only people who understand the power of persuasion. Teachers, parents—and your best friends—try to change your mind about anything and everything from your choice of movies to your choice of books to your thoughts on political issues.

Howard Gardner, a Harvard psychologist and author of *Changing Minds,* [5] has identified seven major factors that help change people's opinions. To check to see which ones might work for you and help you influence your readers' opinions, respond to the following questions:

1. **Reason:** Is the argument rational and logical? Will the idea work? Will the product do what its claims indicate it will do? Is the idea realistic? Is there another side to the position or claim? Do emotionally loaded words attempt to sway your reader's thinking?

2. **Research:** Can you prove it? What does the data say? Where does the data come from? Who conducted the poll? The survey? How current is the information and evidence? Do they present facts or opinions, which interpret the facts? What qualifications do the experts have who provide evidence? Are they credible? Believable? Is the evidence relevant? Or does it detract from the real issues and ideas?

3. **Resonance:** Do you find yourself saying, "Well, I don't care what the evidence says, I just like the candidate, product, idea?" Are you persuaded to buy something, think something or vote for someone because it just "feels right?"

4. **Re-descriptions:** Do the politicians and advertisers sell themselves through a variety of formats: speeches, ads, policy statements, small group meetings or large, controlled group presentations?

5. **Resources: & Rewards:** Are the messages consistent? Do they try to convince audiences in a variety of ways: stories, data, inspiring examples and symbols, ideals of fairness and justice? What promises are made? How will you benefit?

6. **Real World Events:** What is happening in the world that influences and persuades you? Are they controllable? Uncontrollable? Life changing?

7. **Resistances:** What appeals are made to an audience's prejudices and biases? Fears and desires? What kinds of ideas keep you from accepting the views of others? What topics "push your buttons" more than others do? What keeps you from accepting other people's ideas?

> **Your Turn:**
> Read a recent State of the Union speech, or an Inaugural Address. Identify the types of logical, emotional, or ethical appeals used in the speech. Then, apply Gardner's factors and criteria. Does the speech offer reasons, research, resonance, re-description, resources and rewards, real world events or resistance? Do any of them change your mind about the policies and ideas presented in the speech? If so, what examples can you find of each?

How Do I Evaluate an Argument?

Authors might be clear in stating a position, while using information that is not accurate. They might use relevant information but fail to think through the complexities of the issue. An argument might be logical but not significant. As citizens, readers and writers, we need to become adept at assessing the quality of reasoning and the techniques and .strategies used in strong arguments.

Your Turn:

Choose an essay or speech from history. Some good examples from history might include: Patrick Henry's "Give Me Liberty or Give Me Death" speech, Jonathan Swift's satire, "A Modest Proposal," Martin Luther King's "Letter from Birmingham Jail," or Henry David Thoreau's "Civil Disobedience." Then, evaluate the accuracy and honesty of the logic the author uses to present the ideas. Cite evidence from the speech or essay to support your ideas. Use these questions to help you:

1. Is the author's **opinion and purpose clearly stated,** or is it vague, confused, or muddled in some way?

2. Who is the **intended audience** for this argument? Does the author assume the audience will be friendly or hostile to the author's stated/implied purpose?

3. Has the author been **accurate** in their claims and use of evidence? Cite examples from the text.

4. Has the author provided precise **details and specifics** when specifics are relevant? Where? How?

5. Does the author stray from the purpose and introduce **irrelevant** material? If so, where? Cite examples from the text to support your ideas.

6. How does the author convince you that he or she is **knowledgeable** about the subject? Cite evidence from the text to support your opinion.

7. Does the author **project "good sense," "good will" and "good character" (ethos)?** OR does the author attack his opposition's ethics rather than the opposition's argument? Cite evidence from the text.

8. What kinds of **logical support** does the author use? (Personal experience or observation, expert testimony, appeal to authorities or experts, examples, statistics, facts, studies/reports, etc.?) How are they effective? Cite evidence from the text.

9. Has the author said something **significant,** or has he or she dealt with the subject in a trivial manner? Have they tried to appeal to your emotions **(pathos)** or does the author strike a balance between **logical reasoning (logos) and** emotion? Cite evidence from the text.

10. Has the author been **fair,** or have they taken a one-sided, narrow approach? Have the authors depended on **fallacies of logic?** See the next page for a list of the most common "Logical Fallacies."

What Are Fallacies of Logic?

A fallacy of logic—a failure in reasoning—invalidates an argument. Some fallacies are committed intentionally (to manipulate or persuade by deception), others are unintentional due to carelessness or ignorance. When writers and speakers use language aimed at influencing attitudes toward some cause by presenting only one side, we call it "propaganda." As in football—and other games of life—the best defense is often a good offense. When we understand that language can sometimes contain fallacies, then we can better protect ourselves against the use of them as tools of propaganda by unscrupulous writers, speakers and advertisers. Below, you will find a few of the most commonly used logical fallacies:

1. **Loaded words** are words that appeal to your emotions.
   Example: Vote for Jones—the choice of patriotic, religious Americans.
2. **Faulty Cause and Effect** assumes that one event leads to another with no connection.
   Example: They launched a new weather satellite, and it has not stopped raining.
3. **Bandwagon** appeals to the desire to be like everyone else.
   Example: "But, Dad, all the kids are going to the concert."
4. **Testimonial or irrelevant authority** uses a famous person to sell a product or idea.
   Example: A rock star sells a dairy product by wearing a milk mustache.
5. **Ad hominem** diverts attention from issue by attacking the motives or character of a person making an argument.
   Example: His proposal for health care won't work because he's a former alcoholic whose wife just divorced him.
6. **Transfer** shows something most people feel good about and suggests you transfer those pleasant or unpleasant feelings to a product or idea.
   Example: A beautiful girl dressed in a bikini sits on the roof of a car.
7. **Slogans** use catchy phrases to help people remember a product or idea.
   Example: Free your mind. Be colorblind.
8. **Non-sequitur** is a Latin term that means, "It does not follow."
   Example: John Hinkley could not have shot President Reagan because he came from a good home.
9. **Begging the question** restates the original premise in other terms.
   Example: The charges of physical abuse are untrue. The police would never do something like that.
10. **Either-or Fallacy** assumes you only have two choices.
    Example: Either we ban boxing or hundreds of young men will be killed.
11. **Stereotype** is an oversimplified or standardized image of a person or group.
    Example: All "Rap" and "Hip Hop" musicians have low opinions of women.
12. **Red Herring** present an irrelevant topic to divert attention from another issue.
    Example: We should have stricter standards for college admissions. After all, we have a budget crisis and do not want to decrease teachers' salaries.
13. **Hasty Generalization** occurs when conclusions are based on insufficient evidence.
    Example: Smith, a visitor from England, sees two white (albino) squirrels. He calls his wife, and he tells her that all U.S. squirrels are white.

> **Your Turn:**
> Look through a print magazine, an online editorial, blog, or newspaper editorial page and identify examples you find of Fallacies of Logic. Cut them out or copy and paste them into your Writer's Notebook.

Test Your Knowledge: A Quiz

Stereotype Loaded words Testimonial/Irrelevant Authority	Ad Hominem Transfer Slogans Hasty Generalization	Faulty Cause Effect Non-Sequitur Either-Or Fallacy	Bandwagon Mud slinging Begging the Question

1. Politicians and people who run for public office are all crooked.

2. If we can send a man to the moon and communicate with him there, then surely we can communicate with government leaders in other countries.

3. Our football team had a winning season because of the new weight program. Before this new program, we had lost 10 consecutive games.

4. Visit Splash and Sun, where all the most popular kids at school spend their summer weekends.

5. Vote for Senator Jones—the choice of patriotic, church going Americans who have real family values.

6. Ozzy Osbourne wears a milk mustache and says, " Milk is the best choice for growing children."

7. Free Your Mind. Be Color Blind.

8. "Don't listen to her. She's a ditzy blonde."

9. "If such actions were not illegal, then they would not be prohibited by the law."

10. Karen won't be a successful lawyer. No one in her family has ever amounted to anything

11. Phone America is better, cheaper and simpler to use than U.S. Phone Co.

12. Either we allow everyone to carry guns, or the crime rate will increase dramatically.

13. Little children playing in the sunshine appears in an ad for a candidate. Little children sitting in the squalor of a backyard appears in an opponent's TV commercial.

Answers: 1. Stereotype; 2. Faulty cause-effect; 3. Non-sequitur; 4. Bandwagon; 5. Loaded words; 6. Faulty testimonial; 7. Slogan; 8. Ad Hominem; 9. Begging the Question; 10. Mudslinging; 11. Hasty Generalization; 12. Either-or; 13. Transfer.

> **Your Turn:**
> Listen to a political debate, or news programs on Fox, CNN or MSNBC where candidates, or their representatives make a speech or discuss current issues. Find and list your own examples of "Fallacies of Logic" and "Propaganda Devices" in your Writer's Notebook

LESSON 9: POETRY—
THE "VOICE" OF IMAGINATION

Antony &
Cleopatra

Tristan & Isolde

Adam & Eve

Samson &
Delilah

Elvis &
Priscilla

Abraham &
Sarah

Romeo & Juliet

Minnie &
Mickey

"Language developed as a way for men to woo women."
—Robin Williams in "Dead Poets' Society"

What is Poetry?

A Few Poetic Definitions [1]

Poetry—
A lake where each word
Is a pebble
Thrown by the poet
Into the water.
~**Megan Nayak**

Poetry is a day on the ranch.
The rhythm of a hammer or a dog barking
Poetry is an axe coming alive as it chops away,
The bellow of cattle during a round-up,
Horses' hooves pounding green grass,
I believe poetry is all of these.
~**William Nestor**

Poetry is expression of artistic balance,
A view of a world behind the violence,
Behind the thinking barrier.
Reading poetry puts me in a room of glass,
Without walls, a door of steel,
That can be broken by a needle,
But not by human touch.
Poetry is a maze in a pyramid,
A secret world which opens up
Through reading and writing.
~**Steve Matthews**

Catcher

To make some light,
We tear out Catcher's
First chapter and burn
It up in a few minutes.

I need the fire to write down
an idea that may turn to poetry.
You need the flame to sketch
a figure that may turn to paint.
~**Matt Walsh (1995:1)**

Abraham the Poetry Analyst

Poetry, fear me.
My mind is now in arms
forged by the modern Intellectual Smithy,
honed by fires
that burn cold, lacking
desires and passion—
a steely blade
no longer even
content to cut
while you lay etherized on a table.
I open you live on my Dachau desk
to see what I can find
with the Intellectual Smithy
leering behind.

I am a Twentieth Century
Hippocrates
abducting Zeus from his Olympian home.
Sacrificing my god
upon his marble monoliths
dissecting his immortal heart
and naming every bone
proudly explaining, he was not sick,
But I have found what made Zeus tick.
and the god lies dead upon the stone.
Poetry, forgive me,
I am a reluctant assassin
but my trigger finger is quick
and my desk is covered in books
and bones.
~**Justin Storms (1996:1)**

Effective writers of prose
write—and think—like poets.

Essay: "Creating a Live Poets' Society"[2]

Students instinctively know what poetry is; in the form of nursery rhymes, poetry is often one of the first experiences children have with literature. Today, young people hunger for poetry. Publisher's lists show an extraordinary upsurge in the number of poetry books in print, and youngsters are helping to create that demand. We can hear poetry in their music, read it in their graffiti, see it on their faces when they pass it to us—or each other—on crumpled pieces of paper. They seek the rhythms, passion, and universality of poetry. They like poetry that speaks in bold, blunt voices like the ones they hear at home and school, and they want poetry to connect and relate to the worlds they know.

However, many teachers fail to give students a sense of what a poet does with language, and how image, sound and form combine to make meaning, so they teach poetry badly or indifferently, or not at all. Teachers, however, need to throw out the old rules and help students find poetry in themselves. Students will forget the technical aspect of rhyme and meter, and the formulas for writing poetry, but they will remember the experiences they have with it.

Every student writer starts from a different point and travels in a different direction. The universal language of poetry helps bring all those different kinds of writers together. Writing poems gives students a feeling of control over the English language. Because students work with a limited number of words and lines in a poem, teaching students to revise is not such a chore. Working on a poem filled with action verbs all in the same tense can help them understand the problems with shifting verb tenses. Reading poems aloud helps them understand the uses of punctuation and the value of writing parallel constructions.

Writing poems help students become more conscious of specific word choice, denotation and connotation. Because they work with fewer words when writing a poem, students find it easier to use a dictionary and thesaurus for spelling and building vocabulary through synonyms. In his book, *On Writing Well*, William Zinsser writes, "Rhythm and alliteration are vital to every sentence because readers read with their ears more than we imagine. Good writers of prose must be part poet, always listening to what they write."

> **We have become a society fearful of revealing who we are. We have evolved a language of impersonality.**

We have become a society fearful of revealing who we are. We have evolved a language of impersonality. However, good writers' individual voices are always visible just behind their words. If writers are not t allowed to use the pronoun, "I," they should at least think in the first person when they write drafts which will help warm up an impersonal style. They can always edit the "I's" later. All teachers of writing recognize that students write more willingly when they write about experiences that touch their lives; motivation is at the heart of all writing assignments. Writing a poem as prewriting for a composition can bring warmth, humanity and poetic expression to student prose.

Poetry is the dessert of literature. Like chocolate-covered cherries, poetry tastes sweet and satisfying as a special treat. Like candy, students should taste poetry in small, sweet, stolen pieces and little bites. No matter what a class is studying, teachers can find a poem that fits, and poetry scattered in mini-lessons throughout the school year whets students' appetites for more of it. One problem with teaching poetry involves decisions about how to evaluate it. I wanted to encourage students to do all the things I thought writing a poem could do, but I also wanted them to know there is a difference between good, great and average poems. To help students evaluate poetry, I shared the criteria for effective poetry before they chose a poem to revise. After reading so many poems throughout the year, they began to understand that pretentious, overly sentimental poetry or "preachy" poetry would not be appropriate for publication.

Studying poetry in bits and pieces throughout the year prepared students for the final stage—submitting their poems for publication. They began this preparation by reviewing all the poems in their portfolios—everything they had written during the year. Next, we spent a week writing poems based on universal themes. We tried to write two or three poems during a class period, remembering Robert Frost's advice, "The freshness of a poem belongs absolutely to its not having been thought out and then set to verse."

After students selected their best poems, they revised them using the same process they used to revise prose. They eliminated passive verbs, substituted vivid words for weak words, corrected tenses and other usage problems and then proofread their poems for spelling and punctuation. They read them aloud to check where lines should end for emphasis and meaning and then they prepared their final pieces for submission to our school's literary magazine.

Several principles of teaching poetry can guide teachers as they motivate students and generate enthusiasm for language in their classrooms. First, teachers who are not readers of poetry should not pretend to teach it. If they do enjoy reading poetry, then they should teach only those poems they really love. They should encourage students to have a chance to choose their own poems to read and discuss. Teaching poems in "little bites" must replace the two-week poetry unit taught at the end of the year. Above all, teachers must stop over explaining and intellectualizing poetry.

Finally, teachers should write some poetry with their students. Words are the biggest tools we can give our students. We can help them learn to use them with originality and care; we can teach them to value them for their strength and infinite diversity. When they read their poems aloud, student writers become aware that somebody out there is listening—they become physically and emotionally involved with the ideas expressed in their poetry. They may not stand on their desks and salute you as, "Oh, Teacher, My Teacher," but they may   write you a poem.

Student's Voice: Poetry Personified

Does she know how much I admire
Octagonal rhythms, lines that
Zephyrly breathe
      through every punctuation
In subtle harmony?
Every idea echoes resiliently
      gloriously on the page
      of her face. Does she
Realize how she inspires?
      --Alison Boye [3]

Your Turn:
In your Writer's Notebook, define the term, poetry," or "poet" in a poetic way. Or answer this question, "Is poetry still alive in the U.S. today?" so your response looks like a poem. Then, create a poem by writing an "Acrostic" poem. Write the letters of your last name vertically on the left side of a sheet of paper. Then, begin a line of poetry with each of the letters. Surprise your readers! Surprise yourself!

"What Is Poetic Freedom?"

Ryan Anderson (1998:54)

May I suggest poetry?

No, you did not hear wrong. I did, in fact, say, "Poetry." Most teenagers express themselves visibly: through fashion, trends, clothing, and attitudes. This is not wrong, but it has no lasting form. It leaves fossilized remnants to be unearthed in the future, and therefore separates these teenagers from their past. They will never dig up a piece of poetry they created in high school and shout, "By all that is mighty, I wrote this!" People without these experiences are incomplete.

Poetry enters the equation here. Not only will writing poetry leave something to mull over when they are out of school, but it will also invite them to express themselves now. For example, I wrote, "I Hoped a Butterfly" this year to open another window of my personality to my friends:

> I hoped a butterfly, painted blue and green,
> The colors of the sea,
> Would float past the pink azaleas
> Blooming in my mother's garden,
> And land on my knee,
> So I could pull its wings off.

This isn't conventional, but it's part of me, and something I created. I will be happy to look back on it in following years...

What if Bill Clinton and Saddam Hussein sat each night in their studies and pumped out poetry? Would that make them more influential or would the act of poetry change them? ...It is obvious that poetry has earned its place as a viable and recognizable form of expression in America today, but I feel concern for the many who still choose to ignore it. All I can say is try it, poetry is not such a bitter pill to swallow.

Some Myths About Poetry	(Possible) Truths About Poetry
1. If it rhymes, it must be poetry.	1. Poetry occurs when imagination overcomes habit.
2. If it feels good, it must be poetry.	2. Poetry often results from frustration and impatience.
3. If I make it up, it must be poetry.	3. Poetry often happens when we are farthest away from a piece of paper and pencil.
4. If I like it, it must be poetry.	4. Poetry involves making new combinations.
5. If my friends tell me it's good, it must be poetry.	5. Poetry is the great "a-hah!"
6. If it's about my emotions, it must be poetry.	6. Poetry means getting out of the way.
7. If no one understands it, it must be poetry.	7. Poetry involves all of who and what we are as humans.

> **Your Turn:**
> Would writing poetry change the attitudes of politicians towards war? Write your answer in the form of a "Question/Answer poem"?

What Are A Poet's Bill of "Writes?"

Many writers have defined poetry, and each of their definitions has contributed to this oldest form of writing. For this lesson, however, we should think of poetry as a genre of literature in which a writer uses tiny explosions of experience to communicate an insight, tell a story, or comment on the human condition. I'd like to define poetry as, "a writing form that uses a minimum amount of words to create a maximum impact on readers." As you write some poems and think about your readers, you might consider the following "Bill of Writes:"

1.   Your voice has a right to be heard.
2.   You can discuss a poem without making comments directed towards the poet.
3.   You have the right to write anything you think or feel in any style you wish; however, your readers have the right to dislike what you have written.
4.   You have the right to say what you want to say in the way that works for you. If you cannot   say what you want to say because it won't fit into a particular style or form, then you can try another style or form. If you do not   believe in your own voice, how can you convince your readers? (eecummings is not Emerson is not Frost is not Hughes is not YOU!)
5.   You have the right to write bad poetry. Writing a poem never wastes time because:
     a.   sometimes it can be fixed with a little editing;
     b.   sometimes you can take the idea and make a better poem;
     c.   sometimes the poem is bad but there are one or more good images or phrases which you can use to build a better, stronger   piece of writing.
6.   You have the right to change your ideas about poetry. As we mature, we re-evaluate the world around us based on new information. Your views will change; however, your old poems will remain the same, reflecting the old you.
7.   You have the right to ignore any suggestions made by your readers whether they are friends, teachers, or other writers. However, it is always a good idea to study the advice before you disregard it.
8.   You have the right to like particular writers and respect their styles. However, sometimes poets you don't like will show you another way, so try to keep an open mind.
9.   Not all poems contain rhyme. If you choose to use rhyme, remember that you have to be a very good poet or your poem will sound "childlike" or even worse, "childish."
10. You have the right to carry a poem in your pocket at all times, and you have the right to share it with your friends and family.

---

imitating eecummings

e e cummings
i make make peace with you
the same way pound
did with Whitman.
you wrote
without uppercase
and
        spaced
for
        effect.
but when I imitate
you cummings,
all I get
are tiny soldiers
with no swords
marching off to war.
    —Jessica Wilson
    (2005:55)

Your Turn:
Add your own poetic "write" to the list and then write a poem that   declares your independence from all the beliefs you previously held about poetry.

What Are Rules for Writing Poems?

Poets and professors have tried for years to determine a common set of rules for writing poetry; you can find about 32,000,000 links on the Internet when you use the keywords, "How to write a poem," to search for suggestions for writing the perfect poem. While I certainly don't claim to have all the answers, I do believe your poems can benefit from some of the same suggestions I would provide for writing any interesting, thoughtful, effective composition. You can find a few suggestions below:

1. **Write old things new.** Avoid drab statements about the obvious. Avoid trite, threadbare images, clichés and gushy, mushy, overblown language.

2. **Be original and creative.** Don't tell it, SHOW it by saying something in a new way, but don't force readers to guess at the meaning.

3. **Be specific.** Choose concrete, specific nouns over abstract and general ones. Choose active verbs over passive verbs. Pay close attention to detail. Avoid wordiness and redundancy. Be concise. Write Tight.

4. **Use your "voice."** The best poems show signs of a mature individuality and style—the presence of a unique voice, a new way of thinking about the topic of the poem.

5. **Strive for universal appeal.** The best poems contain elements of universality—a common human element that arouses appreciation, wonder and sensitivity in readers.

6. **Restrain your "I."** Write your poems with restraint and originality instead of with soap opera melodrama. Focus on the topic of the poem, rather than yourself. When you overuse the pronoun, "I," your poem can become self-centered, self-indulgent and self-pitying.

> **Tortilla Memories**
>
> At the stove inside,
> Momma cooked
> Spanish rice and warm
> tortillas.
> Grandma sewed
> Abuelo's jeans
> Though long since torn.
> Cousins played
> In the sun.
> And the tios
> Talked of better days.
> **—Alyse Fullum**
> **(2004: 40)**

7. **Center attention on the poem.** Avoid obscenities, intellectual snobbery, soapbox posturing, ungrammatical rebellion, typographical oddities and messy manuscripts.

8. **Name your poem.** To call a poem "untitled" still gives it a name, just a ridiculous and useless one.

9. **Craft your poems.** After the first "inspiration," and several drafts, let the practical, grammatical, rule-conscious part of the brain take over and perform its technical editing duties.

10. **Follow the rules.** Review the rules of the contest you're entering, the guidelines for the publication seeking submissions, and the traditional rules of good writing: grammatical correctness, clarity, unity, coherence, conciseness, neatness, originality and significance.

11. **Don't quit.** Try writing poems again and again….and again.

> **Your Turn:**
> Choose one of the poems you have written in your Writer's Notebook. How many of the suggestions above did you observe as you wrote it? Which suggestions can help you revise it?

How Do "Narrative" Poems Tell Stories?

Do you remember an important piece of advice you received from your first boss, coach, teacher or parent? Well, Frank, the speaker in the poem, "About Peas," does, and he shares his memory in a conversation between himself and the owner of Willy's Groceries in the narrative poem below:

About Peas

No, Frank, the peas go on the
top shelf.
There ya go. Geez, that's a
good job
you're doing there. You remind me of myself
back in the day. I started as a stock boy
back in 1924. Yep, I was the best damn
stock boy at Willy's Groceries.
Man, I could stack a display of castor oil
like nobody's business, and don't even ask
how long it took me to sack groceries.

And Willy was good to me, too.
When he passed away he gave me
his old grocery store and a little advice.
He says to me, "Ed, put the peas
on the top shelf. I know it sounds strange
but when I started this business,
the very first day I opened my store,
I put the peas on the top shelf,
and for some reason, I have ever since.
And ever since, I ain't ever had a worry
in the world o' mine. Never went hungry,
or went without a roof over my head."

Yep, that's what he said to me.
And, though I changed the name out front
from Willy's to Ed's, and no, you can't buy
live chickens here anymore,
I'll be damned if I don't put the peas
on the top shelf. Just the way Willy liked it.
And I'll be damned if I ever go a day
without a bite to eat
or a roof over my head.
~**Jay Galik (1996: 55)**

Your Turn:
Use boxes like these to sketch the events that occur in the poem.

☐ → ☐ → ☐

Then, use the questions below to help you discover the poet's purpose and meaning in "About Peas:"

1. In your own words, who is involved in the story? Where and when does it take place? What happens?
2. What event have you experienced that might be the basis for a similar story?
3. Why do you believe the poet wrote about this incident? How does the poet want his readers to feel or think about after reading the poem?
4. What details does the poet use to help you visualize the events that occur in the poem? How do they contribute to the meaning of the poem?
5. How does this poem remind you of a movie, a song, or another story?
6. What does the poet do to make this event sound realistic?

Your Turn Again.
Write your own poem about a first job, or a time when you received some good advice from an adult.

How Do "Lyric" Poems Express Emotions?

Hayti, Missouri 1959 [4]

Outside the room,
 an old man rocked all day on his porch.
Miss Cora had purple-blue skin;
 a bent, broken Negro man cut her lawn.
Girls in tight jeans blew smoke rings
 in the last booth at the drug store.
Boys tried to put their hands
under blouses in the back seats of cars.
 In the kitchen, parents drank in silence.

Inside the room
Errol Flynn rescued me from sultans,
pirates and evil plantation owners.
Carefully spaced charcoal drawn eyes
stared from a sketchpad.
I traveled to Atlanta, Spain and Russia
 in books hidden under the bed.
 The Virgin Mary watched from the wall,
palms and fingertips placed together.

Morning hung like wet wool
on backyard clotheslines.
Days stretched from here to there
in ribbons of sunlight and shadows.
Plastic curtains waved in windows,
while attic fans whirred
and hummed with importance.
Secrets lived in houses on streets
shaded by dust and decay.

~Lynne Dozier

Your Turn: Use the "map" below to describe emotions in the poem, "Hayti, Missouri 1959":

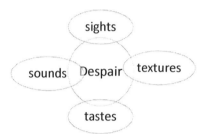

Use the questions below to help you discuss the emotional tone conveyed by the poet in the poem.

1. In your own words, who seems to be the "I" in this poem? Do not assume the poet is the narrator.
2. What is happening in the poem?
3. What emotion have you experienced that might be the basis for a similar lyric poem?
4. Why do you believe the poet wrote about this town? How does the poet want his readers to feel or think about after reading the poem?
5. What details does the poet use to help you describe the emotions that occur in the poem? How do they contribute to the meaning of the poem?
6. How does this poem remind you of a movie, a song, or story about the same emotions?

Your Turn Again:
Write your own poem about a place you loved or hated. Do not name your feelings about the place in your poem. "Show. Don't Tell." Read it aloud to a teammate, and ask them to draw an illustration to accompany the images in your poem.

Where Can I Find Poems?

Naomi Shihab Nye, an Arab-American poet, lived in St. Louis, Missouri, Ramalla, Palestine, the Old City in Jerusalem and in San Antonio, Texas where she earned her B.A. in English and World Religions from Trinity University. She has authored several books of poetry and when asked how she found poems, she replied, "I'll tell you a secret: poems hide. In the bottom of our shoes, they are sleeping…They are the shadows drifting across our ceilings the moment before we wake up…Maybe if we re-invent whatever our lives give us, we find poems. Check your garage, the odd sock in your drawer, the person you almost like, but not quite" ("Valentine for Ernest Mann." www.poets.org)

What can we do with a poem when we find it?

• Unfold it.	• Share it.
• Touch it.	• Sing it.
• Read it.	• Draw a picture of it.
• Think about it.	• Find a poem hiding inside it.

Finding a poem in prose has several advantages: You don't have to start   from scratch since the words you use are already there; it celebrates plain language and words found in ordinary conversations while it avoids fancy "poetic" words, words with too many syllables, hollow words (happiness, sadness) that mean too many things to too many different people. As you read, look for words in books, newspapers, on walls, in junk mail, or even other poems. Keep track of where you find the words so you can give the source credit.

What Are the Ground Rules for Writing a "Found" Poem?

Step 1. Find important words you like—that really interest you—the "good stuff."

Step 2.   Copy the words in the order you found them. Double space between lines.

Step 3. Study the words you copied. Cut out everything that's dull or sounds bad.

Step 4. Read your "cut down" version aloud. You can add 2-3 of your own words to the original.

Step 5. REARRANGE WORDS AS YOU READ ALOUD.

Step 6. Try to end lines with key words—usually a noun or a verb. Make some lines long and some lines short. You might want to put

key

words

on lines by themselves.

Step 7. Make other "little" changes in verb tenses, punctuation and capitalization.

Step 8. Give credit to the source of words you used in your poem.

Thirteen Ways of Looking at a Grandchild

(with a nod of appreciation to Wallace Stevens)

I.
Grape jelly
On a grandchild's cheek
Makes sweet kisses.

II.
A grandchild asks, "Why?"
And when I answer,
Asks, "Why?" again.

III.
When we cross the street,
A grandchild holds my hand
And tells me to look both ways.

IV.
Birds sing in the trees
And azaleas on the back fence
Watch a grandchild run across the grass.

V.
Asleep between us,
A grandchild stretches—
Feet in my back,
Head resting on your arm.

VI.
Among thirty wooden pews,
I hear a grandchild praying.

VII.
A son and a daughter
grow into parents.
A mother and a father and child
create children and grandchildren.

VIII.
Clouds filled the grey skies
With rain.
The whispers of a grandchild
Shared secrets
Of fairies and princesses
Walking in magic forests.

IX.
The wind is blowing.
Somewhere a grandchild must be crying.

X.
I understand the beauty of logic,
 and the images of poetry,
But I understand, also,
That a grandchild understands love.

XI.
A teacher told me
God didn't give her grandchildren,
But He blessed her with teenagers.

XII.
Listen, generals and presidents,
  Do you hear
The sighs of a grandchild
When you make
Decisions about war?

XIII.
Morning wakes with sunrise,
And the clock ticks on the mantle,
And the moon sits on a tree limb.
A grandchild reads
A book while sitting in my lap.
          ~Lynne Dozier

Waiting
Birds sing in trees
and azaleas on the back fence
watch children run across the grass.
 Clouds and rain fill the grey skies.

Sunrise wakes morning,
the clock ticks on the mantle,
while the wind blows.
and the moon sits on a tree limb.

Listen, generals and presidents,
Do you hear their sighs
 Or hear the praying voices of children
 in thirty wooden pews
when you make decisions about war?
          ~Lynne Dozier

I "found" my poem by imitating Wallace
Stevens'"13 Ways of Looking at a Blackbird,"
but now I can keep, "Waiting" as my own.

Your Turn:
Find an object or person you care about and describe it
in 13 different ways. Number each of the ways. Then,
find another poem inside the first poem you wrote.

What Can I Write Poems About?

Poems   Secret Places
Fathers, Mothers   Food
Brothers, Sisters   Sports
Extraordinary people   Fishing
Pollution   Crows, Sparrows, Robins, Bats
Custer's Last Stand   Arithmetic
A Coyote's Song   Music
War   Space
Confessions—big and small   Schools
Grown Ups /Children
Underground Railroad
Jobs/Professions   Almost Anything!
Heroes/Villains
Streets, Roads

Poets and critics have identified more than 55 poetic forms, including odes, sonnets, ballads, limericks, haiku, sestinas, elegies and epigrams. A few of our favorites included in *Getting the Knack: 20 Poetry Writing Exercises*,[5] edited by Stephen Dunning and William Stafford, are:

"Found" & Headline Poems
Letter poems
Acrostic & Recipe Poems
Dream Write Poems
List/Catalogue Poems
Imitation Poems
Memory Poems
Question/Answer Poems
Dialogue Poems
Confession Poems
Monologue Poems
Pantoums
Syllable Count Poems

You can learn more about poetic forms, by visiting www.poets.org

Your Turn:
Jump into the poetic waters! See the next page for more suggestions. And, have some fun! Poetry, the oldest form of literature, can still inspire, entertain and enlighten. You might find a new way to accomplish these miracles.

Any Other Suggestions for Writing Poems?

1. Go back as far as you can remember, and visualize the first place you slept. Draw a map (or floor plan) of the room. Start with the walls, the windows, the door. Put in the closet, stairs, furniture. When you finish the map, show it to a classmate. Write a poem of three stanzas. The first stanza should show (actions, dialogue, concrete details) objects you remember. The second stanza should describe the place. The third stanza should show your attitudes you have towards the room and your memory of it. Write the poem in present tense. It does not have to rhyme.

2. Draft a poem made up exclusively of a title and dialogue between two speakers. Use no speaker tags ("he said," "she said"). Do not use narration or description to explain ("They shook hands on the driveway"). Ask each character to speak 5 times. Use punctuation to indicate change of speakers. Let their words show their relationship and personalities.

3. Find 50-100 words that really interest you in a newspaper, short story or book you're reading. Copy the words in the sequence you find them. Then try to eliminate half of them. Arrange them on a fresh sheet of paper so they LOOK and SOUND good. Supply your own punctuation and capital letters. At the bottom, write the name of the newspaper, short story or book where you found the words.

4. Pretend you are weather (a raindrop, snowflake, wind, hail, lightning, sunshine, earthquake, tornado). You can go or fall or drift anywhere you want. What noises do you make? What do you see on your way to earth? Where do you land? What do you do when you land? How do you affect the place you land? Where do you go when you are finished?

5. Pretend you are a season or holiday. How old are you? Are you male or female? What do you wear? What do you do? Think? Say? Feel? See around you? Why are you important?

6. Write a poem describing the sounds made by an ordinary scene (a cat eating dry pet food, a city street, a drummer practicing). Try to use onomatopoeia to echo the sounds you hear.

7. Write a 6-8 line poem using the same letter to start as many words as possible. Read it aloud to a friend to see who can read this "tongue twister" the fastest without making a mistake.

8. Think of three people you would like read your poems, describe them and their reactions to your poems when they read them.

9. Find a poem you really like by a famous poet, and write an imitation of it.

10. Draft a poem that shows 3 images you might see as you glance in a mirror. In the last line, show how the images made you feel about yourself. Do not use the pronoun, "I."

> **Your Turn:**
> Look around you. Walk in the woods or in your neighborhood or down your school's hallway, or along the fence of a sports field.   Jot down everything you see, hear, smell, taste, taste or touch…Somewhere, you will find a poem of your own.

How Do I Revise Poetry?

Richard Hugo volunteered for World War II where he served as a bombardier in the Mediterranean. Hugo flew thirty-five combat missions and reached the rank of first lieutenant before leaving the service in 1945. Like other World War II pilots, he would later recount his experiences in his poetry (www.poets.org). He offers the following suggestions for revising poetry:

- Make your first line interesting. When the poem begins, things should have already happened.
- Don't erase. It's gone then. Cross out. You may want to reconsider.
- Avoid semicolons.
- If you want to change something—first try leaving the same words, but play with the arrangement of the words on the page.

- Use strong, action verbs. (Enough said!)
- Maximum sentence length: 17 words.
- Minimum sentence length: 1 word.
- Use words you "own." If you don't love them enough to own them, you have to be very clever to write a good poem.

- End more than 1/2 your lines with words of one syllable.
- When rewriting, write the whole poem again.
- Make sure each line is at least four words longer or shorter than the one before it.
- Do not use more syllables, or more words, than you absolutely need.
- Beware of words necessitated by grammar (meanwhile, as, during, and, that, which). They may dilute the poem's impact and drama.

Peer Editing
1. Exchange poems with a partner.
2. Find imagery—words and phrases that create pictures in the reader's mind. In the margins, draw illustrations for them.
3. Underline Verbs.
4. Circle Nouns.
5. Put brackets around [figures of speech].
6. In your own words, write a summary. What is the poem about? What is happening?

How Do I Evaluate Poetry?

GREAT "A" POETRY:

    1. Engages readers in responses to Images, Words, Sounds, Rhythms and INTELLECT;

    2. Does not merely entertain—rather it brings readers fresh, renewed important and universal insights into the HUMAN EXPERIENCE.

    3. Does not insult readers by simply TELLING—rather it involves the readers in the poetic experience, and the reader discovers the meaning.

GOOD ("B") POETRY APPEALS TO:

    Our senses and imagination
    and succeeds in its poetic purpose.

AVERAGE ("C") POETRY:

    1. Indulges sentimentality, emotionalism and self-pity.

    For Example:

> I wish
> that we were
> as one again;
> my love for you
> is as high
> as any mountains
> up above the clear
> blue sky.
> I say this because
> I love you.
>
>   —a Valentine's greeting card

    2. Has teaching or preaching as its primary purpose.

    For example: Early to bed and early to rise,

> Make a man healthy, wealthy, and wise.
>
>   —Benjamin Franklin

I.	**II.**
The spoken or written word	The written word
Should be as clean as a bone,	As clean as bone,
As clear as is the light,	As clear as light,
As firm as is a stone.	As firm as stone,
Two words will never serve	Can stand alone.
As good as one.	

Your Turn: Read both poems aloud. Which of the above versions of a poem is better? How do you know? Choose one of the poems you have written this year. Is it an "A," "B" or "C" poem? Write a justification for your decision.

Poems in Your Pocket

More than 230 years ago, John Adams, in a letter to his son,   John Quincy Adams, wrote, "You will never be alone with a poet in your pocket." In 2003, the Academy of American Poets began to sponsor   a national "Poem in Your Pocket" Day to encourage people to share poems with friends, coworkers, family members and classmates. Today, many students and their parents carry poems in their pockets to their schools and workplaces to celebrate the importance of poetry. Below, you can read some of the poems my students wrote to carry in their own pockets:

Eye Creases

Poetry
is all the sticky stuff left
on the lunch table
from the spilled Dr. Pepper
that gets
on your elbows
and makes you curse
and it's the condensed version
of the lint between my toes
and it's the flaked
day-glow orange nail polish
scattered on the carpet under my desk
and it's that one time,
well maybe two,
when I would've been home on time, but...
~**Kristen Ortwerth(1999:61)**

The Written Word

We sit here silently
 under water fountains of light,
Crystal prisms above.
Below we wipe the mud
Off our feet
Onto ornate designs that bleed
Symmetrically over the carpet,
Closed in with walls
Where golden leaves shine off
Brass branches.
The odor of new binding
smells like fresh air.
A plastic tree, in the corner,
Breathes while
An army of chair soldiers salute
In attention, facing, listening
To a bearded man
Talk of poetry.
We look around for unwritten books.
~**Dan Heilbrun (1997:1)**

Missed Memo

Beneath the telephone,
a crumpled detail
skips across the tiled countertop
            and
                    falls.
~**-Emily Caulfield (2002:81)**

The Inheritance

Dust fell from grey curtains
as the sun danced on broken chandeliers
hanging from vaulted ceilings.
Rainbows kissed
the aged portrait of a young girl,
golden hair shadowing turquoise eyes.
The rosewood clock stood frozen
beneath a veil of cobwebs.

Tapestry chairs huddled
around a black walnut table,
polished surfaces faded.
The marble fireplace coughed
years of stale air.
Mahogany bookcases
flanked the fireplace,
while Dickens and Austen
stood beneath the family Bible.

Shadows moved across papered walls,
their hand winding the rosewood clock.
The wood floor moaned
as the grand piano shifted
towards stained glass windows.
Gilded couches blinked
as tattered sheets rippled
leaving dust suspended in air.
~**Melissa Watkins (2005:41)**

LESSON 10. STYLE—
THE "VOICE" OF PERSONALITY

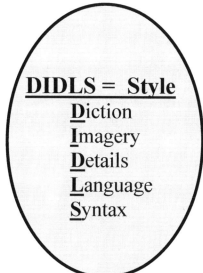

DIDLS = Style
 Diction
 Imagery
 Details
 Language
 Syntax

> **"Proper words in proper places make the true definition of style."**
> ~Jonathan Swift, 1720

What is Style?

What makes Walt Whitman sound like Walt Whitman? eecummings sound like eecummings? Martin Luther King sound like Martin Luther King? What makes YOU sound like YOU when you write an essay, report, a poem, or a story? The answer: these writers have achieved an individual "voice"— personality and STYLE—by choosing words, using language, creating images and writing sentences that readers have learned to associate with a unique and individual point of view, ideas and attitudes. As you discover your own "style," think about the different ways famous writers, thinkers and scholars might have answered the question, "Why did the chicken cross the road?"

Plato: It was for the greater good.

Karl Marx: It was a historical inevitability.

Darwin: It was the logical next step after coming down from the trees.

Emily Dickinson: Because it could not stop for Death.

Ralph Waldo Emerson: It didn't cross the road. It transcended it.

Henry David Thoreau: To live deliberately...and suck all the marrow out of life.

Chaucer: So priketh hem nature in hir corages.

Howard Cosell: It may very well have been one of the most astonishing events to grade the annals of history. A historic, unprecedented avian biped with the temerity to attempt such a herculean achievement formerly relegated to homo sapiens pedestrians is truly a remarkable occurrence.

Paul McCartney: (from the other side of the road)
Yesterday… all our chickens were so far away.

Mark Twain: The news of its crossing has been greatly exaggerated.

Dr. Samuel Johnson: Sir, had you known the Chicken for as long as I have you would not so readily enquire, but feel rather the Need to resist such a public Display of your own Lamentable and incorrigible Ignorance.

Isaac Newton: A chicken in motion tends to stay in motion.

Ernest Hemingway: To die. In the rain.

For more examples, see: http://fusionanomaly.net/whydidthechickencrosstheroad.htm

Achieving a style is not an easy task. You have to "shop" at many places, try on many writers, twist and turn to look at yourself in the mirror of opinion, and finally become comfortable with the techniques, strategies and choices that work for you.

To connect with readers, writers need to establish a personal and true style.

Hearing Student Voices:
"The 3 Ps: Prose, Poetry and Profits"[1]

Many years ago, when asked to teach a creative writing class, I suggested to our school's principal that I would like to sponsor a literary magazine as an extra-curricular activity, open to all students in the school, rather than limit it to pieces submitted by students in the class as part of the curriculum. I promised her that, "we may not win any awards, but we will make a lot of noise." And we did.

For almost twenty years, students have written, produced and published *Aquilae Stilus*, "the eagle's pen." We had an exciting, always challenging history. The first editor, Chris Noellert, begged to become the editor, "I'll do anything you want: cut your grass all summer, wash your car weekly, paint your house. Just, please, give me this chance." I couldn't refuse him so he took the helm of the first issue. Chris asked his friend, Vicki Black, a gifted writer and artist to be assistant editor. One day, I grabbed the arm of Yolim Khoo, a former student, drew him into my classroom and told him, "Yo, we need you. We're planning to put out a student literary magazine—like nothing that's ever done before—and we need your vision." Together, they gave the magazine a name, ("Latin is such a classy language"), designed a logo, interviewed and "hired" a staff, set goals and standards, advertised and then marketed and sold the award winning student art/literary anthology.

The first year was not without turmoil. A few staff members, eager to have "literary magazine" on their high school résumés, quit when they realized how many hours after school, evenings and on Saturdays, they would spend reading, typing, editing, designing a layout and formulating an advertising campaign. None of us knew what we were doing. Only Chris had any knowledge of computer technology; Vicki, because of her art talents, became "his eyes." Yolim and I considered ourselves "technologically challenged," but we, too had purposes—his to preserve the integrity of the vision—and mine to worry. The bill for printing the first year was more than $2700.00. When they began this adventure, they had only $300.00 in their account, a gift from the English and Art department budgets. I thought we'd be mopping floors in the lunch room to meet the costs of publication; however, they assured me, "If we write it, they will buy." *Aquilae Stilus*, after all, had become their "Field of Dreams."

> *Aquilae Stilus*, after all, had become their field of dreams..

They were right. That first year, they covered all the costs through sales and patronships—donations from parents, community and local businesses. The magazine received recognition from the National Council of Teachers of English, and several writers received awards from the Texas High School Press Association. Chris, Vicki and Yolim earned the admiration and respect of students in our high school who elevated their status to those of football and basketball athletes. Through their efforts to share the writing and artistic talents of all students, writing had become a vibrant part of something big and important at our school.

When they finally finished the typesetting and the layout on one of the first Apple computers, a square box, with a 12"x11" screen, I told the six students who stayed until the bitter end, "Publishing AQ (by now, a favored acronym) is like having a baby. It takes many months, the labor is painful, and you scream a lot at the people you love the most. Then, when you see what you have created, you smile at each other and say, 'Wow! Isn't she beautiful? Let's make another one.'"

Aquilae Stilus reflected the cultural and socioeconomic diversity of our high school. In less than five years, student minority population had increased from 2% to cultural and socioeconomic diversity of our high school. In less than five years, student minority population had increased from 2% to more than 68%. Today, students represent 54 different countries, every major religion and a per capita income that ranges from extremely low to extremely high. The anthology contains short stories, essays, poetry, art and photography from special education, foreign language classes and all levels of English and Art classes. At our school, a sense of audience has fostered a community of writers and artists. Most mornings, lunch periods and after school, students filled my classroom to read each other's pieces, discuss the art and craft of poetry, the use of imagery, details, dialogue and description in their own stories, as well as the 200-400 manuscripts submitted each year by students who reflected a variety of styles, cultural and historical influences.

The editors, Chris, Vicki and Yolim, handed over the reins of leadership to the students they had trained while creating the first edition. Yolim, a senior by now, and Harbeer Sandhu, a member of the first manuscript committee, returned as editors to help make the transition. The second edition continued its award winning ways and the training program was in full bloom. The editors interviewed twice as many people for staff positions, and each editor began mentoring an underclass staff member for a future editorial position. The legacy and heritage of *Aquilae Stilus* began to form.

During the third year, the editors, feeling totally empowered to produce the magazine, visited other schools and made presentations that showed how teamwork and goal setting could inspire creativity in students. They had learned marketing, advertising, financing, and interpersonal skills necessary for success of any organization. The budget had grown to $8,000.00, a quantum leap from the beginning. The third edition was named "Outstanding Literary Magazine in Texas" by both the Texas High School Press Association and the NCTE, and was featured in the November, 1995 edition of *The English Journal.*

That year's banquet celebrated the success of their vision, and they knew nothing could stop them now. They announced the next year's editors, who knew "they had their work cut out for them." With the glow of success fresh in their minds, the new staff dedicated their year to having fun—and so they did. Beside the tradition of excellence, they also continued the tradition of "marshmallow fights," outrageous publicity stunts, entertaining school announcements that the whole school woke up and listened to—and parties. Oh, yes, the editors and staff loved parties: dinner at my house, the "New Member Welcome, the "Send it to the Printer" parties, and their own get-togethers at coffee shops, poetry readings and concerts. Since its beginning, *Aquilae Stilus* had evolved into a fully functional, totally empowered student entrepreneurship, and as important to the school as the band, drill team and sports teams. They now had a Mission Statement:

To create an anthology of prose, poetry and art
that reflects the most creative minds of Klein Forest students.

Producing *Aquilae Stilus* was a labor of love. I loved the young people who sacrificed their spare time to create it; they loved each other as they worked together, and the students at our school loved the expression of their ideas, their voices, and the changing personality of their high school contained in its pages.

How Do Writers Develop "Style?"

Students in classes today   come from a wide variety of religious, economic, cultural, racial and historical backgrounds, and they reflect a wide range of knowledge generated from their families and past educational and community experiences. If teachers and professors expect anything when they read essays and compositions from students, they look for the real "YOU" behind the words you use, the grades and test scores. So, here are some tips that will help you develop a writing style that reflects your personality:

Be Honest. Be Yourself.

Ernest Hemingway lived in Spain, hunted animals in Africa, and drove a World War I ambulance in Italy; Emily Dickinson, a recluse, rarely left her home or talked with other people. Martin Luther King marched with thousands in the Civil Rights Movement; Henry David Thoreau lived, quietly, on a patch of land beside Walden Pond; Jack London worked in canneries and factories in Alaska; F. Scott Fitzgerald attended fancy parties with his wealthy wife and friends during the "Roaring Twenties." All of these writers found "voices" in their varied experiences, saw life from different points of view and created writing styles that distinguish them as unique and important influences in American literature. As they probably did, ask yourself these questions:

1. What distinguishes YOU as an individual?
2. What events and experiences have provided "hallmark" stories for YOU?
3. What are YOUR goals, aspirations, worries, ideals, values and principles?

Write in a clear, natural voice.

We have few seventeenth-century scholars left in the world; don't write as if your favorite tool on the computer is the "Thesaurus." Don't use the word, "amongst" when you mean, "among," or "nostril" for "nose," or "shall" for "will." But, don't be too informal either. Take care when using slang, profanity or colloquialisms. Instead,

1. Write to convey YOUR ideas clearly and easily; do not write to "impress."
2. Write about what's specific to YOU—not what you think we want to hear.
3. Express YOUR individuality; could your parents and friends pick out your essay
    from a pile of fifty others? If they did, why would they want to read it?

Remember that every effective piece of writing has a beginning, middle and an end.

After you have thought about **what** you want to say, think about **how** you want to say it. You have as many ways to present your ideas as there are ideas. Generally, though, you want to present them in an organized, coherent fashion so readers understand what they are reading. You should also remember, that composers have only eight notes, but the way they use them creates a symphony, a country song, or rap and hip-hop.   A writer has only eight parts of speech and many choices to make involving **diction, images, details, language and syntax (DIDLS).** Always remember to think about your audience's needs and your purpose for writing.

> ### Your Turn:
> Read passages from 3 different writers from three   different time eras. Retype them and then use the Grammar Checker to check Reading Level for each. What differences do you see in their choice of words, pictures they create, details they use (or leave out), sentence patterns and length,   and level of language in each.

DIDLS: Diction and Denotation

Diction refers to the writer's choice of words, usually dependent on situation, audience and purpose. Generally, linguists have identified five levels of diction [2]:

A. **Frozen:** Printed language that does not change (Pledge of Allegiance, Biblical quotations, The Declaration of Independence).

B. **Formal:** Language focused on form and one-way participation, no interruption. Technical vocabulary or exact definitions are important (Presentations, Lectures, Introductions and Legal briefs).

C. **Consultative:** Conversations in instructional settings involving two-way participation (Memos, emails, schools conferences between teacher/student, doctor/patient, expert/apprentice).

D. **Casual:** Conversation between friends in a social setting. May contain ellipses, Slang (Personal letters, anecdotes, stories, jokes).

E. **Intimate:** Non-public between spouses, twins, sweethearts, Private vocabulary. Also includes non-verbal messages (Private notes, diaries and journals).

Denotation is the dictionary meaning of a word. **Connotations** are the emotional associations of words that go beyond their literal, dictionary denotations. Adjectives, for instance, make judgments—one reason why writers should choose them carefully. For instance, a conceited comedian might say:

"Your jokes are funny." (neutral judgment of a friend)

"My jokes are hilarious." (positive judgment of self)

"Their jokes are absurd." (negative judgment of others)

The following groups of sentences describe the same church breakfast, but each group communicates a different attitude. As you read, highlight the adjectives that contribute to each writer's attitude towards the scene.

> **Neutral** (unbiased, impartial and factual): Every Sunday, between church services, the women of the congregation serve a breakfast of scrambled eggs, bacon, grits, biscuits, juice and coffee for $1.95.
>
> **Positive** (optimistic, warm and friendly): Every Sunday, between the uplifting church services, the faithful ladies of this charming congregation offer an appetizing brunch of fluffy scrambled eggs, crisp bacon, butter-laden grits, light, hot scones, fresh, frothy nectar, and steaming café au lait for a reasonable $1.95.
>
> **Negative** (downbeat, hostile and cynical): Every Sunday, between the deadening and dreary services, the female do-gooders of this dull-witted congregation ladle out a nauseating mess of leathery scrambled eggs, limp bacon, soggy hominy grits, heavy, cold, stale bread, flat juice-flavored water, and tepid java for an exorbitant $1.95.

> **Your Turn:**
> Take an ordinary object, scene, or person and write three different descriptions— neutral, positive and negative for three different audiences. Choose your words carefully to maintain the tone and attitude you want to communicate. As you write, think carefully about the level of diction appropriate for each reader.

What Words Describe a Writer's Diction?

At some point, an instructor might ask you to describe how writers choose the words they do, and how their diction contributes to the meaning, message and their attitudes towards a specific topic. Below, you can find words to help you do this:

1. **Colloquial:** Everyday, common spoken and written language

2. **Old-Fashioned, Archaic:** words not commonly used in present day language

3. **Informal:** Conversational

4. **Formal:** Literary and historical

5. **Connotative:** Suggestive, emotional meaning

6. **Denotative:** Exact dictionary meaning

7. **Concrete:** Specific, factual, detailed

8. **Abstract:** General or Conceptual

9. **Euphonious:** Pleasant Sounding

10. **Cacophonous:** Harsh sounding

11. **Monosyllabic:** words with one syllable

12. **Polysyllabic:** words with more than one syllable

> **Your Turn:**
> Choose ten of the words from the list of words that describe diction and create an example of each for your Writer's Notebook. Then, review one of the pieces you have written and identify the kind level of diction you used. How would you describe your own choice of words?

13. **Jargon:** language associated with a profession or job

14. **Euphemism:** words that make something unpleasant sound pleasant

15. **Gobbledegook:** words meant to deliberately confuse and distort meaning

16. **Idioms:** phrases and sayings natural to native speakers of a language

17. **Dialect:** words used by a people from a certain geographic area

18. **Slang:** words used often as part of a fad or special group—teenagers, for instance

19. **Profanity:** abusive, vulgar and unworthy words

20. **Epithet:** places an object in a distinct light—words often used as forms of abuse

21. **Acronym:** words made from first letters of other words NASA, snafu, radar

22. **Stream-of-consciousness:** a type of interior monologue characterized by chaotic leaps in syntax and punctuation because the words reflect fragmented thoughts and random emotions

23. **Esoteric:** words understood by a select few who have special knowledge

24. **Bombastic:** full of high-sounding words meant to conceal a lack of ideas

25. **Trite:** lacking freshness because of constant use of repetitive and common phrases

dIDLS: Imagery Appeals to the Senses

Imagery is a technique writers use to paint pictures of scenes and characters in the minds of their readers. As you learned in "Lesson 6, Description," objective description works well in some instances, but writing that uses strong imagery takes description to an entirely new level. When an author correctly uses imagery, readers can feel as though they are actually *experiencing* the place and time of the scene. Read this piece below and identify as many images as you can:

One Day She Fell in Love

Summer. She could smell Freedom. Playtime had ended; her brothers and friends trailed into the house, and she was left alone outside where she could smell warm grass, sweat, and dust in her face. Her tired body wandered; her mind flew. She found herself lying in bed, a bed firmer and more comfortable than any Sealy. Her head rested on Tree's root, and soil hiding beneath the lawn embraced her back. Grass held her in his arms. She slept.

Gradually, Sun woke her, warmth dribbling away from her skin. Thinking how the Ground had contoured to her body, she focused above on Tree's branches into the light blue Sky as it became pinker and deeper until stars marked it. She felt connected to Sky and Earth and Tree and everyone else.

Her fingers tickled Grass and she sat up, refreshed. A cool, night breeze blew across the yard, over to her house, and she snuggled against the landscaping. "Hi, Tree! Night sure is beautiful tonight, isn't it?" Wind and Plant whispered their approval. One by one, she held each in her arms. "Sleep tight. I'll see you tomorrow."

The porch lights flashed on, reminding us that privacy is temporary. Her mother's voice quivered, "Karen...Karen...have you been outside this whole time? It's 9:30...what are you doing…?"

She couldn't respond to her mother or to the rest of my family. She floated up the stairs, into her bed and opened her window. Nature sang her a lullaby as she drifted back into my dream.

—Karen Cullinan (1995:122)

<u>**Your Turn**</u>:
Choose a painting created by a famous American artist (John Singer Sergeant, Norman Rockwell, Winslow Homer, Andrew Wyeth, Edward Hopper, for example). Then, write a story that connects to the painting. As you write, incorporate details and images depicted in the painting. Then, use them to create a plot, conflict and characters. Try to focus, as you write, on showing what is happening during the few minutes shown in the scene depicted by the artist—a turning point or a moment of decision, for instance.

Read your story aloud. Cut all adjectives and adverbs unless they are pure "gold." With a friend, review several paintings and then ask your friend to determine the painting that inspired your story.

How Do Figures of Speech Create Images?

Figures of speech involve the comparison of two dissimilar things, and in doing so, they help readers create pictures in their imaginations. Scholars have identified hundreds of figures of speech; you can find the most common ones and examples listed below:

1. **Allusion**—a reference to a historical, mythological, Biblical or literary figure
   "I am Lazarus, come from the dead," (T.S. Eliot)
2. **Anaphora**—repetition of words or expression at the beginning of successive phrases, clauses or sentences
   "We cannot dedicate, we cannot consecrate, we cannot hallow this ground," (A. Lincoln).
3. **Apostrophe**—words used to address an inanimate object
   "Oh, Liberty, what things are done in thy name," (Carlyle).
4. **Anachronism**—outdated and old-fashioned use, relating to a more primitive time.
   He steered his 8-cylinder chariot away from the mountain's rim.
5. **Chiasmus**—inverted relationship between elements of parallel phrases
   "Ask not what your country can do for you, but what you can do for your country." (John F. Kennedy)
6. **Metaphor** (direct, implied)
   Winter is mittens; summer is sand. (direct)
   The black clouds of God's wrath covered the December day. (implied)
7. **Metonymy**—a word represents something else, which it suggests.
   "They fought for lands belonging to the crown."
8. **Oxymoron**—the use of contradictory terms
   "Feather of lead, bright smoke, cold fire, sick health!' (*Romeo and Juliet*)
9. **Paradox** —a statement that seems to contradict itself
   "It was the best of times; it was the worst of times." (*A Tale of Two Cities*)
10. **Personification**—giving human characteristics to something nonhuman
    A tree looks at God and lifts her leafy arms in prayer.
11. **Pun**— word is used to convey two meanings at the same time
    "Ask for me tomorrow and you shall find me a grave man," (*Romeo and Juliet*)
12. **Simile**—a comparison indicated by the words, "like" or "as."
    Nancy's voice sounds like a car riding on a tire rim.
13. **Symbol**—when a concrete object represents an abstract idea or emotion
    Each morning we show our patriotism when we pledge allegiance to the flag.
14. **Synecdoche**— a part of something represents the whole thing.
    Washington and Tehran both claim support for their positions.
15. **Hyperbole**—a gross exaggeration.
    The backpack weighed a ton.

Your Turn:
In your Writer's Notebook, create original examples of five figures of speech in the list above. Save them for use in either prose or poetry as you continue writing in these lessons.

DIDLS: Using Concrete Details

Details are facts writers use to convey judgments, meaning and attitude. The number of details a writer chooses is less important than their quality and appropriateness. Effective writers select and use those details relevant to their purposes and needs of their readers: For example:

"Kilimanjaro is a snow-covered mountain 19,710 feet high, and is said to be the highest mountain in Africa. Its western summit is called the Masai, Ngaje Ngai," the House of God. Close to the western summit there is the dried and frozen carcass of a leopard. No one has explained what the leopard was seeking at that altitude. "
—Ernest Hemingway. "The Snows of Kilimanjaro."

.

Your Turn:
The following basic simple sentences lack concrete details. Take each   sentence, and develop the idea expressed in the sentence with relevant and important details. Use the questions following the sentences to help you gather details to use. Then rewrite them in your Writer's Notebook.

For Example:
    1. Simple sentence: Marvin hit a home run.
Questions to Generate Details: How old was he? How was the game going? What was the effect? How often had he hit home runs? How did he feel about it?
        Revised Sentence: (one possible revision)
        To his parent's delight and his coach's surprise, Marvin, an eight-year-old Little Leaguer, hit his first game-winning home run.

Now You Try It.
    2. Simple Sentence: Pollution is a solvable problem.
Questions to Generate Details: What kind of pollution? Where is the   pollution? How is it solvable? How will pollution affect the future?
    3. Simple Sentence: The river is low.
Questions to Generate Details: What river? How low is it? What is its normal level? What is the effect? What caused it be so low?
    4. Simple Sentence: I was late to class.
Questions to Generate Details: When were you late? What class was it? How often were you late? How late were you? Why were you late? What happened as a result?

Next, review one of your drafts you have written.   Find sentences that lack concrete details. Revise them by supplying information appropriate for your purpose and necessary for your audience's understanding. Use some of the questions in this exercise to help you revise your own draft.

How Do I Add Concrete, Specific Details?

Using the questions in The Reporter's Formula (Lesson 4: Narration) can help you add specific, concrete details to your sentences. As you write a sentence, continually ask yourself, "Am I providing enough details so my readers know Who? What? Where? When? Why? How many?"

General	Specific, Concrete
The handbook provides a good guide for documentation.	The **MLA Handbook** provides a **thorough and accurate** guide for documenting **Works Cited.**
General The governor vetoed legislation that increased the amount of federal aid to public schools.	**Specific, Concrete** The governor **of Texas, John Smith**, vetoed legislation that increased the amount of federal aid to public schools in **low-income districts.**
General We watched the sun set.	**Specific, Concrete** **On the bow of the ship,** we watched the sun set **into the English Channel on the last day of our two-week cruise**.
General Members of the Student Council were absent, and the motion did not pass.	**Specific, Concrete** **Because thirteen** members of the Student Council were absent **at the monthly meeting,** the motion **for increasing dues** did not pass.

Your Turn;
In your Writer's Notebook, respond to the following questions.
- What do you believe are the 5 most beautiful words in the English language? Why?
- What do you believe are the 5 ugliest words in the English language? Why?
- What do you believe are the 5 most useful words in the English Language? Why?

Write sentences that use the specific words and provide concrete details in each of the sentences that help SHOW.

DIDLs: Using Language Effectively

Thoughtful ideas, logical organization, well-developed paragraphs, interesting sentences, do not guarantee exceptional results in an essay. The effective, purposeful, and overall use of language conveys a writer's thoughts with vigor and vitality. The main purposes of writing—to tell a story, describe, explain, inform and persuade—can't be achieved if a writer's language is murky or misleading. As you review the language you use in your essays and composition, you should consider:

The Need for Clarity
Realize who your readers and listeners are and aim your words towards them. Don't take them for granted. Don't write so simply that you talk down to them. Define words that may have unfamiliar or specialized meanings. Develop a double vision—look inward to see what the words mean to you and outward to see what they might mean to your readers or listeners.

The Need for Appropriateness
Often, audiences do not know you, and so, they judge the sophistication and maturity of writers' ideas by the sophistication and maturity of their writing styles.

The Need for Economy
When writing academic or personal essays, your writing must communicate everything necessary to help readers understand completely, so it's important to omit every unnecessary word, phrase and sentence. Achieving economy in writing is like dieting: the purpose of both is to remove fat. What's left should be strong, firm and muscular. These reminders might help:

♦ **Communicate in Natural Language—Rely on short, simple, plain words.**
"We have nothing to fear but fear itself."
--Franklin Roosevelt
"Mankind must put an end to war, or war will put an end to mankind.
--J.F. Kennedy

♦ **Listen to every sentence to determine if it sounds like you are "talking."**
Original: In view of the scare number of vocational opportunities that appear to be available to all members of the feminine sex in the community where I reside, my expectation for success were at a minimum.
Revision: Because few jobs were open to women in my hometown, I expected little success.

♦ **Use Concrete, Specific Nouns**
General: I fed my pet.
Less General: I fed my dog.
Most Specific: I fed Brandi, my white, toy poodle.

♦ **Avoid Overworked Verbs and substitute lively, specific verbs for general, lifeless verbs.**
Dull: The teacher looked at the student.
Lively: The teacher (glared, glanced, peered) at the student.

♦ **Substitute action verbs for the "be" family of verbs.**
Before: He is a pitcher for the Houston Astros.
After: He pitches for the Houston Astros.

Replace clichés and other trite expressions with your own figurative language.

Often student writers turn to tried but true phrases that one may have been as pretty as a picture, but now are as old as the hills. These students may think they are being sharp as tacks, but the expressions, to make a long story short, are as dead as a doormat, and as ugly as sin.

A Special problem— "I"

Feel free to use the first person pronoun, "I," but keep an eye open to see that it doesn't sneak in at the beginning of several sentences, let it appear only when you need it to appear. Remember, every time you use the word, "I," the reader focuses on the writer, rather than the ideas, actions or mood the writer is trying to convey.

Email/Blog Etiquette

Consider the following rules, especially when the email's recipient is a superior and/or someone who does not know you:

1. Include a meaningful subject line to help clarify your message and help the recipient prioritize reading your email
2. Open your email with a greeting like "Dear Dr. Jones," or "Ms. Smith:"
3. Use standard spelling, punctuation, and capitalization. THERE'S NOTHING WORSE THAN AN EMAIL SCREAMING A MESSAGE IN ALL CAPS.
4. Write clear, short paragraphs and be direct and to the point. Don't write unnecessarily long emails or otherwise waste the recipient's time
5. Don't try to joke around. Jokes may not come off appropriately in email.

He-Mail (aka Experiments with Technolocheese)

I've been #ing my head
On your jpeg
Trying to stay com…
But, you've caught me in the net.
Searching your eyes,
I start to :-)
I send you a @-- ` - -
You tell me to :-*your*
You and I used to click..
Now I feel like the host
Of a virus…
A love virus…:-(
                    ~Alison Ditto (1997:4)

Your Turn:

Send your English teacher, or another adult, an email in which you summarize the information about using language effectively on these two pages. Remember, to use language that is appropriate for your subject, occasion, audience and purpose.

How Do I Describe Language?

Describing a writer's use of language, particularly the English language can provide some interesting challenges. How can you discuss the use of language in these sentences?

1. The soldier decided to desert his dessert in the desert.
2. Since there is no time like the present, he thought it might be time to present the present.
3. If teachers taught, why don't preachers praught? If a vegetarian eats vegetables, what does a humanitarian eat?
4. English is a crazy language. Eggplant does not contain egg, nor is there ham in hamburger. However, a few words below might help you describe the English language—the most versatile language in the world:

Artificial	false
Literal	apparent, word for word
Bombastic	pompous, ostentatious
Moralistic	puritanical, righteous
Obscure	unclear
Obtuse	dull-witted, undiscerning
Ordinary	every day, common
Cultured	cultivated, refined,
Pedantic	academic, scholastic,
Detached	cut-off, removed, separated
Didactic	preachy, teaching a lesson
Plain	clear, obvious
Emotional	expressive of emotions
Poetic	lyric, melodious, romantic
Precise	exact, accurate, decisive
Pretentious	pompous, gaudy
Exact	verbatim, precise
Provincial	rural, rustic, unpolished
Scholarly	intellectual, academic
Sensuous	passionate, luscious
Grotesque	hideous, revolting
Homespun	folksy, homey, native, rustic
Idiomatic	Peculiar, vernacular
Insipid	uninteresting, tame, dull
Trite	common, banal, stereotypical
Informal	casual, relaxed, unofficial
Learned	educated, experienced
Vulgar	coarse, indecent, tasteless

Search for Missing Youth[4] (courtesy of Channel 2 News)

Apparently, he slipped out the back
door   with calculator and car keys
and didn't bother waking his mother
or calling his father
to tell them where he was going.
So now he is missing,
and the cold front is coming
with snarling teeth like the dogs
on the search team.
He did, however, bring
his brown backpack
full of books and notes
and logical problems to solve
until his location is known,
which hopefully will be in time
for his test on Tuesday.
        ~Justin Cone (1994:16)

Your Turn:
How would you describe the language in Justin's poem? Why do you suppose he chooses the words he chooses? What is his purpose? How does he want you to feel about the youngster in the poem?

DIDLS: Syntax—Sentence Functions

When you first learned to write, you learned to write complete sentences. As you mature as a writer, you should also learn to classify sentences   according to their function or purpose in a piece of writing.   Understanding the functions of sentences can improve the effectiveness of your writing style since readers enjoy reading a variety of sentences; each sentence should have a definite purpose and function. If a sentence does not have one of the functions mentioned below, then it might not even be a complete sentence.

- **Declarative Sentences** state an idea.
  > "Krebs went to the war from a Methodist college in Kansas."
  > —Ernest Hemingway, "Soldier's Home"

- **Imperative Sentences** give an order or direction. The subject is "you."
  > "You will make all kinds of mistakes, but as long as you are generous and true,   and also fierce, you cannot hurt the world or even seriously distress her."
  > —Winston Churchill in his autobiography, *My Early Life* (1930)

- **Interrogative/Rhetorical Sentences** imply or demand an answer.
  > "Although they should be used only occasionally in other kinds of writing, what could be more natural than a few questions in autobiographical writing?"
  > —Michael Adelstein in *The Writing Commitment* (1997)

- **Sentence Fragments** can shock or emphasize an idea.
  > "The teacher thought I was stupid. Couldn't spell, couldn't read, couldn't do arithmetic. Just stupid."
  > —Dick Gregory in his autobiography, *Nigger* 1964)

- **Active Sentences** show the subject performing the action.
  > "Crashing water echoed over the mountainside ahead."
  > —Melissa Watkins, "Jewel in the Mountains," *Aquilae Stilus* (2004)

- **Passive Sentences** show the subject receiving the action.
  > "Failed metaphors must be scraped from the bottom of the pan."
  > —Emily Caulfield, "Literary Cuisine." *Aquilae Stilus* (2002)

- **Dialogue Sentences** indicate conversation.
  > "Rube," he said, "there's an elderly gentleman outside who wants to see you. He says he's your father from Cleveland."
  > "He's not my father," I said. "My father wouldn't go across the street to see me. But you go out and get his autograph book and bring it in, and I'll autograph it for him."
  > —Rube Marquand, "I Become a Big Leaguer"

> **Your Turn:**
> Choose a passage from your favorite writer (other than yourself) and copy it in your Writer's Notebook. Then color code each sentence according to its function. Red=Declarative, Blue=Imperative, Yellow=sentence fragment, etc.

DIDLS: Syntax:—Sentence Structures

Although all sentences have the same **SUBJECT-PREDICATE** structure, a number of basic sentence structures are possible within that structure. These   basic types comprise the building materials for constructing all the possible sentences in the language.

Conjunctions: coordinate (FANBOYS—for, and, nor, but, or, yet, so) & subordinate (that, which, because, until, though, when, who, while, as if)

Phrases (a group of related words**)**

Clauses [a group of related words that contain a subject and predicate.] They may be independent or dependent.]

Proficiency in sentence construction is, perhaps, the most important aspect of effective writing. Look at the variety of sentence structures E.B. White uses in his essay, "Once More around the Lake"
http://www.moonstar.com/~acpjr/Blackboard/Common/Essays/OnceLake.html

A **simple sentence** consists of one independent clause..
["We had a good week at camp."]

A **compound sentence** contains two or more independent clauses, joined by a comma and a conjunction *or* by a semicolon.

["We would walk out with the bottle of pop apiece]*, and* [sometimes the pop would backfire up our noses and hurt."]

A **complex sentence** contains one independent clause and one or more dependent clauses.

["When the others went swimming,] [my son said he was going in too."]

A **compound-complex sentence** contains two or more independent clauses, and one or more dependent clauses.

["We explored the streams, quietly,] [where the turtles slid off the sunny logs *and* dug their way into the soft bottom;] *and* [we lay on the town wharf *and* fed worms to the bass."]

Your Turn:
In your Writer's Notebook, create a variety of sentence lengths on a topic of your choice by imitating the structures in the models presented by E.B. White in his essay, "Once More Around the Lake."

DIDL**S**: **S**yntax—**S**entence Patterns

Writers can manipulate the basic sentence structures to create variety for their readers and to emphasize the most important ideas by changing positions of words, phrases and clauses. Understanding sentence patterns also helps readers look for the most important ideas so they can read more efficiently.

Periodic Sentences
(most important clause comes at the beginning of the sentence)

Klein Forest is majestic and stately when the students have left and few teachers sit at their desks.

The Indians stood silent and intent, facing the wind, feathers ruffling, their eyes turned upward.

Cumulative Sentences
(most important clause comes at the end of the sentence)

When the students have left and few teachers sit at their desks, *Klein Forest is majestic and stately.*

Facing the wind, feathers ruffling, their eyes turned upward, *the Indians stood silent and intent.*

Balanced Sentences
(Important information equal on both sides of conjunction)

"Old wrinkled hands ran through thin white curls *while* ripped brown loafers tapped to a sassy beat."
Alyse Fullum, *AQ,* 2004

"I jumped off the swing *and* I sprinted through the woods."
Madison Houston, *AQ,* 2004

Sentences with Bound Modifiers
(modifiers stick to nouns)
In his *lunch* box, he carried *ten, purple* marbles.

Free Modifiers
(modifiers "float" in a sentence)

He forgot the *only* assignment.
Only he forgot the assignment.
He *only* forgot the assignment.
He forgot the assignment *only.*

Writing Hint:
To convey your ideas clearly, you should consider the various ways of manipulating sentence structure:
- Reordering words, phrases & clauses
- Combining simple sentences.
- Converting passive sentences to active and vice versa.

Your Turn:
Choose a section from an essay you wrote and "reorder, combine, or convert" the patterns in the sentences. If you don't like the sentence after you change it, remember, you can always "hit" the "undo" button.

DIDL**S**: **S**yntax—Parallelism

Parallelism—the repetition of words, phrases, or clauses that have similar grammatical structures—brings rhythm, style, and cadence to language and writing. Each of the passages below from Jefferson's "Declaration of Independence," demonstrate this element of style. Identify parallel structures by underlining words, putting parentheses around phrases, and brackets around clauses. Notice, also, the use of the ellipsis to indicate words left out.

Models:

1. ["...we mutually pledge to each] (other our lives,) (our fortunes,) and (our sacred honor.")
2. ["He has combined with others to subject us to a jurisdiction] (foreign to our constitutions) and (unacknowledged by our laws.")
3. "But when a long train of abuses and usurpations, begun at a distinguished period and pursuing invariably the same object, evinces a design to reduce them under absolute despotism, it is their right, it is their duty to throw off such government."
4. "We have reminded them from time to time of attempts by their legislature to extend a jurisdiction over these our states. We have reminded them of the circumstances of our emigration and settlement here…"
5. "He has constrained our fellow citizens taken captive on the high seas, to bear arms against their country, to become the executioners of their friends and brethren, or to fall by themselves by their hands."

Review the following sentences and their corrections. Which one sounds better?

Not Parallel: John enjoys swimming, movies and to play video games.
Parallel: John enjoys swimming, attending movies and playing video games.
Not Parallel: My friend not only likes to read, but write poems.
Parallel: My friend not only likes to read, but she also likes to write poems.

Your Turn:

Fill the blanks in the following sentence stems so the sentences contain parallel structures:

1. As soon as I saw my grades were in trouble, I _____ ,

   I _____ , and I _____ .

2. Snow lay everywhere. I covered the _____ filled the _____

   and _____ .

3. One candidate promised to _____ , to _____ , and

   to _____ while his opponent promised to _____ ,

   _____ , and _____ .

LESSON 11: SATIRE—THE "VOICE" TONE AND ATTITUDE

> "I have often thought that the best way to define a man's character would be to seek out the particular mental or moral attitude in which, when it came upon him, he felt himself most deeply and intensely active and alive."
> --William James, *The Letters of William James.* (1920)

What is Satire?

A man slips on a banana and falls down. Sometimes this scene makes people laugh. But is it satire? No. If the man is labeled "consumer" and the banana peel is labeled "government anti-inflation policy," then the fall becomes satirical. When the goal of humor involves an implied criticism or social comment, then we call it "satirical."

Anything, or anyone, can become the target of satire: powerful institutions and individuals; social and sexual traditions and values; hypocrisy, politics, war, education, racism, urban problems, etc. Satirical pieces are usually short and entertaining; they are always critical and one-sided. A person's response to satire—humor that ridicules, criticizes and attacks chosen targets—is especially subjective. In taking on the "powers that be" and Everyman's dislike of criticism, the satirist is often a lonely figure.

The first major satirists (that we know about) were Roman and Greek —Horace, Juvenal, and Petronius— and they wrote gentle, amusing satires or bitter and contemptuous satires. Satire can either be "direct," with a first person narrator, or "indirect" which might involve a story with cast of characters who comment on the state of affairs. "Romantic" satire features other-world characters and exotic, far-removed places and eras. "Realistic" satire contains true-to-life, down-to-earth details and events. In fact, the original Latin meaning of the word "satire" (*satura)* is "medley," or "hodge-podge."

Humor is subjective and personal; what is funny to one person may leave another cold. Some people criticize satire because it presents a distorted, exaggerated view of reality and brings out the worst in its readers—we enjoy secret impulses to join others in tearing someone or something down. Satirists, however, are not primarily social reformers or moral commentators. They are artists, motivated by their individual needs for self-expression as much as they are motivated by righteous indignation. To appreciate satire, readers should be wary of materialism, corruption and dehumanization in society. Satire, when we understand its goal and purpose, makes us feel morally and intellectual superior as we take sides with satirists against whatever topics they are mocking. We understand a point of view that should be obvious to all, but usually isn't. And, we don't feel obligated to do something to correct the problem the satirists challenge and depict.

Do you ever imitate teachers when they leave the room? Deride unfair school requirements or practices like cafeteria lunches? Exaggerate the acting, or playing style of a favorite actor or musician? If you do any of these things with a sense of humor, and without hurting anyone's feelings, you might qualify as a satirist.

Writers have attitude when they develop a point of view.

Satire: "A Recommendation Letter"

When Jim asked me to write a letter recommending him for admission to Rice University, I wanted to make sure he would remember it—and me—for a long time. I thought he might enjoy a satire because, as a student, he had keen antennae for detecting hypocrisy, pretentiousness and false piety. He took authority figures (especially me) with a grain of salt and enjoyed watching me squirm when he asked a pointed question or challenged me on a point. So, I wrote the following letter, and when he began to read it, I hoped he would find it funny. He did, and after we finished laughing, I gave him a copy of the "real" letter I wrote for him. He asked if he could keep the one below to show to his mother, who he thought would "get a kick out of reading it." As with all satire, there's enough truth in the letter below to make the exaggerations more humorous.

Dear Scholarship Committee:

Jim _____'s reputation preceded him, so when he strolled into my AP Language & Composition class, I knew I would experience an interesting, mind warping, and personality changing year. Jim is an arrogant, pseudo-intellectual and an academic snob, and if I managed to teach him anything he did not already know, I consider it a miracle. Of course, he qualifies for a scholarship, and receiving the money he needs to go to college would certainly help him leave our neighborhood and inflict his charms upon a larger academic community.

Jim brings an encyclopedic mind to all his endeavors. He has a broad range of reading interests and happily shares his opinions with anyone who will take the time to listen to him. He uses books and words like weapons, and in a college environment, no professor will be safe from his sharp sense of irony and his ability to challenge every point on every assignment to enhance his academic advantage. Jim is a capable writer, but he cannot take criticism and refuses to revise anything he has written. The best essay he wrote in my class made all the girls cry and brought tears to the eyes of his one best friend. In detailing his grandmother's premature death, he managed to bring pathos to a lie, and of course, greatly disturb his parents and grandmother and destroyed her golf game for several months.

Jim believes his leadership alone caused the phenomenal success of the baseball, Academic Challenge and Decathlon teams. If you ask him, or even if you do not ask him, he will gladly share his lists of awards and honors: Baseball Team Captain, Perfect Score in Speech Competition, and a total of nineteen medals in academic competition. He loves to brag that he is the only freshman and sophomore team member in our high school's history.

Jim is one of those lucky people who instinctively know how to take tests. He is a National Merit Scholar, and the College Board designated him as an AP scholar. His classmates voted him "Most Versatile," after he distributed several hundred $1.00 bills to students at lunch. *Aquilae Stilus,* our school's nationally recognized literary magazine, published one of his pieces because his parents made an extremely large contribution to help underwrite the costs of printing.

In summary, Jim is a sexist, politically incorrect individual, motivated by greed and self-promotion. His favorite writer and literary hero is Ayn Rand, and so we understand his commitment to selfishness and ego. A scholarship will enable him to pursue his goal: an education at Rice University where his vast knowledge and caustic wit will make his classmates feel inferior.

Jim has the potential and character to be president of the United States, and I cannot believe I suffered through a whole year of experiences with him.

Sincerely,

Lynne Dozier

Why Should I Understand Humor?

During the first weeks of school, I made sure that students understood the importance of enjoying a good laugh every once-in-a while. I told them, "A sense of humor is a sign of intelligence, and when you laugh at my jokes, you'll show me how smart you are." So, why should students enjoy humor? Laugh, occasionally, in a classroom?

1. Analyzing humor helps students understand why they laugh at David Letterman's Top Ten Lists and develops an appreciation for subtle, mature forms of humor. Analyzing humor makes us feel morally superior when we side with comedians against whatever subjects they are mocking.

2. Analyzing humor helps develop effective communication skills and provides release from stress in most careers and occupations. Imagine firefighters, policemen—and yes, teachers—who could not laugh at work.

3. Analyzing humor gives students practice in creative problem solving. Studies show that the body retains adrenaline after a hearty laugh, which makes students more alert and able to think better—form ideas "out of the box."

4. Analyzing humor helps students consider the relationship of censorship to such terms as good taste, appropriateness, tolerance, kindness, respect, sensitivity and political correctness. What is funny in one situation might be hurtful in another.

5. Analyzing humor as a social tool helps bring people together by providing comfort and joy while exploring cultural differences. Smiles are stronger than frowns.

What Makes Us Laugh? Some "Pattern" Jokes:

1. "Tom Swifties"
   > "My name is Tom," he said swiftly.
   > "Would you like another pancake?" she asked flippantly.

2. License Plate Humor
   > 10SNE1 = Tennis, anyone?
   > RM4U2 = Room for you, too.

3. Light Bulb Humor
   > "How many New Yorkers does it take to screw in a light bulb?"
   > "Three—One to do it and two to criticize."

4. "Short of…" Insults
   > "…a few bricks short of a load."

5. Good News/Bad News Stories
   > "Have you heard the good news/bad news about the year 2020? The good news is that all the sewage water available for drinking will be treated; the bad news is there won't be enough to go around."

> **Your Turn:**
> Choose one pattern and write your own "pattern joke." Share them with your writing group and vote on the funniest one. Groans and "boos" don't count!

How Is A Sense of Humor a Sign of Intelligence?
"SNL," "The Colbert Report," "The Daily Show," "The Simpsons," "South Park"

Some critics and psychologists feel that satire brings out the worst in us—our own sadistic impulses to join en masse in tearing something or someone down. They point out that many satires feature a rogue figure who usually gets the best of a fool figure—with the reading or viewing audience's complete approval.

Other critics complain that satirists do not t present solutions to problems. However, most literature exaggerates or uses "tunnel vision" in some way. Satirists are not primarily social reformers or moral commentators. They are actors, comedians, critical commentators motivated as much by their desire to entertain and express their own ideas as they are by righteous indignation.

Mark Twain, a master of satire, began keeping writing notebooks in his teens. His first journal logged his experiences on the Mississippi River as an apprentice steamboat pilot. He recorded every bend, sandbar, farmhouse, doghouse and outhouse on the banks of that mighty river highway. The logbook provided details for *Huckleberry Finn, the* novel that, many people regard as the beginning of all American fiction. We still quote some of his short, humorous, satiric comments. Here are a few examples of Mark Twain's wit and wisdom:

1. "Nothing is made in vain. But the fly came near it."
2. "Man is the only animal that blushes. Or needs to."
3. "There is no native criminal class except Congress."
4. "Patriot: The person who can holler the loudest without knowing what he is hollering about."
5. "I didn't attend the funeral, but I sent a nice letter saying I approved of it."
6. "Cauliflower is nothing but cabbage with a college education."
7. "A classic is something that everybody wants to have read and nobody wants to read."
8. "Man is the only animal that blushes. Or needs to."
9. "The human race is a race of cowards; and I am not only marching in that procession but carrying a banner."
10. "Don't go around saying the world owes you a living; the world owes you nothing; it was here first."

Your Turn:
Choose a narrator, use some of the techniques defined and modeled for you and create your own satire. You may use one of the subjects below or choose one of your own:
1. Discuss the political opinions of prunes regarding health care.
2. Discuss the advantages and disadvantages of being a snail.
3. Defend the moral values and virtues of a marshmallow.
4. Discuss the ethnic and cultural characteristics of penguins.
5. Argue for/against the economic value of eggplants—or other vegetable.
6. Create an editorial cartoon that satirizes some condition or issue in your school that you think deserves criticism. For examples, look at the editorial page in your local newspaper or http://www.ehow.com/how_2171718_draw-political-cartoon.html

How Do I Recognize Satire?

"Writing humor is serious business," says William Zinsser in *On Writing Well*. A satirist can direct the satire toward one individual, a whole country or even the world. It is sometimes serious, acting as a protest to expose a problem, or it can be comical when used to poke fun at something or someone. Some examples of satire in today's media include:

TV/Movie Title	Subject of Satire	Comment or Criticism
"Weekend Update" from "Saturday Night Live"	Television news shows	Makes fun of human flaws and vices related to politics, entertainment and current events
"Scary Movie"	Horror Movies	Exaggerates film techniques used in horror movies to scare audiences
"Austin Powers"	1960's spy movies	Ridicules sexism towards women, improbable escapes by spies and evil villain's stupidity
Political cartoons	Politicians and political issues	Mocks policy decisions and personality traits of elected officials
Songs by Weird Al Yankovich	Musicians and music videos	Derides excess, simplicity and immaturity of modern musicians and their lyrics

Consider, for example, the attitude of a student in my class towards writing:

How many students does it take to screw in a light bulb?
Just one. But the student has to describe the texture, smells, tastes and colors of the light bulb, explain how and to screw in the light bulb, and why it should be screwed in anyway, share an anecdote about the first time he/she screwed in a light bulb, analyze its brightness, and evaluate the result of screwing in the light bulb on the people in the darkened room.
—Joey Chance [1]

Your Turn:
Write a paragraph in which you use exaggeration and hyperbole to make fun of one of the subjects above. Do not forget to be outrageous and remember that you are presenting a distorted, exaggerated view of reality, not reality itself.

What Techniques Do Satirists Use?

Throughout this book, we have discovered that writers have many techniques and strategies from which they can choose to communicate an idea, attitude or mood to an audience—or to achieve any of the other many purposes available to a writer. Besides using the diction, figures of speech, language and sentence structures discussed in "Lesson 10: Style," writers use several other techniques to create satire:

1. **Satire**—both a genre and tone—a literary work holding up human vices and follies to ridicule and scorn; works through subtle attack and biting wit.
2. **Sarcasm**—a tone created through scornful, taunting contemptuous language.
3. **Reduction ad absurdum**—distortion and exaggeration to the point of absurdity.
4. **Incongruous and inconsistent contrasts**—comical and tragic elements, formal and slang language, odd groupings.
5. **Invective**—vehement denunciations and vituperation.
6. **Puns and twisted clichés**— "He who hesitates is sometimes saved" (James Thurber).
7. **Epigrams**—terse, witty sayings. "Conscience: the inner voice which warns us someone is looking," (H.L. Mencken).
8. **Paradoxes**—contradictory statement that may be true, either in fact or in a figurative, metaphorical sense. "It was the best of times; it was the worst of times." (Charles Dickens)
9. **Verbal Irony**—when words spoken communicate the opposite of what's really meant
10. **Dramatic Irony**—when what happens turns out to be the opposite of what was expected to happen.
11. **Cosmic irony**—when fate and the gods seem to play havoc with human plans and destinies.
12. **Hyperbole**—a figure of speech that describes something MUCH MORE than it is.
13. **Understatement**—a figure of speech that describes something MUCH LESS than it is.
14. **Litotes**—a form of understatement that says the opposite of what is intended. (Allison is not a bad singer.)
15. **Caricature**—a picture or verbal description which exaggerates the features and characteristics of a person but keeps the identity intact.
16. **Allegory**—a literary work that contains characters and settings that represent philosophical concepts and moral qualities.
17. **Parody**—Making fun of a style of a person or work of literature.
18. **Reversal**—to present in the opposite of normal order. Reversal can focus on the order of events—dessert before the main course— or hierarchical order—for instance, when a young child makes all the decisions for a family or when an administrative assistant dictates the decisions and actions of the company president.

> **Your Turn:**
> With your parent's permission, watch one of the television shows mentioned in this lesson, and see how many examples you can find in an opening monologue, or a comedy sketch. What seems to be the target of the particular comedy event or routine? How do you know?

How Do I Analyze Satire?

Satire represents a variety of genres—fable, movies, poems, cartoons, song lyrics, newspaper articles, as well as books, essays and stories. Below, you will find a list of some of the most popular writers—and examples—of satire in literature:

Essays	Novels
"A Modest Proposal," Jonathan Swift	*Animal Farm*, George Orwell
"Good Souls," Dorothy Parker	*Catch 22*, Joseph Heller
"Advice to Youth," Mark Twain	*A Clockwork Orange*, Anthony Burgess
	Gulliver's Travels, Jonathan Swift
Satirical Short Story Authors	**Movies/Films**
O. Henry	"Airplane," Jerry Zucker, Director
Mark Twain	"Caddyshack," Harold Ramis, Director
Ambrose Bierce	"Dave," Ivan Reitman, Director
James Thurber	"Mash," Robert Altman, Director

No matter whether you read or watch satire, you should ask these questions to test your understanding of this important literary and language form:

1. What qualities does a person need to be a good satirist? Do you think you would feel comfortable or uneasy sitting and talking with the satirist?
2. Why should satirists usually feel detached from their subjects? Do you think satirists can write easily about someone or something they deeply, personally feared and despised?
3. Since satirists are primarily creative artists, and since creative artists often perceive the world differently from the rest of us, why should we accept their views as valid?
4. What genre (story, novel, poem, essay, drama) did the writer choose? How does it communicate a message? Why is it an effective choice?
5. Do the satirists speak in their own voices, in a pretended first-person voice, or through a cast of characters?
6. What is the tone of the satire—gentle and amused or scornful and contemptuous?
7. What are the targets and messages of the satire?
8. What satirical elements and techniques are used and how?
9. Does the satirist imply a solution to the problem? What is it?
10. How do the satirists stack the deck in their favor? What details or circumstances favorable to the target do they omit?
11. Does the satirist's message convince you? Does it make you laugh? Why or why not?
12. Does the satirist seem aware of the audience? Consider their ideas, prejudices and biases?

> **Your Turn:**
> With your parent's approval, read one of the stories, books, or see one of the films listed above. Then, write an essay that shows what the authors or satirizing and why. The questions above will help generate ideas for your analysis. Be sure to cite examples from the literature that support your analysis.

How Do I Write a Parody?

Parody is a special kind of satire that makes fun of a particular literary style or work through imitation and exaggeration. Parody usually imparts a completely opposite message from the one intended in the original work. Parodies of idyllic and romantic pieces, like *Romeo and Julie,* for instance, become cynical, sarcastic, or humorous in message and tone.

Parody has long been a favorite of moviemakers. In 1940, Charlie Chaplin created a comedy satirizing Adolf Hitler with the film "The Great Dictator." About 20 years later Mel Brooks started his career with a Hitler parody as well. After "The Producers" (1968), Brooks became one of the most famous film parodists and did spoofs on many kinds of film genre. "Blazing Saddles" (1974) is a parody of western films and "Spaceballs" (1987) is a science fiction spoof. The British comedy group Monty Python is also famous for its parodies, for example, the King Arthur spoof "Monty Python and the Holy Grail" (1974), and the satire of Jesus in "Life of Brian" (1979).
To read some more examples of parodies, check out:

- http://www.shakespeare-parodies.com (scenes from Shakespeare's plays);
- http://urbanlegends.about.com/od/historical/a/twas_the_night.htm (Clement Moore's famous, "The Night Before Christmas);
- http://www.amiright.com/parody/misc/mothergoose7.shtml (Mother Goose rhymes in a whole new way).

Your Turn:
Below are twenty-one familiar targets for satire. Choose a topic that interests you, and find (or write yourself) a "serious" example of such writing. Then, write a parody that imitates and exaggerates the tone, style, subject, and word choices of the original work. You'll find that parodies are fun to write, and entertaining to read—especially aloud.

1. Advertisements—house-cleaning products, cars, cosmetics
2. A horoscope column
3. An advice column
4. A fan story in *People* magazine
5. A movie review
6. A weather report
7. A TV cooking demonstration show
8. A sportscaster's broadcast
9. A coach's pep talk
10. A political speech of a school or government office seeker
11. A door-to-door sales clerk's pitch
12. A boring teacher's lecture
13. A pompous sermon
14. A popular song lyric
15. A scene from a novel you were assigned to read

Remember that your purpose is to make fun of a style of speaking or writing. As with anything you write, think about your purpose, your audience and your tone of voice. What might seem funny to one person might be hurtful to another.

Why is My Tone and Attitude Important?

Tone is the sound of the writer's voice, as it communicates the writer's attitude towards the subject or topic of the piece of writing. When speaking, we use voice inflections, facial expressions and body language to show how we feel about what we are saying. We might lower or raise the sound of our voice, scowl, raise our fist, or shake our head. We might cross our arms or shrug our shoulders to communicate the way we feel about a subject—an idea, place, or even a person. Writers can only use words, but we can "infer" the tone behind the message.

Readers often confuse **mood** with **tone.** Mood, however, suggests a sense of place and atmosphere, while tone suggests the author or speaker's attitude. Mood often complements tone. For instance, "dull," "dark," and "dreary," suggest the mood of an oppressive place; "vacant eye-like windows" might suggest the somber attitude towards that place.

Most young children can sense a speaker's attitude in the tone of voice. For that matter, even dogs understand the tone of their master's voices. "You lazy old mutt, how are you doing today? Did anyone tell you you're absolutely useless?" The dog wags his tail, enjoying the attention and kindness of its master's voice despite the <u>**literal meaning**</u> of the words the master has just used.

Writers manipulate language in an attempt to achieve the same effect. Writers' tones depend on the choices they make about diction, images, details, language and syntax. As readers, and writers, we cannot say we understand any piece of writing, or work of literature until we have sensed, understood and inferred the writer's tone—the emotion behind the words and between the lines—the <u>**figurative meaning**</u> implied by the writer.

> ### Your Turn:
> Choose one of the poems below as a model, and then write a few sentences of your own. Show some attitude! Save it in your Writer's Notebook so you can find it easily.

Anorexia Nervosa

You are the second girl
that I've seen in the mall today
sitting with her model perfect boyfriend,
nibbling on a spring roll
from his mound of Chinese food.
I watched you over my burrito,
you with your long blonde hair,
tight black sweater,
and your impossibly thin waist.
                    ~**Jessica Wilson (2005:104)**

Devil in Texas

Is Texas getting hotter?
I'll be damned if Texas
isn't getting closer to hell,
and the roadside churches
are finding their white wood
 panels cracking from the heat
 of the winds blowing
 from the south
as if from the sigh
 of a lazy devil's open mouth.
                    ~**Erica Wilkins (2004:38)**

How Can I Describe Tone and Attitude?

Once again, let's define tone in a written composition as what the author (rather than the reader) feels about the subject. (What the reader feels about it, by contrast, is referred to as the mood.) Tone is also sometimes confused with "voice," which can be explained as the author's personality expressed in writing. For instance, you might describe your mother's personality as "caring, kind and thoughtful," but if you come home late after your curfew, her tone—or attitude—might be harsh, demanding and angry—which would affect your mood.

Tone is the attitude writers take when they write about a subject—the sound of their voices if we could hear them speak. Tone is established when the author answers a few basic questions about the purpose of the writing: Why am I writing this? To whom am I speaking, or writing? How do I feel about my topic? What do I want the readers to learn, understand, or think? How do I want them to feel, or do, after they've read it?

Tone and voice, two features of writing that go hand in hand, create the STYLE for a piece of writing. The attitude and the personality — two other ways to describe tone and voice — could also be said to blend into a flavor of writing. Whatever your attitude, choose the diction, images, details, language and sentences (DIDLS) and then, make a conscious decision about tone based on the purpose, the audience, and the desired outcome of your work.

When you read, if you misinterpret tone and mood you can misinterpret a writer's meaning and message. For instance, if readers miss irony or sarcasm, they may find something serious in subtle, veiled humor. When trying to describe a writer's tone, here are some words and phrases you can use:

Objective	Sympathetic	Pleading
Solemn	Pious	Patriotic
Playful	Straightforward	Ambivalent
Ironic	Sincere	Satiric
Sarcastic	Hopeful	Sardonic
Critical	Nostalgic	Whimsical
Reverent, irreverent	Loving	Hopeless
Philosophical	Forgiving	Dejected
Humorous	Admiring	Derogatory
Affectionate	Compassionate	Cynical
Approving	Moralistic	Worried, yet resigned
Mocking	Didactic	Fearful and searching
Sentimental	Conciliatory	Indignant and spiteful
Disgusted	Exuberant	Remote and disinterested
Tragic	Elated	Outraged and intolerant
Angry	Passionate	Elevated and authoritative
Mournful	Fervent	Thinly veiled contempt

> **Note:** Try to use a phrase when describing tone because most writers use a combination of tones to communicate meaning.

LESSON 12. MEDIA LITERACY—
THE "VOICE" OF ANALYSIS

YouTube,
Facebook,
Internet, Google
it!
Twitter,
Instagram
,I-Think?

Buy Something!
Buy
Anything! Buy
for America!
Elect My
Candidate!
Charge! Charge!
Charge!

"You can tell the ideals of a nation by what it advertises."
—Norman Douglas, *South Wind* [1917] Ch. 17

What is Media Literacy?

"Tired of the same old assignment? Has studying zapped your strength? Caused bad breath and loss of hair? Looking for a writing assignment that can turn you into an executive with three sports cars and a summer home? Britney Spears and Ozzy Osboune swear this assignment will bring you riches and make you famous. With this assignment, you can also fight terrorism, forces of evil, and join your patriotic friends who love America, want freedom and need less government. Follow us on Facebook and Twitter. When you receive this email, send this announcement to 10 of your best friends. Good luck will follow."

****

We receive much of our information about the world through visual images and media "sound bytes" that shape our views and opinions. As a form of persuasion, advertisers, politicians and media representatives achieve their goals in advertising by considering what a certain group of people need, want or desire. Then, they combine specific words and images to appeal to that group's emotions, prejudices and attitudes. In today's world, technology—through the Internet, YouTube, Facebook, Twitter, and Google—spread those images and words from nation to nation, people to people and neighbor to neighbor with the speed of light.

Interestingly, the best ads on television and the Internet are those that entertain us by making us laugh, frighten us or seem to be about something else other than the idea or product they are really promoting. As consumers, advertisers often hook, trick and cajole us into spending our money for items that harm our health, overload our charge accounts and waste our days and leisure time. Because of advertiser's creativity, we often forget Henry David Thoreau's wisdom, "That man is richest whose pleasures are the cheapest." As citizens, we often make choices in the voting booth based on our "gut instincts," rather than facts and information. In his timeless 1946 essay "Politics and the English Language," George Orwell condemned political rhetoric as a tool used "to make lies sound truthful" and "to give an appearance of solidity to pure wind." When that happens, argument becomes persuasion, and persuasion becomes propaganda.

As you learn to write—and THINK—more effectively, you should become conscious of the differences between a sound argument, effective persuasion and propaganda—especially if it involves visual images, graphics and "sound bytes." Becoming media literate—acquiring the ability to use, understand, analyze and create media—can help you discover the differences between persuasion and propaganda so you can protect yourself against those who might want you to buy more and think less.

Writers Influence Attitudes, Judgments and Values of Society.

Essay: "Idioms, Idiots and Ideas"[1]

In 1960, my first college English professor, Dr. John Bierk, discussed the themes of George Orwell's novel, *Nineteen Eighty-Four*. During that fall semester, Orwell's fictional account of life twenty-four years in our future seemed improbable, impossible and highly imaginative.

The vocabulary Orwell associated with totalitarian control of a population—"mini-plenty, newspeak, oldspeak and thoughtcrime"—reminded me of Lewis Carroll's the "sound and feel" words in "Jabberwocky," where he tells readers to "Beware the Jubjub bird, and shun/ the frunious Bandersnatch!" The idea that a Big Brother could use those words to watch us, that the Thought Police would read our minds, and that the we'd have a government where the "Party controls the people by feeding them lies and narrowing their imaginations through a process of bewilderment and brutalization that alienates each individual from his fellows and deprives him of reasoned inquiry" (Hintzsche 2) could never happen in the United States—or so I thought.

When the year 1984 actually arrived, however, Ronald Reagan was president and the "Me Generation" spoke the language of "Reagonomics": "golden parachutes, supply side and trickle-down economics, debit cards, hostile takeovers, leveraged buyouts," and "insider trading" (Lederer 46). The National Council of Teachers of English began its Annual "Doublespeak" awards; citizens listened to political leaders in "sound bytes;" many newspapers closed their doors, the victims of 24 hour TV news programming; and Rupert Murdoch and Ted Turner formed media conglomerates that owned and controlled most television, movies, and magazines. Today, millions of people, driving home from work, listen to Rush Limbaugh, and trust him when he tells them, "Don't bother reading the newspapers. I'll read them for you and tell you who to believe and what to think."

Orwell, in his essay, "Politics and the English Language," published in 1946, twelve years after he first published *Nineteen Eighty-Four,* "The decline of a language must ultimately have political and economic causes" (527). He blamed most of the decline on the "staleness of images" and "the lack of precision" (529). Orwell's prediction in his dystopian novel *did* not prevent his vision from happening when the year 1984 arrived.

> After World War II, English with a twist—American jargon and slang—circled the globe, boosted by U.S. economic and political power.

To understand the present, we need to examine the past. English, now spoken worldwide, began as a rude language spoken by obscure German tribes who invaded England in 1066. It spread with the British Empire during Elizabeth I's reign, aided by the invention of the printing press and influenced by Shakespeare, Milton and *The Bible.* After World War II, English with a twist—American jargon and slang—circled the globe, boosted by U.S. economic and political power.

Today, English has become to the modern world what Latin was to the ancients, and it dominates our planet as the standard for communication in science, technology, commerce, tourism, diplomacy and "pop" culture. Today, almost 750 million people, one of every 7, claim some knowledge of English. It is the native language in 12 countries, official or "semi-official" language in 33 countries and widely studied in 56 other countries. Today, the English language represents 80% of the information stored in computers around the world (McBee 52).

Millions of people overseas struggle to master the irregular verbs, strange idioms and irrational spelling of English words. In Japan, businesses offer high salaries to anyone who can write technical manuals in plain English. A few years ago, Sony Corporation placed this ad in Tokyo newspapers: "Wanted: Japanese who can swear in English." In Germany, scientists first publish in English because as one official said, "If you write in German, you get read in Germany, but nowhere else." Even in France, 83% of students choose to study English over German. Signs reading, "Hi-Fi," "Fast Food," and "Le Scoop du Jour," or "today's special," appear in French store windows (McBee 50).

Books, television and the U.S. Information Agency have helped spread American English across continents. Instant communication across the world through e-mails, fax machines and the Internet have stimulated a whole new vocabulary of acronyms (NASA, sonar, radar, FAQ, CD-ROM) which threaten to overwhelm us. Space and computer jargon have encouraged the publication of a multitude of dictionaries to explain their definitions. The word, "Google," has become a verb with past, present and future tenses.

People in other countries often mangle the English language as they stumble over pronunciation, idioms, jargon and slang. For instance, a Chinese guide, when explaining the pressures of population growth, said, "the city is pouring out of its skirts," and in Tokyo, a store sign advertised, "Hair Saloons." Sometimes, an idiomatic "goof" can lead to a diplomatic blunder. Once, a Soviet envoy raised his glass in a toast at a Washington dinner party, and instead of toasting, "Bottoms up," he said, "Up your bottoms" (McBee 52).

In his book, *On Writing Well,* William Zinsser registers concern about the overabundance of jargon, and euphemism occurring in the English language, the ailment the National Council of Teachers of English calls "Doublespeak." Today, for instance, in many schools, libraries have become "learning resource centers" and jails have become "correctional facilities," implying they should, and could do more than detain criminals.

Government, possibly the result of "stonewalling" during Watergate, calls a morning invasion of Marines a "predawn vertical insertion," and civilian deaths lack the impact of headlines and aren't newsworthy when referred to as "collateral damage." A "wood interdental stimulator" is more expensive that a toothpick; a housewife gains status but does not earn more money as a "domestic engineer," an elevator operator is a "vertical transportation corps member," and in medical jargon, a "therapeutic misadventure" saves a malpractice lawsuit when the patient dies. In April 2003, President George Bush, a favorite target of claims of "doublespeak" because of his "Bushisms," said in 2003, "I reminded [the soldiers] and their families that the war in Iraq is really about peace" (Bush, George).

The real danger of English writing today is not grammatical flubs, but clotted and convoluted expression that makes ideas needlessly complex. In *The Elements of Style, E.*B. White writes, "Vigorous writing is concise. A sentence should contain no unnecessary words, a paragraph no unnecessary sentences, for the same reason that a drawing should have no unnecessary lines or parts" (23). The value of "writing tight," making every word count in a coherent, correct and concise piece of writing reaches across continents. When writers "click and send" an email to Japan, or any other place in the world, they cannot afford to be misunderstood in translation.

As long as English continues to dominate business, technology, politics and media, speakers and writers should value the strength, diversity and flexibility of our language. Educators, especially English teachers, should continue to influence the language habits of their students by creating a consciousness about the way the English language works and its inherent power to influence, inspire and affect worldviews. Awareness will enable students, our future voters, to defend themselves against the propaganda of ideas in Orwell's *Nineteen Eighty-Four* like "WAR IS PEACE. FREEDOM IS

SLAVERY. IGNORANCE IS STRENGTH" (164). Citizens who understand the way language can work to manipulate and persuade will realize that "Power is not a means; it is an end...The object of power is power" (217). With an understanding of language, particularly "political language designed to make lies sound truthful and murder respectable" (220), we might avoid a future where we can "imagine a boot stamping on your face forever" (242). Today, fifty three years after Dr. Bierk's class lecture, Orwell's future no longer seems improbable, impossible or imaginative.

Works Cited

Bush, George. April 11, 2003. CNN Interview. (http:transcripts.cnn.com/ TRANSCRIPTS/0304/11/se.05.html. 2 August. 2012.

Hintzsche, Daniel. (November 2, 1999). "A Glance. 1984." Review. Enu.net/archive/ books/cult_etc.html. (August, 2012).

Lederer. Richard. (1991). *The Miracle of Language.* New York: Simon & Schuster.

McBee, Susanna. (February 18, 1985). "English: Out to Conquer the World.'" *U.S. News and World Report: 49-2.*

Orwell. (1946). *Nineteen Eighty-Four.* _New York: Harcourt, Brace, Jovanovich.

Strunk, William and E.B. White. (1979). *The Elements of Style.* New York: Macmillan Publishing.

Zinsser, William. (1994). *On Writing Well.* New York: Harper Collins.

They are coming…

Ahhhh!
The world is going to end,
The Carrots told me

Of the   Evil that will befall
The world if they are given
A chance to rise.
They are coming…

They are coming
To take over the world
And force the poor pacifist
Fruits and Junk foods to work
In vegetable gardens,
While the humans
Consume only veggies!

They will torture
The humans
Making year round
Schooling and other
Horrendous nightmares.

The only vegetables
That would do such
A vile thing are…
The Cucumbers! And
Their mischievous accomplices
The Brussel Sprouts,
Whose only goal in life
Is to rule the world.
                    ~Jennifer Wilson (2001:66)

Your Turn:
Use the Internet to find at least 6 examples of "Doublespeak" in politics, advertising and media today. What is the "hidden message" behind the examples? How do they "clot and confuse" communication? Be sure to document your sources correctly (See Lesson 10: Synthesis).

What is "Doublespeak?"

In Orwell's classic dystopian novel, *Nineteen Eighty-Four*, Newspeak," became the official language of the county Oceania, and developed to meet the needs of "Ingsoc," a shortened version of "English Socialism." In the novel, "Newspeak" replaces "Old speak," or Standard English, by 2050. To serve the needs of the totalitarian government, and dystopian society, "Newspeak," according to Orwell's view, [2] helped:

- promote ideas and philosophy of Ingsoc;
- make all types of thought impossible except those ideas promoted by Ingsoc party members;
- discourage all divergent thinking;
- eliminate political and intellectual freedom by cutting down choice/number of words;
- eliminate undesirable words—abstract nouns and words that had multiple meanings.

In the novel, to achieve the goals of total control, government leaders invent new words (miniplenty"), combine old/new ("thoughtcrime") create euphemism (Ministry of Plenty), and slogans ("War is Peace"). They strip words of multiple, secondary, unorthodox meanings (adjectives like "free"), cut choice of words to bare minimum ("times 3.12.83 bb dayorder,") and create three distinct and separate A, B, C categories of vocabulary:

1. The A vocabulary consists of the words needed for the business of everyday life— eating, drinking, working, putting on one's clothes, riding in vehicles, gardening, and cooking, and the like. Composed almost entirely of words like *hit, run, dog, tree, sugar, house, and field* — with rigidly defined definitions. All ambiguities and shades of meaning are purged out of them.

2. The B vocabulary consists of words constructed for political purposes—to impose a desirable mental attitude upon people using them. Without a full understanding of the principles of Ingsoc, it is difficult to use these words correctly. The B words are compound words consisting of a noun-verb, and inflected according to ordinary rules. The word *goodthink* means, "'to think in an orthodox manner," for instance. As an adjective, it becomes "goodthinkful," and "goodthinkwise" becomes an adverb.

3. The C vocabulary consists entirely of scientific and technical terms. Scientific workers or technicians can find all the words they need in the list devoted to the scientific specialty, but he seldom had more than a smattering of the words occurring in the other lists.

The word "doublespeak," coined in the early 1950s never actually appears in *Nineteen Eighty-Four*. Doublespeak may be considered, in Orwell's lexicography, as the vocabulary of Newspeak, words "deliberately constructed for political purposes: words, that is to say, which not only had in every case a political implication, but were intended to impose a desirable mental attitude upon the person using them," according to William Lutz.[3]

> **Your Turn:**
> Write an essay in which you agree or disagree with this statement:
>> "As societies grow decadent, the language grows decadent, too. Words are used to disguise, not to illuminate, action: you liberate a city by destroying it. Words are to confuse, so that at election time, people will solemnly vote against their own interests."
>> —Gore Vidal, author, playwright, novelist and social critic

Linguistic Self-Evaluation Experience
(Duh? You mean, like a quiz?)

In his bestselling book *Doublespeak,* William Lutz [4] notes that doublespeak is not an accident or a "slip of the tongue." Instead, it is a deliberate, calculated misuse of language. Doublespeak is language which pretends to communicate, but really does not. For fun, and for practice, match the following "doublespeak" phrases containing euphemisms, gobbledygook and jargon with their Plain English definitions:

Plain English	Doublespeak
1. Used car	A. Non-goal oriented member of society
2. Pig pens and chicken coops	B. Single-purpose agricultural structures
3. Bum, street person	C. Downsizing personnel
4. Firing employees	D. Advanced downward adjustments
5. Budget cuts	E. Collateral damage
6. Bank robbery	F. Experienced automobile
7. Civilian casualties	G. Unauthorized financial withdrawal
8. Grocery store checkout clerk	H. Kinetic kill vehicle
9. Anti-satellite weapon	I. Ultimate high-density warfare
10. Nuclear war	J. Career associate scanner

Your Turn:
A few years ago, an email from an employee of the U.S. Public Health Service discussed a sure-fire way to create jargon. This "Methodical Government Expression Projector," below employs a glossary of thirty carefully chosen "buzzwords." To see how it works, think of a three digit number (phone, social security, driver's license—1-2-6), and then select a corresponding "buzz" word from each column.

After you have created "doublespeak" phrases, write a definition for each of them. For example, a **"total monitored time-phase"** might be the "number of hours in a shift at a fast food restaurant. Then, you, too, can drop these phrases, or "systematized logistical projections," into any report to make you sound like an important government official.

1. Total	1. Organizational	1. Flexibility
2. Systematized	**2. Monitored**	2. Capability
3. Parallel	3. Reciprocal	3. Mobility
4. Functional	4. Digital	4. Programming
5. Responsive	5. Logical	5. Concept
6. Optional	6. Transitional	**6. Time-phase**
7. Synchronized	7. Incremental	7. Projection
8. Compatible	8. Third generation	8. Hardware
9. Balanced	9. Policy	9. Options
10. Integrated	10. Management	10. Contingency

Answers: 1 F, 2 B, 5 A, 4 C, 5 D, 6 G, 7 E, 8 J, 9 H, 10 I

Argument? Persuasion? Propaganda?

Before you try to understand the power of advertising and the impact of visual media in our daily lives, let's consider some important definitions:

- **Media Literacy (n.)** 1: The process of asking questions about what you watch, hear, see and read. 2: Literacy skills applied to mass media culture and information technology, messages. A necessary skill for life in a media saturated society.
- **Advertisement**—1. The act of advertising, a notice designed to attract public attention and promote sales.
- **Propaganda**—1. Systematic propagation of a doctrine or cause: 2. material disseminated by the advocates of a doctrine or cause.
- **Logic**—1. The study of the principles of reasoning, valid reasoning, esp. distinguished from invalid or irrational argumentation.
- **Fallacy**—1. A false idea or notion, 2. Incorrectness of reasoning or belief.

	Argument	**Persuasion**	**Propaganda**
Goal	Discover "the truth."	Promote an opinion or position rooted in truth.	Offer "political opinion or position" that may distort the truth and include false information.
Purpose	Show certain ideas are valid and others are not.	Move an audience to action or to change its beliefs.	Used by certain groups to persuade or scare others into adopting their political, religious or philosophical beliefs.
General Technique	Offers sound reasoning and evidence that appeals to audiences' logic.	Uses personal, emotional or moral appeals to convince audiences to adopt a particular point of view.	Relies on emotions and values of audience to accept a position regardless of facts and evidence.
Methods	Considers other perspectives on an issue; Offers facts that support the reasons; Predicts and evaluates the consequences of accepting the argument.	May consider other perspectives on an issue; Blends facts and emotions to make a case, often relying on opinion; May predict results of accepting a position, especially if the information will help convince an audience to accept an opinion.	Focuses on its own message, without considering other positions; Relies on biases and assumptions, may distort or change evidence to make a case; Ignores the consequences of accepting a particular position.

How Are "Needs" and "Wants" Different?

Abraham Maslow, an American psychologist, formulated a theory of behavior based on a hierarchy of needs [5], which he believed all humans have when they are born. Trying to satisfy and fulfill those needs at each of the levels motivates and influences behavior and human relationships. He arranged the needs into a pyramid based on their importance to human beings' growth and maturity.

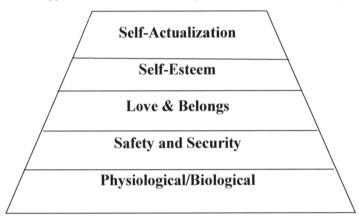

Self-Actualization

Self-Esteem

Love & Belongs

Safety and Security

Physiological/Biological

Level 1: The most important needs for survival—basic biological, physiological requirements for food, air, water, sleep.

Level 2: Once individuals fulfill basic biological needs, they can concentrate on the second level, the need for safety, security, order, and predictability.

Level 3: Next, humans have a strong need for love and belonging—friends, companions, companions, a supportive family, and identification with a group.

Level 4: Then, according to Maslow, humans need self-esteem—recognition from other people that result in feelings of prestige, acceptance, status, competence, and confidence. Maslow believed that unfulfilled esteem needs results in feelings of inferiority, discouragement and disillusionment.

Level 5: Finally, self-actualization occurs—the need to acquire and understand knowledge and the need for beauty, balance and harmony— which sits at the top of the pyramid.

As you think about advertising and the influence of film, television, radio and the Internet on our choices in products, lifestyles, and yes, political candidates, ask yourself, "How do advertisements, commercials and the voices heard through media outlets manipulate my emotions? How do they appeal to basic needs? Do I need this product? Or do I just want it? If I purchase this product, or vote for this candidate, will it be because I feel "unsafe," or because I believe the candidate will make my community a more harmonious place to live?"

> **Your Turn:**
> Sit for one hour in front of a television set. Count the number of ads shown during that time. What categories of products are most often advertised? What audience are advertisers most interested in purchasing their products? How do you know? Do the ads appeal more to emotion? To reason and logic? Are they more persuasion or propaganda? How do you know? What examples can you provide as evidence?

How Do I Analyze The Power of Advertising?

Ads create a culture of discontent. They imply we need something to make us feel better, behave better, look better or perform better. We see ads everywhere. Advertisers strategically place products in movies; the Internet contains ads that "pop up" in all kinds of unexpected places. We wear advertisements on our clothes and see them on stadium billboards, fences, and on the sides of school buses. Musicians and athletes endorse shampoos, tennis shoes and pills for arthritis and other medical conditions. Advertising, using our talents for art, design, creativity and storytelling have become so much a part of everyday life that we rarely stop to think about its effect on human behavior, citizenship and society. The questions in this section will help you "take apart" an advertisement or commercial.

Your Turn:

Choose an advertisement from either print or media, and on note cards, or separate sheets of paper, take notes on each of the following questions for paragraphs you will write later:

Media Literacy: Subject

What item is advertised and what role does it play in American culture and society? What action is taking place in the advertisement and what significance does it have? (This might be described as the ad's "plot.") What theme(s) do we find in the advertisement? (The plot of an advertisement may involve a man and a woman drinking but the thematic idea might be aligned with jealousy, faithlessness, ambition, passion, etc.)

Media Literacy: Occasion

What is the occasion of the advertisement? (What is happening in the world at large that influences the use of/need for the person/product/service? BE SPECIFIC.) What does the background/setting tell us? Where does the action in the advertisement take place and what significance does this background/setting have for the participants? For the audience?

Media Literacy: Audience

Who are the imagined consumers/users of the product/service? What do the advertisers seem to know about an audience's age, sex, race, and education? What do they assume are their needs? Wants? Motivations? Goals? Aspirations? Ambitions? What do the advertisers believe their audience values and respects?

Media Literacy: Purpose

What is the purpose of the ad? To convince viewers, readers to do what? What about the purpose of the language used? Does it essentially provide information or does it try to generate some kind of emotional response? Or both? What sociological, political, economic or cultural attitudes are indirectly reflected in the advertisement? An advertisement may be about a pair of blue jeans but it might, indirectly, reflect such matters as sexism, alienation, generational conflict, loneliness, elitism and stereotypes.

Media Literacy: Techniques

Images? Size? Objects? Colors? Product and Logo placement? Spacing? Numbers? Websites? Email addresses? Quotes from authorities? What have advertisers left out? What haven't they told you about their product, candidate or ideas? What questions can you ask that advertisers might not want to answer, like cost or side effects? Is it mostly facts? Or mostly opinions?

Media Literacy: Implications and Conclusions

What kind of person does the advertisement tell viewers they can become if they purchase the product, accept the idea or vote for the candidate? What is the general ambience of the advertisement? What mood does it create? How does it do this? Finish this sentence starter: The advertisers imply that buying this product, using this service, voting for this candidate will

_____

_____

_____.

Your Turn Again:

Combine the information and ideas the questions above generated into a five or six-paragraph essay that analyzes the power of advertising. Determine the "real" meaning behind the images and actions. In addition to selling a product, service, or candidate, what do the advertisers try to sell you about yourself? What are they trying to show about Americans? If you had never visited the United States, what would the ad you've chosen tell you about our values, attitudes, problems and beliefs?

What is "Election Speak" Jargon?

Jargon is the specialized vocabulary of a profession, technology, or field of academics. While specialized words may communicate effectively within a field, they can confuse and obscure meaning to readers and listeners outside a profession. Below is a glossary of political terms that can get you through a campaign and Election Day. Define as many as possible. You may need to use online dictionaries since many words have not found their way into standard usage dictionaries yet.

Landslide	Polls	Stump speech
Blue State	Primary election	Youth vote
Red State	Pundit	Money Race
Conservative	Popular Vote	Soft Money
Liberal	Electoral Vote	Swing Voters
Ticket	Orator	Caucus
Exit Poll	Rhetoric	Partisan
Independent	Swift-boating	Inside/Outside The Beltway
Neo-Con	Attack/Negative Ads	Voting Rights Act
Robocalls	Battleground States	Redistricting
Blank Check	527's	Gross Domestic Product (GDP)
Front Runner	Lame Duck	Gross National Product (GNP)
Incumbent	Lobbyists	Absentee Ballot
Fat Cat	Mudslinging	Delegate
PAC, Super PAC	Reagan Democrat	Entitlement
Turnout	Soccer Moms	Bipartisan
Spin Room	NASCAR Dads	Grass Roots
TEA Party	Platform	Sound Bytes

Your Turn:
After defining these words, look for them in a national magazine, newspaper either in print or online. Underline them. Do some math. What is the percentage of "Election Speak" used in the article?

How Do Clichés "Sell" Candidates?

Political campaigns often fill the airwaves with clichés, or overused phrases that lull the voting public into a somnolent slumber—a numbing of intellect and emotions. Below, you will find phrases that campaign managers and advertisers use to describe their candidates. Substitute "she" for "he" wherever appropriate.

Candidate Descriptions

He has a clear vision for our future.	His record on the issues is clear.
He is a man of character and integrity.	The voters can identify with him.
He is a candidate for the people.	He understands the middle class.
He is running a grassroots campaign.	He's willing to stand up to Washington bureaucrats and insiders.
He cares about children and family values.	He won't back down to special interest groups.
He has demonstrated real leadership.	He stayed on message and got out the vote.
He is good for the country.	

Brochures, Town Hall Meetings, Debates and "Sound-bytes"

We will build a bridge to the 21st Century.	Together, we will make America great.
We will grow the economy.	We are the defenders of freedom around the world.
We are going to change government.	Let us celebrate our diversity.
We will reach across party lines.	We are a better, more prosperous country than we were four years ago.
We are here to serve the American people.	Are you better off today than you were four years ago?
We will fight for working families.	We will find out how great a nation like ours can be.
We must put our people first.	

Your Turn:
Create a brochure for a student running for president of your school, your grade or your class. Fill it with as many clichés as you possibly can. Make sure your brochure is red, white and blue and contains flags and other U.S. state or school symbols.

How Does "Election Speak" Sell Candidates?

During election years, you will encounter all sorts of political language on television, online, and in magazines and newspapers. The activities below will help you understand the "real message" behind the words of political candidates, their "surrogates," and the "pundits" when they appear in speeches, debates, news and "talk" shows.

Completing Political Sentences

Directions: The sentences below have missing words commonly used in election campaigns. Complete the sentences by using words from the vocabulary word bank. Feel free to change the tense or form of the word to fit the sentence.

Eloquent	Charisma	Gracious
Bunk	Canvas	Declare
Controversy	Veto	Adverse
Candidate	Strategy	Jubilant

1. At 9:00 p.m., the Governor _____ the nominee a winner.

2. Such an absurd claim was plain _____.

3. Wasn't it a brilliant _____ to offer free perks?

4. The President claimed he would _____ the bill.

5. She was always an _____ and forceful speaker.

6. The _____ crowd roared its approval.

7. Her _____ and kind attitude have tremendous appeal.

8. His manager feared an _____ reaction to the policy.

9. There was an _____ over the ballot count.

10. Volunteers were glad to _____ the area for votes.

11. With her _____ and appeal, she would be elected.

12. The _____ crisscrossed the country to register voters.

> **Your Turn**:
> With a partner, create a fictional political candidate for a local election. Then, create a short speech for the evening news. Use as many clichés and examples of jargon as you can to sell your candidate and the issues. Don't forget to create a slogan! Have someone "act" as the candidate and deliver the speech with a straight face and proper gestures.

Student Voices:

Miss Your Light

Put my poem
On a street light in Austin,

The one smothered
In promotional gimmicks
For a concert
For one of those wannabee bands
Hoping to make it big.
Maybe people will stop and read it
And see something,
Learn something
And feel something—
And miss their light
To cross the street.

~-**Tawny Hammett (2008:35)**

Gilded Gold

Let's put America back together again.
When Blues weren't Democrats,
Reds weren't Republicans,
And whites weren't the only people
who care to vote.
Let's sew the whole flag back together,
Like the Red, White, and Blue we loved.
Let's put the heart back
in the chests of cowards,
The tin men we call soldiers,
The brains back in our scarecrows,
In addition, give some bravery to our lions.
Bring families back home.
A home where immigrants aren't a burden,
A cockroach in society,
But a handy blend of work and culture.
A gilded age of gilded men and women
Lies upon us now.
And ordinary people act as weak metals
Covered in shiny glasses.

~**Leonora Varvoutis**
(2008:48)

The Tissue

What about the tissue?
A fly swatter, a paper towel.
Eyeglass cleaner, and a duster
All in one.
The tissue's soft texture
Makes it smooth on noses.
Those fancy boxes
Revolutionized the cold experience,
And to make a tissue dance,
Put a little boogie in it.

~-**Nicole Lowman (2008:90)**

Casualty of War

His muddy boots
touch the melting runway pavement.
His camouflage uniform now
covered in a thin blanket of foreign dust,
along with a few holes
around his knees and elbows.

Eighteen months ago,
he boarded a plane with flawless skin
the color of peaches and cream.
Now, that skin holds wrinkles
around his North Carolina baby blues,
and a two inch scar above his left eyebrow—
his face once young and innocent,
now aged and guilty.

As his boots mark toward her,
she finds herself standing
before a stranger.
his eyes grey and empty;
his face dark and cold.
Salty streams trickle down her cheeks
as his whisper floats in the air—

"My body may be home, Mama
But my heart is still at war."

~**Sara Childs (2008:40)**

Your Turn:

Create a "print" ad or a commercial that takes a stand, presents a point of view that convinces an audience to accept your opinion, buy a product or calls people to act in some way. Consider the use of propaganda in your advertisement.

LESSON 13. RESEARCH—
THE "VOICE" OF SYNTHESIS

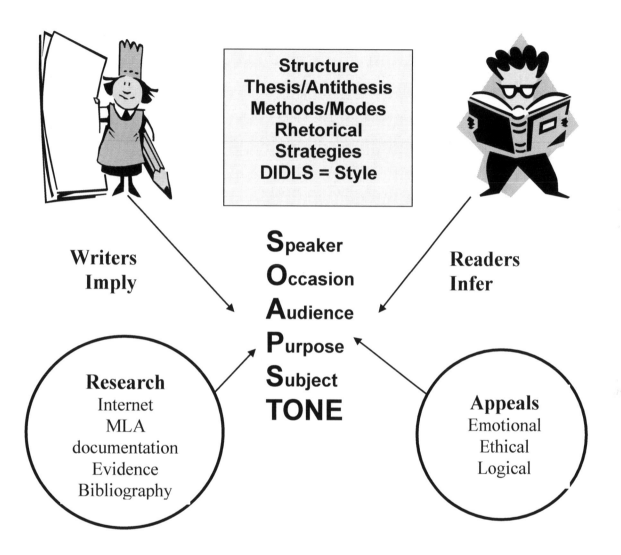

Structure
Thesis/Antithesis
Methods/Modes
Rhetorical
Strategies
DIDLS = Style

Writers
Imply

Readers
Infer

Speaker
Occasion
Audience
Purpose
Subject
TONE

Research
Internet
MLA
documentation
Evidence
Bibliography

Appeals
Emotional
Ethical
Logical

"Information competence is the fusing or the integration of library literacy, computer literacy, media literacy, technological literacy, ethics, critical thinking and communication skills."
--from a California State Polytechnic University Report
http://www.education-world.com

What Is a Synthesis Essay?

Take a minute to review all the types of essays and compositions you have drafted in the "Your Turn" exercises in *The Writer's Voice* so far. How many times did you have to read something to get ideas for an essay? Interview or talk with someone who had some information you could use? How many times did you have to look up facts to make sure that you understood the topic—and more importantly—could explain it to someone else? How many times did you rely only on your own observations and experiences without checking those observations and experiences or verifying them with someone else?

In academic and workplace situations, you will often need to use and combine information from several sources to make a case or support your own opinion. The "synthesis essay," by definition, combines information from several sources, but writing an effective, coherent and convincing essay also depends on your ability to infer relationships between those sources and the information they provide. People synthesize information naturally to help others see the connections between things they learn. For example, you have probably stored up a mental data bank of various things you've heard, or read, about particular cars or sports teams or movies. You will probably use the information you have gathered to help you decide whether to buy a certain car, attend an event with a certain team, or buy a ticket to see a certain movie. Synthesizing sources is a matter of pulling them together into some kind of harmony so you can achieve the purpose of supporting a thesis, assumption, theory or proposition.

Because a synthesis essay is based on using two or more sources, you will need to be selective when choosing information from those sources. In a history class, for instance, it would be impossible and unwise, to try to discuss every point about such a large topic as the Depression that several authors of several sources have covered in books. As a writer, you must learn to select ideas and information from each source that best support the thesis and purpose of your essay. Writing an effective synthesis essay that uses information from a variety of sources will require you to do several things:

1. Read for evidence;
2. Cite evidence from text correctly;
3. Learn to paraphrase and summarize accurately;
4. Use criteria to evaluate Internet sources;
5. Avoid plagiarism;
6. Use your best writing skills to create a thoughtful, interesting, and informative essay that shows your expertise and power to interpret and analyze information that helps your readers view a topic in a new way.

Writers understand how to combine techniques, methods and resources.

Essay: "Teaching Johnny to Spell"[1]

Ever since I began teaching English in Missouri in 1964, I have agonized over the problem of how to teach vocabulary and spelling to my students.¹ The most common issue parents want to discuss during Open Houses and parent-teacher conferences concern the spelling errors they see on students' tests, essays, and homework assignments. They also want to know how students can improve vocabularies so they perform at higher levels on state standardized tests and national SAT, ACT and AP college admission tests.

In fact, parents —and school administrators—have valid reasons for these kinds of questions. First, readers cannot read poorly spelled papers because misspelled words provide obstacles to comprehension. Secondly, misspelled words create an impression of illiteracy more readily than any other element of writing. Lastly, spelling, vocabulary and other mechanics seem to be the most elementary of skills and mastery of them seems to indicate a higher level of communicating (Irmscher, 127). On the other hand, poor spelling inhibits a student's vocabulary choices so teachers need answers when asked about these closely related skills of spelling, reading and vocabulary development.

Since I always excelled at spelling (I once won a county spelling bee), I believed all my students should turn in perfectly spelled papers that contained broad, rich and varied vocabularies. However, experience has convinced me that traditional methods of teaching spelling do not work. For many years, I watched students, primarily boys, become frustrated when they wrote compositions. Stopping frequently to ask how to spell words or look them up in dictionaries were tedious tasks for students and interrupted their thought processes.

> **However, experience has convinced me that traditional methods of teaching spelling do not work.**

Often, students chose simple words, rather than difficult ones because spelling easier words helped avoid the teacher's "red, bloody, pen." Sometimes, they gave up and turned in assignments, misspellings and all. A few students refused to write more than the minimum, discouraged by penalties and limited vocabularies. The emphasis on correct writing in their assignments, or "products," seldom gave them opportunities or time to improve vocabulary and correct spelling. I tried traditional spelling textbooks, occasionally so difficult, with their emphasis on syllabication, pronunciation and rules, that even I had to check the answer key! I used vocabulary lists, played games and gave quizzes at the end of the week on the assigned words. However, these assignments bored the students (and me) who saw no relevance in them, and most of them scored poorly on the quizzes. Those who scored well by memorizing definitions and correct spellings did not transfer those skills to their writing assignments. I finally abandoned them as a waste of time, and chose, for awhile, to do nothing about teaching spelling or vocabulary skills.

One summer, while attending the New Jersey Project Writing Institute, I discovered many of my ideas about spelling had support. William Irmscher, in his book *Teaching Expository Writing,* writes, "Those who chronically misspell have built up defenses that no teacher is likely to penetrate...in thirty years of teaching I have never known an adult who overcame the problem of bad spelling" (124). However, Irmscher also believed students could overcome bad spelling habits if teachers do not overlook certain facts as they teach students to write in their classrooms:

1. Almost everyone spells more words correctly than incorrectly;
2. Since the patterns of misspelling are individual, diagnosis needs to be done on an individual basis—the worse spelling errors are the ones students repeat over and over again;

3. Every writer has to believe that learning to spell better has positive benefits worth the effort to learn and the time it takes to proofread;

4. The word processor is one of the most overlooked devices for teaching spelling because typing provides a different view of words on a page;

5. Learning to spell is a continuing process because we constantly encounter new words. Accurate spelling requires a keen eye;

6. Millions of people have mastered the English spelling system (125-126).

Research supports the premise that "Children learn to write by writing" (Atkins, 11). Children begin writing with "invented spelling," using personal logic rather than, or in conjunction with, standard spelling. With "invented spelling," children listen to sounds in their words and use the sound-symbol correspondence they know. They work out—unconsciously, of course—the rules and generalizations involved in writing (Atkins, 10-11). "Invented spelling gives young writers early power over words. Professional writers don't worry about correct spelling on their first drafts, and neither should eager, young writers. They want precise and lively words for their stories; they don't want to stop and look up each word in a dictionary," (List 15). Spelling is not an end—it's a tool. From the start, developing writers should focus on language and content during a first draft, and search for correct spellings later on, after drafting and revision, when the piece is almost finished.

The single, most important factor in the development of writers is the teacher-student relationship. My students varied in maturity levels and in writing abilities. Generally, girls were better spellers than boys. Most had more advanced spoken vocabularies than written vocabularies. All of them have access to computer technology either at home or in the classroom.

Teachers can influence the writing skills of students by creating a consciousness about the language they use. The Writing Process helps students craft their writing; the reading/writing connection helps students improve by exposing them to words in print and ideas for writing topics. Students should choose their own vocabulary words, look up definitions, and write them in personal word banks in their notebooks. As they share unfamiliar words, or words used in special ways, they become aware of the role connotation plays in a piece of writing. They can discuss the importance of the "right" word—and most importantly, they have a list of words to use that has relevance for them because they are student-generated instead of teacher-chosen.

Ratiocination—an editing technique—helps students make corrections during the revision stage of the process. During "ratiocination," students color code problem words and phrases (Carroll, 91). Circling "be" verbs, putting wavy lines under repeated words, marking vague, "empty" words with an "x," drawing triangles around pronouns, and highlighting clichés invite students to use a Thesaurus and instill confidence in their abilities to improve and correct their own problems with language. This kind of "hands-on" activity also helps students understand the codes used when they click on "tools" or "review" when using computer spelling and grammar checkers.

However, not all writing assignments give students time to go through all the stages of the process. When students write during "timed" essays, test situations or on homework assignments, they still need to take time to proofread for spelling, grammar and mechanical errors. With instruction and practice, students can learn to proofread and correct errors quickly. . Some tricks can help them focus if they allow five minutes at the end of a "timed" situation to:

1. Read an essay backwards to help isolate words from the context so the writer sees each word individually;

2. Touch each word with a pencil, which causes them to look carefully each word;
3. Correct errors by neatly drawing a line through incorrect words and rewrite them correctly. Most test evaluators see neatly corrected errors as a sign a writer cares enough about expressing their ideas that they took time to proofread and edit.

Now, after 30 years, I can answer questions about improving students' spelling and vocabulary. When asked, I reply, "Student writers can improve through efficient and knowledgeable use of the tools on their computer. They can keep lists of new words in their notebooks. They can read their papers aloud, revising every word that does not t sound or look "right." They can ask a friend to help them proofread. (I have never known a young man who did not appreciate the proofreading abilities of a pretty girl.) During this final stage of the writing process, parents can help as long as they remember that proofreading is the primary job—parental rewriting does not help a student grow in confidence and ability.

If all these suggestions fail to convince parents and administrators, I quote Andrew Jackson who said, "It's a damn poor mind who can think of only one way to spell a word."

Works Cited

Atkins, Cammie. "Writing—Doing Something Constructive." *Young Children.* November 1984: 9-13.

Carrol, Joyce. "Ratiocination and Revision or Clues in the Written Draft." *English Journal.* November 1982: 90-92.

Irmscher, William F. *Teaching Expository Writing.* Holt, Rinehart & Winston, 1979.

List, Hindy. "Kids Can Write the Day They Start School." *Early Years.* January 1984: 14-16.

> **Your Turn:**
> Choose a draft from your Writer's Notebook that you've drafted quickly or a "timed" essay written in class. Proofread and correct your errors using the three steps mentioned above. Make sure that you remember that the "spell checker" does not check homophones—words that sound alike, but have different meanings and spellings like, "their, there and they're."

Does "Synthesis" Mean "Research?"

In a simple word, "yes." When you research the word, "research" in a dictionary, you will discover that it means, among other things, "the collecting of information about a particular subject." Certainly, in high school and college classes, your instructors will expect that a synthesis essay will include the information you have gathered in an insightful, correct, thoughtful way presented in an interesting manner. A few years ago, I surveyed students to find out how they viewed "research." A few of their responses included:

Research: More Than Google

My Questions for Students: What is research? What do you do if you don't know anything about a topic? How do you find out information? What issues in America concern you? What would you like to know more about? What's the difference between facts and opinions? How do you prove your opinions? Why is research important?

Typical Student Responses: "Research is looking up things on the Internet. I usually use Wikipedia and maybe a few other sites the teacher tells us about. I try to change a lot of words so the teacher doesn't think I copied word for word and I use lots of quotes. Teachers like quotes. I usually don't have many opinions, and the Internet has all the facts I need, so I just use what I find on the Internet."

Synthesis, by definition means, "combining information to form a unique product requires that creativity and originality." So, "research means "collecting" and synthesis means "combining." The original product produced when this happens might be an essay, newspaper, proposal for a problem-solution, advertisement, video, new game, blueprint, or even a song, poem or novel. When you "collect" and "combine" information you will need to complete several tasks that require you to:

- **Decide** upon a topic;
- **Formulate** questions;
- **Generate** research plan;
- **Collect** data;
- **Convert** data into written notes;
- **Identify** sources;
- **Differentiate** between paraphrasing & plagiarism;
- **Evaluate** relevance, validity, reliability of sources;
- **Develop** topic sentences;
- **Summarize** findings and make conclusions;
- **Present** findings in consistent format;
- **Use** quotations and other evidence to support ideas.

Your Turn.
Before you work through the following exercises, brainstorm several topics in your Writer's Notebooks you would like to know more about, and beside each topic, write a sentence or two that shows why the topic is important to YOU.

Why Do I Need Research Skills?

In his senior year in college, our son wrote eighteen reports and essays that required research that supported his ideas and opinions. And, those assignments happened in the engineering/business courses he took to complete his Engineering degree and major in Industrial Distribution! When he called home to ask me about metaphors, analogies, and imagery and how to use them in a report—techniques required by his professors, I sent him copies of handouts I used in class.

A few years ago, when I took some college courses, a favorite professor said, "Pick a topic. Do some research, and present it to me in an interesting way. Do not write a boring report." After researching the best ways to prepare a preschooler to read, I created a newsletter for mothers and dads of toddlers and made copies for distribution in neighborhood preschools and early learning centers. I learned about my topic; my professor enjoyed reading it, and preschools in our community still use the newsletter to inform parents.

Success in college depends on acquiring research skills, but they are also important for success in business and professional careers. Executives research markets and analyze them for trends; lawyers track down facts and organize them into briefs and contracts; journalists depend on investigative research to gather materials for articles and reports. Engineers, actors, architects, insurance agents—and yes, teachers—all use research skills to keep abreast of current techniques and update their knowledge. Would you want a doctor who hasn't researched the latest findings about a disease to diagnose your symptoms and make decisions about your health care?

Myths About Research
- Research papers are dull;
- The conclusion has to repeat the introduction;
- The more quotations you use, the better the paper;
- The larger the words, the better the paper;
- No one really checks sources anyway;
- A research paper is like any other paper—just longer;
- Students can write a research paper in one night.

(Possible) Truths About Research
- A writer has a responsibility to make a researched paper interesting to readers.
- Quotations support ideas; they do not replace them;
- Instructors (and other readers) DO check sources;
- Students document using MLA, AP or another recognized format for documenting consistently;
- Presenting research involves multiple tasks and that takes time;
- Last, not all research is presented in a formal essay or composition.

Your Turn:
Review the essays and poems included as examples in *The Writer's Voice*. Which selections might have needed some sort of research? Do some kinds of information come from sources other than just personal experience? Highlight information from personal experiences in one color; highlight information from other sources in a different color? What do you discover about the importance of synthesizing ideas and information from a variety of different sources?

What Does A Synthesis, or Research, Assignment Look Like?

Contemporary life is marked by controversy. In college, you will have opportunities through discussion, essays and exams to confront issues and problems that require you to present effective, ethical and logical proposals and arguments. After college, no matter what profession you enter, you will spend much of your time trying to sell a product, service, idea and—most importantly—yourself.

As a future leader, you have a responsibility to offer solutions to social, economic and cultural problems that confront citizens locally, nationally or globally. Persuading others to consider your ideas requires strong, well-constructed arguments, and skillful presentations of facts and information that support your opinions.

To prepare you for the future, many high school, college assignments and business plans require synthesis and the need for documented research. Some examples might include:

- **Analysis papers to examine causes and effects:**

  Analyze the responses of Franklin Roosevelt's administration to the problems of the Great Depression. How effective were these responses? How did they change the role of the federal government? Use information from several documents   and your knowledge of the period 1929-1941 to construct your essay.

- **Annotated Bibliographies requiring summarizing multiple sources:**

  Explore the Internet for primary, secondary sources and editorial cartoons   that provide information about a current event or problem. For suggested topics,   review the President's State of the Union address.

- **Argumentative papers that compare differing views and offers support for a coherent position:**

  Choose a controversial current problem or issue that interests and impacts   you and/or your family. Then write an essay that cites evidence from at least   three of the sources listed in your annotated bibliography to defend and support the position stated in your thesis/antithesis.

- **Business reports might need synthesis to examine different ideas and blend them into a coherent and usable plan.**

  Discuss some of the plans to improve St. Louis' waterfront to attract more   visitors and increase business opportunities. What other communities have developed successful plans for this purpose? What important factors do you need   to consider?

> **Your Turn:**
> Use one of the samples above and write your own version of an assignment that might include synthesis and research of information from history, politics, government, literature, science or technology. Keep a list of all your sources to use later.

How Do I Narrow a Topic and Form a Thesis?

Many experiences "feed your mind" and help you become an analytical, critical thinking human being. For example:

1. You go places and experience things;
2. You talk with friends and family members who have emotions, ideas and opinions;
3. You see things on television and in movies;
4. You read things in books, newspapers and magazines;
5. You hear things on the radio;
6. You learn things by reading online.

Those influences and experiences affect you and help you make decisions about where you live, what career you might pursue, the candidate you elect to lead your city, state and nation. Once you determine a problem, you need to narrow it to a topic that you can explore and form a thesis/antithesis that clearly states your opinion or supports your decision.

Choosing a Topic

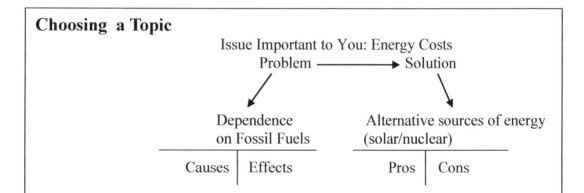

Forming an Opinion

Hypothesis (stated as a question): Can alternative energy sources, especially solar and nuclear power, solve America's dependence on foreign oil?

Thesis: The development of alternative energy sources, especially solar and nuclear power can help solve America's dependence on oil from foreign countries.

Antithesis: The development of alternative energy sources, especially solar and nuclear power, can help solve America's dependence on oil from foreign countries (**although, however, but**) it may increase taxes.

> **Your Turn:**
> Choose a community, city, state, or national problem that concerns or affects you and/or your family, and then write an essay that synthesizes information from a variety of sources that addresses that problem. Make sure that you can also offer a solution.

How Do I Find Evidence?

When confronted with so much information in so many places we can often become confused as to which sources will provide the most accurate, thoughtful and meaningful information. Libraries, today, have become "Discovery Centers," "Learning Resource Centers," and "Reading Rooms." The chart below can help you choose the best resources for the kind of research you need to do.

Library Vs. Online/Web Resources

Go through a review process	No review process
Free, or discounted for use	Some are not free
Organized according to subject and author	Not organized
Meant to be kept permanently	Not permanent, updated frequently
Come with personal assistance from Librarians	On your own
Quality over Quantity	Quantity over Quality

Taking Notes and Finding Evidence from Sources

Prompt/Question: In "The Case for Wal-Mart," the authors, Karen De Coster and Edmonds express the opinion that "If the truth be told, Wal-Mart improves the lives of people in rural areas because it gives them access to a lifestyle that they otherwise would not have." What do you think of Wal-Mart? Do you love it, as De Coster say Americans do, or do you have another opinion of it? In an essay that synthesizes information from several articles, take a position that defends or challenges the claim that Wal-Mart has been good for America. Cite at least 3 pieces of evidence from the articles to develop and support your position. Use the format below to help you take notes on your sources:

Source A: For/Pro/Defend	**Source B: Against/Con/Challenge**
De Coster, Karen and Brad Edmonds. "The Case for Wal-Mart." *Patterns For College Writing.* 652-655.	Featherstone, Liza. "Down and Out in America." *Patterns for College Writing.* 659-666.
"What's more, Wal-Mart management has indeed made decisions to refrain from selling certain items that did not live up to its moral standard—including certain music CDs" (DeCoster, 655).	"Betty Dules points out that Wal-Mart takes out ads in her local paper the same day the community's poorest citizens receive their welfare checks" (Featherstone, 664).

> **Your Turn:**
> Choose a topic that clearly has two different sides. Read at least three primary and secondary sources for each side and take notes. Make sure you document sources correctly.

What Are Primary and Secondary Sources?

Today's students, who do most of their research online, can access a limitless supply of information—much of it from unknown sources. In fact, anyone with an Internet connection and a modicum of skill can disseminate whatever information they choose on any topic. The result is a World Wide Web that contains academic excellence as well as inadvertent ignorance and blatant bias. To succeed in an information-saturated society, we must learn how to tell the difference between credible sources and sources that seek to mislead and distort. In schools and universities, information-literate students should be able to:

- Access information efficiently and effectively;

- Analyze information critically and competently;

- Use information accurately and creatively.

At some point, in a class or business environment, you will need to use credible primary and secondary sources as support in an essay or other composition. So, how can you tell the difference?

Primary Sources—written during a specific time by a participant in the events (memoirs, letters, interviews, speeches, diaries, autobiographies, original prose and poetry), and they reflect the involvement and individual in firsthand accounts of events, experiences and occurrences.

Secondary Sources—accounts written after the fact with the benefit of hindsight. They are interpretations and evaluations of primary sources. Secondary sources can help identify major concepts and references to primary sources. Sometimes, they can provide persuasive and authoritative information, but they should be used sparingly because they comment and discuss evidence. Refer to the chart below to help you tell the difference between primary and secondary sources:

Primary Sources	Secondary Source
Lincoln's Gettysburg Address	Garry Wills' book, *Lincoln at Gettysburg: The Words that Remade America.*
A story, or poem, written by a writer who lived in New Orleans during the Katrina hurricane.	An article in a magazine written by a reporter who visited New Orleans in the weeks and months after Katrina
The text of President Bush's State of the Union address after 911	An editorial in *The New York Times* entitled, "President Blames Axis of Evil"
The figures for Ithaca College found in a table of "Number of Offenses Known to the Police, Universities and Colleges" in the FBI's *Uniform Crime Reports, 2002.*	An article in the *Ithacan* entitled "Study Finds Eastern Colleges Often Conceal Campus Crime."

Your Turn:
Find three primary and three secondary sources on a topic you have chosen. Write a brief summary of each source and make sure you record complete bibliography information.

How Do I Paraphrase A Source?

Sometimes when you need to explain another writer's ideas, you will need to paraphrase or express the meaning of a word, phrase, passage or work in other words that create a fuller and clearer explanation. However, make sure that you always give credit to the person whose thoughts you paraphrased. For more information about paraphrasing, review the chart and examples below:

What is Paraphrasing?

♦ The original quote reflects a complex philosophical ideas as well as the author's style.

♦ The paraphrase takes the idea apart, or "unpacks the ideas," and lays out the elements of reasoning—and therefore expresses the idea in **more,** rather than fewer, words.

Why is Paraphrasing Important?

♦ Practice in paraphrasing stretches the mind, brings us to deeper levels of understanding and helps us take ownership of an idea.

♦ Writing a clear paraphrase shows us we can understand the elements of   logical reasoning: purpose, question, concepts, assumptions, inferences, information, implications and point of view.

Sample Paraphrase

♦ "He who passively accepts evil is as much involved in it as he who helps to perpetuate it."   —Martin Luther King, Jr.

Dr. King believed people who see immoral actions done to others but fail to stop them even though they could intervene, are as immoral as those causing harm in the first place. Through inaction, they demonstrate an acceptance of wrong, anti-social behaviors and allow people to continue them unchecked and unopposed. For example, allowing a child to tease a pet will encourage the child to continue doing it.

A Template for "Unpacking a Thought' and Writing an Extended Paraphrases

1. The subject, or topic, of this quote is….
2. In other words…
3. For example…
4. I can provide a metaphor (or analogy) so readers can better understand my ideas...

Your Turn:

In your own words, what idea does the author below intend to communicate? How do you know? Can you prove it with an example? Make a comparison?

♦ "Universal suffrage without universal education would be a curse."
—H.L. Wayland

How Can I Avoid Plagiarism?

Plagiarism goes beyond the issue of academic honesty. Writers may be inspired by other writers, but taking someone else's words and ideas and passing them off as your own amounts to moral bankruptcy. Plagiarism detection software, Google and Internet search engines can identify plagiarized essays quickly and efficiently. And certainly, your instructors have read enough student papers to recognize the difference between the voice and style of student writers, and the writing of their parents and professional writers. Penalties for plagiarism and academic dishonesty are clearly stated in most high school and college handbooks.

To avoid charges of plagiarism, you should make sure that you cite all sources, either directly or indirectly that you use by following these examples.

Citing Text Directly

In-Text Documentation:

"Women should be required to register for the draft," as **Source A,** in his discussion of the inequalities in the present system argues with such clarity.

Or

Pointing out the obvious inequity in the current system, **Source A** argues that, "Women should be required to register for the draft."

Parenthetical Documentation:

The solution to this inequality is obvious: "Women should be required to   register for the draft," **(Source A).**

Citing Text Indirectly: Paraphrase

Some commentators have argued that one way to resolve the inequalities in the current system is to require women, as well as men, to register for the draft (Source A).

Weak Citations

Source A says, "Women should be required to register for the draft." I agree with this statement.

When Source A says, "Women should be required to register for the draft," I think this is a valid point about the inequality of the draft.

Your Turn:

Take notes on several sources that show different opinions on a topic you have chosen. Some of your notes should cite the information directly and some notes should paraphrase the information. Be sure to list the author, source and page numbers on your notes so you can find them later when you prepare your presentation.

How Do I Evaluate Internet Sources?

When you use the Internet for information on a topic, you should carefully choose and consider the sources and sites that will best meet your purpose. Ask yourself, "Which sources are objective, lacking hidden motives, and fair?" To assure the credibility of information, select web sites that include all of the following information:

- Author's name, title and/or position;
- Evidence of the author's authority, links to other sources;
- Site's organizational affiliation (gov/edu/com/org/~);
- Date the page was created or updated;
- Contact information, such as email address or "snail mail" addresses).

Once you have located sources that appear credible, accurate, reasonable and appropriate, use this chart to determine information quality:

Criteria for Evaluating Web Pages

1. Author: What information is provided about the author's education, background and training? Is he or she a trained expert or uninformed observer? Is the author different from the "webmaster?" How is the person qualified to write this document?

2. Type and Publisher: Does the government agency (gov.), school (edu.), business (com.), nonprofit organization (org.) or person (~) maintaining the site have a particular bias or agenda? Ask yourself, "Why was this page written and for whom?" Does this web page serve as an "infomercial" or a "commercial?"

3. Language: Does the language in the text contain emotional, inflammatory, profane or confusing language? Errors in spelling or grammar?

4. Dates: Is the information current and up-to-date, factual, detailed, exact and comprehensible? Is the information older than 3 years?

5. Graphics: Do the graphics included on the web site convey information, add interest, provide interactivity, or simply distract? Do they take up an unnecessary amount of space?

6. Links: Does the site's bibliography and/or links contain both supportive and contradictory information? Are there any dead links? Are links updated regularly?

Your Turn:
Choose a topic, "Google" it and then evaluate the first ten websites, which "pop up." Which websites offer the most reliable, credible, valid information according to the criteria listed above? Rank them from most credible to least credible.

How Do I Write An Annotated Bibliography?

A bibliography is a list of sources you use, or consult when writing an academic article, report or paper or a list of books or articles an author has published on a specific subject. An **annotated bibliography** includes a brief descriptive and evaluative paragraph (the annotation) for each item in the list. An annotation should include:

1. Complete bibliography information using standard MLA/APA format;
2. An evaluation of the author's credibility, background and point of view;
3. A summary of main ideas in the selection, including the author's thesis (properly documented);
4. Comments about the significance and relevance of the information.

A Sample Annotated Bibliography on a Book

Berliner, David and Bruce Biddle. *The Manufactured Crisis: Myths, Frauds and the Attack on Public Schools.* Reading, Massachusetts: Addison-Wesley Publishing Co.1995.

Dr. Berliner, a professor of education at Arizona State University, and Dr. Biddle, a professor of psychology and sociology at The University of Missouri, have collaborated on a book that reviews the research and politics that have contributed to common ideas about schools in today's media and political arenas.

The authors provide a history of the movement to discredit educators and schools and identify the sources of much misinformation. In matter-of-fact language, graphs and anecdotal research, they refute ideas about student achievement, increased costs of public schools, and the failure of schools to produce workers with good technical skills. For the authors, the real problems evident in American education are: unequal support of schools, expansion and diversity of student populations and societal problems like poverty, drugs, violence, prejudice and discrimination. They believe that, "the American school system is in far shape than the critics would have us believe, and where schools fail, those failures are largely caused by problems imposed on those schools" (241). The authors provide well-documented evidence and a balanced discussion of school reform, vouchers and funding.

Well-organized, with overviews, summaries of each chapter and an extensive bibliography, *The Manufactured Crisis* should have a prominent place in teachers' personal libraries to use as a reference when they write letters, vote in elections and defend their profession against those who seeks to use schools and teachers as political scapegoats for real problems facing America.

Your Turn:
Complete an annotated bibliography for at least six sources for the topic you have chosen. The purpose is to keep track of reading materials and sources so you can use it to document evidence for a report and to prepare a final Works Cited.

How Do I Prepare a Works Cited?

A Works Cited list should appear on the first page after the last page of text, and it will include all the materials that you actually used and cited in your paper or presentation you wrote. You should double-space all Works Cited and alphabetize them according to the author's last name. The preferred format for the social sciences is **APA (American Psychological Association).** The most widely accepted format in the Humanities is the **Modern Language Association (MLA).** You can find a complete guide for documenting sources using APA and MLA formats at http://www.owl.purdue. Be sure to check with your instructor to make sure you are using the preferred format. The most common entries for the MLA format are included in the examples below:

PRINT SOURCES

BOOK BY ONE AUTHOR
Brown, Charles *The Rock and Roll Story*. Englewood Cliffs: Prentice, 1983.

BOOK BY TWO AUTHORS
Coe, Sophie D., and Michael D. Coe. *The True History of Chocolate*. New York: Thames, 1996.

ESSAY IN AN ANTHOLOGY
Grisham, John. "Unnatural Killers." *Patterns for College Writing*. 7th ed. Ed.
    Laurie G. Kirszner and Stephen Mandelkl. New York: St. Martin's. 1998. 570-77.

ARTICLE IN A MONTHLY MAGAZINE
    O'Brien. Conor Cruise. "Thomas Jefferson: Radical and Racist." *Atlantic Monthly*. 1996: 43+.

INTERNET SOURCES

PROFESSIONAL WEBSITE
The American Dialect Society. Brigham Young U. 20 Aug. 1997. 11 Nov. 1997 <http://
    www.et.byu.edu/ ~lilliek/ads/index.htm>

ARTICLE IN A MAGAZINE
Webb, Michael. "Playing at Work." Metropolis Online. Nov. 1997 11Nov. 1997 <http://
    www.metropolismag.com/nov97/eames/eams.html>

PERSONAL WEBSITE.
Lancashire, Ian. Homepage. 28 Mar. 2002. 15 May 2002 <http://www.chass.utoronto.ca:8080/~ian/>.

NONPRINT SOURCES

FILM
"Dances With Wolves." Dir. Kevin Costner. Orion. 1990.

INTERVIEW
Garcetti, Gilbert. Personal Interview. 7 May 1994.

SPEECH
 King, Martin Luther. "I Have a Dream." March on Washington for Jobs and Freedom. Washington,
    D.C. 28 August 1963.

Student Voices:

Who's Up for a Game?

The UN calls it "the greatest
humanitarian crisis in our time."
Children in Africa
Drink water the color of Coca Cola
and veiled women hunch over babies
pestered by blood-hungry mosquitoes.
Muslims fight Muslims in a selfish grasp
for power defying the teachings
of Islam in its struggle
to condemn terrorists that
say they are of the believers.
The people of Darfur, Sudan need
help—lots of it. But they're black.
Who wants to help some black kids
half way across the world pleading
for plastic sheets that'll shelter them
from a merciless rainy season?
Who's up for a game of sleeping
under sheets of pelting water and wind
that whips your face hard?
                    ~Sarah Pacha (2004:67)

Directions

See, class
The truth is that people don't like to read
about that test you failed,
your parents' wiles,
that guy who broke your heart,
or how you smoke
on the weekends and bury the stink with
Febreeze.
The truth is no one cares.
See, there lived a boy named Justin.
who wrote the best damn poetry
I'd ever seen in a Junior class.
He'd write just to piss me off—
and it worked.
Boy, I tell you, the dark abyss you all talk
about like your life couldn't get any worse,
are left out. His grades didn't show
his talent though—he didn't like directions.
He must have read Robert Frost.
Still haven't seen a youngster with the same
Flair? Capacity? Vision?
It's a shame kids can't lose themselves
in poetry and see the world around them.
But, I guess their lives are the lives that matter.
Shoot, who used to say,
"People don't think it's normal to care
about the world, teacher. It's easier
to follow the directions"?
                    ~Sarah Pacha (2004:79)

Your Turn:

Choose a controversial local, state, national or global problem that you care about because it has influenced you or your family in some way. Then, write an essay that cites evidence from at least three knowledgeable, credibly, accurate and specific Primary and Secondary sources to support your ideas and opinions.

Imagine you will present your ideas to an audience of educated, mature and thoughtful readers prepared to understand your position, but who may not be willing to accept your views. Convince your readers that you have a logical, ethical and compassionate position that deserves their consideration. Use a variety of sentence structures, a robust vocabulary and demonstrate control of grammar, spelling and punctuation. Be sure to include a Works Cited of the sources you used   in your essay.

LESSON 14: CRITICISM—
THE "VOICE" OF EVALUATION

"Genius...the capacity to see ten things where the
ordinary man sees one, and where the man of talent
sees two or three, plus the ability to register that
multiple perception in the material of his art."
--Ezra Pound in *Jefferson and Mussolini* (1935)

What Is Literary Criticism?

Why do we take literature, art, music, and film apart? Why can't we just respond emotionally to it? Say, "that was a good book—a fun movie—good music— a nice painting," and let it go at that? The answer—because emotional pleasure is only one aspect of the enjoyment of anything. When we choose a dish from a restaurant menu, we rely on the discriminating tastes which we have developed from years of sampling different foods, and we send compliments to the cook—or chef—who prepared them for our enjoyment. Learned preference, and the people we have eaten with—parents, friends, brothers and sisters—all influence and guide our choice in foods. We can say the same about our choice of films, books, art and music.

We learn to appreciate a piece of literature when we understand the problems writers have and how they solve them. By evaluating and becoming aware of each decision they make and realizing all the possibilities involved in the writing task, we can truly appreciate the difficulty of creating meaning in prose and poetry just as we appreciate the task of preparing a gourmet meal. Learning how to use the techniques of criticism can add dimension to our understanding of all art forms: films, music, painting and photography. When intellectual awareness is increased, so is pleasure. Our choices in films, books, art and music define us and show the world what we value and believe is important.

Criticizing a work of art differs from reporting on it. A report is a more superficial summary of plot and style; on the other hand, critics, authorities on specific genres, have studied the literature, art and music, and the techniques involved in producing it extensively. Literary criticism records successful and effective techniques as well as those techniques that missed the mark. Most critics, today, are more interested in social, political, historical and cultural influences on writers than they are on the writer's personal motivations and experiences. A good critic should concentrate on the literary and artistic elements and skills—not on the opinions of other reviewers or biographical details of the author's life. An effective critic should:

- Weigh the worth and value of the literature, music, film or work of art;
- Evaluate its overall quality;
- Draw inferences from observation and their own knowledge;
- Establish and follow clear criteria for judging excellence;
- Present opinions, supported by evidence from the work of art, clearly and convincingly so that readers can make informed decisions.

Sharpening our critical thinking skills are an important part of becoming discriminating, literate, articulate, intellectual, and sensitive human beings. Our choices in what we read, view or listen to should take the same careful consideration as choosing a meal in an expensive restaurant. Making a choice between "junk food" and healthy, nutritious meals is as important for our bodies as choosing the best books, film, art and must is for our minds.

Writers reflect, create and question the ideas and values of a society.

Film Criticism: Excerpts from "Dances With Wolves: Lessons from Loo Ten Tant's Journal"[1]

When I check attendance, the names sound like a United Nations roster: Shanthi, Anar, Jose, La Quesha, Dedrick, Santa, Jennifer, Steven, Sharaz, Thuy, Sou, Nakry, and Kenisha. During the last five years, minority population at our high school has increased from two percent to over fifty percent. The movie, "Dances With Wolves," (1990), provided an answer to my question, "How can I help these kids from so many different backgrounds learn more effectively?"

In his book, *Reading the Movies,* William Costanzo writes, "Without movies, a good portion of our collective visual memory would have disappeared...It's hard to imagine a world without "Star Wars," "Gone With the Wind," *"It's a Wonderful Life,"* or images of King Kong, or Gary Cooper on a dusty street at high noon, or Gene Kelly 'singin'in the rain'" (8).

Movies in an English Classroom

The universal language of film can touch every student because of the tools of filmmaking: lighting, color, framing, motion, sound, and transitions. Even a "non-native speaker is more like to understand the picture than the word" (27). Teaching students to view "Dances With Wolves," as a piece of literature changed my ideas that:

1. The printed word is the best way to learn;
2. Students like classes that use film because they are easy;
3. To be a valid part of a curriculum, film must reinforce literature;
4. Film is not an art form worth study;
5. Only teachers who want to "wing it" or want rainy day activities use film.

Teachers have a responsibility to help preserve the literary art of film and provide tools so students can evaluate them. Costner's "love letter to the past" (Landau 1990, 1) added to students' visual memories and helped them become more discriminating moviegoers.

Furthermore, watching the movie encouraged reluctant readers to read the book. After watching "Dances With Wolves," Justin, a seventeen-year-old in my ninth grade English class told me, *Dances With Wolves* is the first whole book I've ever read." Watching the film helped students to evaluate and analyze the differences between books and films. "For all critical complaints that 'the book was better,' three out of four Academy Awards for Best Picture have gone to adaptations" (Costanzo, 1992, 20).

Watching "Dances with Wolves" provided a neutral ground for discussing cultural differences, prejudice and intolerance among students. Joy Harjo, a Native American poet, writes, "Indians are not all alike! Yet, I believe there is a common dream, a common thread between us, mostly unspoken (Coltelli 1990, 32). Even though the Native American population of the United States is less than one percent, students identified with John Dunbar's relationships with the Indians because it reflected their relationships with each other.

Movie Appreciation

Dances With Wolves by Michael Blake (1988) is a high-interest novel. *Publisher's Weekly* reviewed it as a "first novel of quiet adventure. These Comanche Indians could have been models for Rousseau's Noble Savage philosophy ...a pleasant escape into a mythical love story ("Dances with Wolves," 1989, 88). The movie, based on Blake's screenplay, won seven Academy Awards including Best Picture, Best Director and Best Cinematography. It received recognition from the New York Critics Association, Chicago Film Critics, and National Board of Review. The Sioux Tribal nation honored Kevin Costner, Mary McDonnell, and Michael Blake for outstanding representation of the Lakota Sioux Nation.

The movie's visual impact totally absorbed students: "Dances With Wolves" recounts the wide open spaces that have been lost to American movies since the Western genre collapsed" (Denby 1990), 107). They enjoyed the "understatement and touch of self-mockery" of Lieutenant Dunbar. They cheered "for a soulful hero, a man who realizes there's more to life than looking out for No. 1" (Ansen

1990, 68). John Bary's musical sound track, which they listened to while writing in their journals, establishes the movie's moods of spaciousness and harmony. The details of costumes, weapons and rituals "set a standard" and are "as authentic as Hollywood can get" (Berkman 1991, 22). The subtitles for the native Lakota Indian language required the students to "read" at some points in the movie.

The image of Dunbar, arms "raised in a final gesture of farewell to this life" (331), in an attempt to "do something worthy of a soldier before he died, something he'd be remembered for," (Landau, 4), and praying, "Forgive me, Father," show him to be capable of great sacrifice. A survivor, "alone, all alone" like the Ancient Mariner, he stops to watch "a pair of water snakes twisting ecstatically in the shallows of the stream," (52). A disciple, he leaves at the end of the film to carry a message, "I must go...I must try to talk to those who would listen." Dunbar follows his dream "to see the vast expanses of prairie and sky before the Frontier disappears." He accepts the responsibility of "clean up duty," takes command of his post, protects his family and friends and writes in his journal, "The country is everything I dreamed it would be."

Lt. Dunbar's words and the sketches he makes show students the importance of keeping a journal as "a trail for people to follow." He settles in alone at the deserted fort, "Thoreau-like, recording his impressions in a diary observed only by a solitary wolf." When students heard Dunbar read in a quiet, monotone voice, "The strangeness of this life cannot be measured," they saw experiences and emotions spanning generations as well as cultures. When he put on his uniform and rode out to meet the Indians for the first time, "he understood what it was like to be an intruder," (Blake 103).

The film, "Dances With Wolves," promoted harmony, expanded thinking skills, and generated enthusiasm for storytelling in my classroom. Knowledge replaced prejudice, and students looked past skin color to find friendship and respect in the class, just as the Indians and Dunbar did in the movie.

At the end of the film, Kicking Bird, the wise "holy man," says to his new "soldier friend," Dances With Wolves, "I was just thinking that of all the trails in this life, there is one that matters more than all the others. It is the trail of a true human being. I think you are on that trail." Watching this soon-to-be classic can help students and audiences to follow a trail to acceptance, tolerance and harmony among peoples.

Works Cited

Ansen, David. 1990. "How the West Was Lost." *Newsweek* 116.21 (19 Nov.): 67-68.

Coltelli, Laura. 1990. *Winged Words: American Writer's Speak:* Lincoln: University of   Nebraska.

Costanzo, William V. 1992. *Reading the Movies*. Urbana: NCTE.

"Dances With Wolves." 1990. Dir. Kevin Costner. Orion.

Denby, David. 1990. "How the West Was Lost." *New Yorker*. 23.45 (19 Nov.): 107-09.

Landau, Diana. 1990. *Dances With Wolves*: The Illustrated Story. Newmarket Press.

Criticism: Webster's Definition

1. The act of making judgments or criticizing; 2. A passing of unfavorable judgments, censure, disapproval. **3. The art, skill, or profession of making discriminating judgments and evaluations, especially of literary or other artistic works; 4. a review or other article expressing such judgment and evaluation;** 5. the detailed investigation of the origin and history of literary documents.

Who Was Aristotle?
And What Does He Say To Us Today?

Aristotle, the most important philosopher in ancient Greece, was the first to classify areas of human knowledge into distinct disciplines such as mathematics, biology, and ethics, classifications we still use today. Plato, a student of Socrates, considered Aristotle as his most brilliant pupil. Together, they laid the foundations of Western philosophy and science.

Aristotle tutored Alexander the Great, and when Alexander became king, Aristotle opened his own school where he continued to teach and study for many years. Aristotle's school has been described as "peripatetic," (from the Greek word, *peripatein,* which means, "to walk about") because Aristotle and his pupils discussed philosophy and the sciences while walking around the Lyceum, a shady tract of land in Athens. They used a form of inquiry, which encouraged vigorous debate, the Socratic Method, named after Socrates, who had also taught Plato.

In more than 200 treatises, Aristotle radically transformed most of the knowledge he touched. Aristotle's numerous writings, appearing in books about the time Jesus lived, form an encyclopedia of classic Greek knowledge, and his ideas had a profound impact on both Christian and Islam philosophy. His reputed polished prose style attracted many great followers, including Cicero, the Roman orator, writer, and political official. The most influential treatises are:

- "Organon" which deals with logic and explores the science of reasoning. His ideas about deductive reasoning were hardly questioned for 2,000 years.
- "Metaphysics" studies the nature of "being" and St. Thomas Aquinas used it as a basis of Christian theology.
- "Physics" is the science of all things knowable, divided into matter, form and motion.
- "Politics" teaches that the state sets the standards for each man's virtue, and the basis for the state is the virtues of a middle class family.
- "Poetics," a treatise on literature, marks the beginning of literary criticism and has served as a guide for later critics and key to the purposes of essayists, dramatists, and poets. [2]

The principles of criticism, set forth by Aristotle, apply to all works of art, including film, literature, poetry, art and music. In this lesson, we will apply Aristotle's principles to film criticism.

When the Olympics Were Commercial Free

On a balcony, cold and cracked in Athens, wine was sipped and laughing voices sang until the sun disappeared behind the Acropolis. Then, it got cooler and thick cotton sweaters were dragged out—wrinkled—from the bottoms of suitcases. Eyes watched as Athens glowed and hummed, never looking at the time, never thinking of home. They made excuses to play the part of different people in this, the city of gods; for immortals were made as they finished the last drops of wine, and shed thick sweaters for cool cotton sheets.

—Jessica Moore, (1998: 42)

How Does Literary Criticism Reflect Aristotle's Principles?

When taking literature apart, it helps to have some principles to guide your thought processes and critical comments. The questions below, based on both Aristotle's philosophy and the levels of critical thinking in Bloom's Taxonomy, ("Lesson 7: Exposition"), can help you write thoughtful, insightful and interesting literary analysis of many different forms of art and literature.

Hexagonal Analysis

I. Literal Association (Aristotle's "definition," Bloom's "knowledge")
Write the title, author and other bibliography information. Then summarize the most important events in the book, story, poem, essay or film. What is the most significant, climactic experience, or main point? Why is it important? How does the event affect listeners, readers or viewers? How does it affect the characters, or people involved? How does it affect the writer?

II. Personal Association (Aristotle's "relationship," Bloom's "comprehension")
Explore and explain your personal connection. How does the literature remind you of some event, person, problem, or situation in your life? Why are those experiences meaningful? What have you learned from your response to the events, characters, and ideas in the literature? How have they changed, or affected you? Helped you grow and mature?

III. Thesis/Theme (Aristotle's "circumstance," Bloom's "application")
Infer the literary purpose of the writer, artist or filmmaker. What are they trying to show about human nature? Human relationships? Human emotions? Human ethics, principles and values? Life and all its processes and problems? What examples, quotations, anecdotes, and illustrations can you provide as evidence for your assertions and opinions?

IV. Interpret Techniques and Style (Aristotle's "consequence and degree," Bloom's "analysis")
Break the literature or art apart. What is the significance of the title? Who is the narrator? Who is the audience? What rhetorical devices does the writer use to enhance the meaning and message? How does the author or director use connotations, light and color, details and dialogue to convey mood and tone? What other strategies best convey the purpose of the literature? How do diction, imagery, detail, syntax and language contribute to the piece? What other creative elements are used?

V. Literary Association (Aristotle's "comparison," Bloom's "synthesis")
Determine literary connections. What books, films, poems or stories does the literature remind you of? How? Can an allusion to a mythological, Biblical or historical figure help explain the motivations or strengths and weaknesses of ideas or story lines? **Note: Television shows and music videos are not considered "literary."**

VI. Evaluation (Aristotle's "testimony," Bloom's "evaluation")
Judge the merits and quality of the literature. Why is this literature important to study? What is its cultural impact and historical significance? How does it challenge audience's intellects? Emotions? Perceptions? Why does it have lasting value? Can you cite specific examples that support your opinions?

What Criteria Defines A Quality Film?

The American Film Institute is a preeminent national organization dedicated to advancing and preserving film, television and other forms of the moving image. AFI's programs promote innovation and excellence through teaching, presenting, preserving and redefining this truly American art form. The AFI helps moviegoers to understand the difference between attending a movie and "viewing a film," which can help   audiences make better choices. A committee of American Film Institute critics, film scholars, screenwriters and directors chose Top 100 films based on the following criteria [3]:

1. **Feature-length Fiction Film**—Narrative format typically over 60 minutes in length;
2. **American Film**—English language film with significant creative and/or financial production elements from the United States;
3. **Critical Recognition**—formal commendation in print;
4. **Major Award Winner**—Recognition from competitive events including awards from organizations in the film community and major film festivals;
5. **Popularity Over Time**—including figures for box office adjusted for inflation, television broadcasts and syndication, and home video sales and rentals;
6. **Historical Significance**—A film's mark on the history of the moving image through technical innovation, visionary narrative devices or other groundbreaking achievements;
7. **Cultural Impact**—A film's mark on American society in matters of style and substance.

You can also apply most of the same criteria to stories, poetry, novels, art, music and drama. Before you read another book, see another movie, or listen to music, ask yourself these questions: Is it original and creative? Critically acclaimed? Has it stood the test of time because of its historical significance or cultural impact? Alternatively, is it just junk food? A "movie" instead of a "film?" For more information about film, and its place as literature, you should visit the AFI web site: http://www.afi.com/tvevents/100years/100yearslist/aspx

> **Your Turn:**
> Use this chart in your Writer's Notebook to choose films from the AFI list, which you would like to see. Then, write an essay that review of one of the films on your list. Plan to share your carefully researched and thoughtful analysis to your classmates in a round table discussion format.

Films I want to see immediately:	Films I'd like to watch when I have time:	Films I'll probably never watch:	Films I think should be on this list—and aren't:

How Should I Choose a Film to Review?

One important note: The American Film Institute List of Top Films is not all-inclusive. Just like any list of outstanding books, most important historical events, best presidents, or top students, there are areas of disagreement—and disagreement and dissent represent the American way. The Motion Picture Association has rated most of the films on the AFI list "G" or "PG". However, some of them received "R" ratings, an indicator that students under 17 should not view them without the company and/or permission of parents.

The films on the AFI list do not represent my personal views or opinions. Even though I have seen almost all of them, the list contains some films, which I have chosen to avoid because of the language, content and graphic violence. I do not recommend them to students. For more information, reviews, summaries and complete rankings of films, please visit the American Film Institute web site.

Students should always check with their parents or guardians before they watch any film. John Milton wrote, "Where there is much desire to learn, there of necessity will be much arguing, much writing, many opinions, for opinion in good men is but knowledge in the making" (*Aeropagita, 1644*). Whatever films students choose to watch, they should share their ideas, evaluations, and criticisms with the adults important in their lives.

AFI Looks at Major Themes in   Films

Against The Grain—inspiring heroes in lonely, dangerous opposition: *High Noon, On the Waterfront, Easy Rider, To Kill a Mockingbird, Dances With Wolves, Schindler's List* **Beyond the Law—Public enemies and private nightmares:** *The French Connection, Bonnie and Clyde, Fargo, The Godfather (Part One), Goodfellas* **Family Portraits—Challenges that face our most treasured and vulnerable institution:** *Shane, Rebel Without a Cause, The Sound of Music, Guess Who's Coming to Dinner, American Graffiti, The Godfather (Part Two), Giant* **In Search of —buried treasure and states of grace and security:** *Ben-Hur, Rocky, Rear Window, The Searchers, Forrest Gump, Raiders of the Lost Ark* **Crazy in Love—snappy, scrappy and sappy love stories:** *Singing in the Rain, A Place in the Sun, West Side Story, The Graduate, Annie Hall*	**The Wilder Shores of Love—Unlike lovers swept up in exotic times and places:** *Wuthering Height, Gone With the Wind, Casablanca, An American in Paris, My Fair Lady, A Streetcar Named Desire* **War and Peace—the horrors of weaponry, conflicts and effects on human emotions:** *The Best Years of Our :Lives, The Bridge on the River Kwai, Dr. Strangelove, Patton, Apocalypse Now, Platoon* **Out of Control—creatures and science on a rampage:** *Frankenstein, King Kong, Psycho, Manchurian Candidate, Jaws, Amadeus* **The Anti-Heroes—the outcasts who make their own rules:** *Citizen Kane, Butch Cassidy and the Sundance Kid, M*A*S*H*, Unforgiven, Taxi Driver* **Fantastic Flights—voyagers in space and time, sometimes surreal and dreamlike.** *The Wizard of Oz, Snow White, Fantasia, 2001: A Space Odyssey, Star Wars, E.T., Close Encounters of the Third Kind*

How Should I Watch a Film?

Writing about films affords much creative latitude because we expect film critics to be colorful and individualistic. Before you begin to write, watch the movie carefully, rewinding and fast forwarding often to allow enough time to take notes and study the film from several different angles and points of view. Personal prejudice should not influence a critic's judgment of a film. Remember, as a critic, you have an obligation to write without bias.

The critic should also understand the tools of the writer's trade since all films begin with the written word. A critic does not always use these literary terms when writing criticism. However, understanding and recognizing them in literature will enhance the discovery process and help make your ideas as a critic more credible. The following questions should help you focus your attention on the techniques of filmmaking and generate information to include in a film review and to help you take notes as you watch the film from a critic's perspective:

1. **Genre:** Comedy? Thriller? Drama? Adventure? Western? Epic?
2. **Screenplay:** Original? Based on a book? Can you briefly summarize the plot?
3. **Character Development:** How do characters change? What motivates them? Why do we care about what happens to them? Who is the protagonist? The antagonist? Do they share any of the same qualities?
4. **Acting:** Which actors seem well cast? Why are they believable? How do the actors react to each other?
5. **Dialogue:** What lines are memorable and quotable? Are there any clichés?
6. **Cinematography:** How are scenes shot so they are believable? How do colors and lighting affect the mood of the audience?
7. **Direction:** How do the scenes flow together? Are transitions smooth or abrupt? How are shots/angles set up?
8. **Musical Score:** What type of music accompanies the scenes? Where is it especially appropriate?
9. **Special Effects**: Do explosions, fires and out-of-the ordinary events and scenes look believable? Is it obvious the car is not moving, or that the clouds are painted on a backdrop? How do special effects enhance the story, or do they replace and become the story?
10. **Themes:** What universal themes dominate the film? What does the film show about people? Society? Issues? Humanity?
11. **Narrative Elements:** What elements dominate the film? Setting? Plot? Character? Conflict? Theme? Point of View?
12. **Point of view:** What is the identity and position of the person telling the story?
13. **Imagery:** What are particularly strong sensory pictures and scenes? When you leave the theater, or the film ends, which scenes stay in your memory?
14. **Symbolism:** What objects seem to represents a concept or idea?
15. **Archetype:** Is there a classic example, or prototype, that goes beyond personal experience and draws upon the experience of the entire human race? The "hero," "mentor" and the "patriot" are examples of archetypes.

Your Turn: Watch the film you have chosen from the American Film Institute Top Film list and use the questions above to take notes on the important elements of filmmaking.

How Do I Write a Film Review?

After finishing a book, listening to a song, or seeing a movie, we either like it or dislike it, enjoy it or not enjoy it, consider our experience time well spent or time   wasted. To translate this gut reaction into specific areas to discuss, thoughtful, intellectual audiences analyze the work, interpret its messages and evaluate its significance. Effective, skilled writers, artists and musicians understand the value of criticism and learn from it.

You should plan to research, synthesize and use outside sources through credible websites to support your ideas and provide background information on the film. Just like any other kind of writing, the changes in technology have influenced techniques of moviemaking, and films reflect the culture, history and political ideas of a specific time period. Remember, your purpose is to show why the film has received acclaim by reporting what the film does, judging how well it does it, and providing enough historical background and evidence from the film to support the judgments which you, as a reviewer, have made. The following "tips" may help:

♦ Keep your ego out of it. Make your points without using the pronoun "I." In drawing attention to yourself, you draw it away from the film.

♦ Don't start with a synopsis of the film. That reads like a high school book report.

♦ Support your main points with sound examples. Integrate important "bits" of dialogue, a sentence or two that illustrates the essence of the film.

♦ Master metaphors. They can trigger instant understanding and evoke a reaction in your readers.

♦ Use action verbs and concrete, specific nouns. Eliminate weak adjectives and flabby adverbs. (Get the picture, yet? Nouns and verbs count so make them strong!)

♦ Don't forget to report. Who did what? Where and when? Why did they do it? How well? Why was it worth doing?

♦ Offer other possible viewpoints and counter them with your own.

♦ Don't waffle. State your position with confidence and conviction.

♦ Put the movie in a historical context. Give your readers background of the performers and the ideas in the film. Explain how they relate to the present.*

♦ Study related works, including books and other films, so you will have a valid basis for comparison.

♦ Make sure you understand the social, political and artistic perspectives that affect the film and the film's producers and director.

♦ Try to understand the filmmaker's intentions; then assess how well they achieved it and whether it was worth achieving.

♦ Remember that your opinion is only an opinion, not a judgment from God. Do not forget that your readers don't mind being entertained. Show some attitude and style!

Note: Support your opinions with sources from credible sources and authorities on filmmaking. Use the Internet wisely. See "Lesson 13: Research" to review ways to evaluate and document your sources. Make sure you keep a list of all your sources for your Works Cited.

> **<u>Your Turn:</u>**
> Write a film criticism that uses Aristotle's Principles of Criticism to help structure your essay so that it has six sections: Literal, personal, theme, interpretation, literary connection and evaluation.

Techniques of Filmmaking
Camera Shots

1. **Close-Up:** a shot showing a detail only (ex. face or hands only)
2. **Cross-Cutting:** cutting back and forth between two or more events or actions taking place at the same time, but in different places.
3. **Cut:** an abrupt transition from one shot to another.
4. **Cutaways:** a shift from the primary subject to something the filmmaker has decided is equally or more relevant at that time.
5. **Dissolve:** an overlapping transition between scenes where one image fades out as another fades in. Editors often use this to indicate a change in time or place.
6. **Establishing Shot:** a shot, taken from a distance that establishes for the viewer where the action occurs and the spatial relationship between characters and their setting.
7. **Extreme close-up:** a detail of a close-up (mouth or fingers only)
8. **Fade In:** a shot that starts in darkness and gradually lightens to full exposure
9. **Fade Out:** A shot that starts at full exposure and gradually fades to black.
10. **Jump Cut:** a cut where two spliced shots do not match in terms of time and place.
11. **Long Shot:** a shot taken at a considerable distance from the subject. A long shot of a person is one in which the entire body is in the frame.
12. **Medium Shot:** a shot framing a subject at a medium range, usually a shot from the waist up.
13. **Reverse Cutting:** a technique alternating over-the-shoulder shots showing different characters speaking—generally used in conversation scenes.
14. **Sequence Shot:** an entire scene or sequence that is one continuous shot—no editing.

Other Useful Terms:

- **Aerial Shot:** shot taken from the air or from a camera mounted on a crane.
- **Dolly:** a camera term referring to when a camera moves in or out of a shot. There are two dolly moves, "dolly in" and "dolly out." A dolly camera is usually mounted on wheels or tracks depending on the budget of the film.
- **Key Light:** The key light is the brightest light and casts the main shadows in a scene. It gives the sense of directionality to the lighting in any given scene.
- **Pan:** a broad horizontal movement on a fixed camera mount, sometimes used as transition between scenes
- **Rushes (dailies):** The director's work prints are usually called rushes or dailies, because a film development lab can produce them so quickly. A day's rushes are usually viewed the following morning or evening after the shoot.
- **Slow Motion:** a shot that makes people or objects appear to move more slowly than normal.
- **Soft Focus:** reducing the sharpness of the image by changing the lens or placing material such as gauze between the lens and the object of the photograph.
- **Tracking Shot:** a shot in which the camera moves from one point to another—either sideways or in an out.

> **Your Turn:**
> With a friend, watch a movie currently available and as you watch, rewind and fast forward film sequences to identify the types of camera shots the filmmakers use most often. If you're really brave, choose one of the stories you have written this year, and make a short film to show to your classmates.

A Scene from the One Act Play, "Aftertaste"
Brad Southerland (2005:69-72)

Lights up. SETH, 19, sits alone in his dorm room. He waits for something. After a few beats, someone knocks at his door, and he jumps up to get it. He opens the door to see an attractive girl of the same age. Her appearance surprises SETH; she looks tired. She has no luggage, just car keys in her hand. They hug and stare at each other for a beat until...)

KRISTA: (*Quietly*). I look great, don't I?

SETH: Never better. (*With slight humor in his voice.*) Thank you for coming.

KRISTA: Hey, I have nothing else to do. I really did mean to call you, I just...

SETH: Don't worry about it. I should have called the first night I got here.

KRISTA: Sounds like we're both doing great.

SETH: *(a beat)*. I'm not.

KRISTA: Me either. *(She sounds like she might cry.)*

SETH: Come here. (*He hugs her again, this time longer as they talk.*)

KRISTA: I don't know what I'm doing anymore.

SETH: What do you mean? Doing here?

KRISTA: Here. Back home. In life. Where am I going?

SETH: Me too.

KRISTA: But you're here. You have a future. This is the beginning of your life, Seth, be happy about it. *(She releases him from the hug)*.

SETH: Yeah, that's what everybody seems to think. *(Quickly)*. But we can talk about me next. What do you need me to tell you to make this better?

KRISTA: I don't know. Just be my friend. I miss you. It's so Longley now; I don't ever have anything to do anymore.

SETH: Everybody didn't leave.

KRISTA: I know, but it was so much more when you were here. We had fun together, alone, it's not the same. It's lonely.

SETH: Here, sit down. (*He sits on the side of his bed; she sits facing him on another bed.*)

KRISTA: Thanks, that's just what I need after that car ride. More sitting.

SETH: Yeah, the drive is a little brutal.

KRISTA: It was relaxing though. I never have anything to do and I just stay at home but...it's not relaxing. I feel like I should be doing something.

SETH: You should.

SETH: College. Go to college, Krista.

KRISTA: *(laughs softly).* Yeah, you know I just don't think I'm the university type.

SETH: Well, the, what do you want to do?

KRISTA: I don't know. But what am I going to do with a college degree? Get a job, okay. Get married, all right. Then, I'll have kids, but am I going to tell them about my life?

SETH: That you went to college and go a degree and then you met…

KRISTA: No. No. My dad had so much to tell my sisters and me. You, out of everybody, know that. His life was so great and it made us want to live up to it. He made us think that there was actually something wonderful out there for us. (*A beat.*) I don't know what I did wrong, but I haven't found it yet. And I want to have something to tell my kids.

SETH: Then do something you're proud of. Something that makes you happy.

KRISTA: I'm trying, but I don't think there's anything left. Seth, I haven't told anybody this so don't freak out.

SETH: What…

KRISTA: I think I might enlist in the Navy, or the Marines. At least I could see the world, you know? Doing something that I could feel good about.

SETH: (*He thinks carefully before…*) Krista, I don't know. I've never understood why people say that about joining up. Like it's some big vacation. I don't think it would be. I guess it could be, but it could also be miserable. And, once you sign those papers you can't turn back. I mean, let's face it, you're not the most decisive person.

KRISTA: That's why I'm thinking about it. I feel like I don't have any other option besides just wasting away by myself. I'm thinking about it. Hard. And, if I decide I want to sign those papers, I'm not going back.

SETH: I...I guess that's good. But you never know what's going to happen once you get started. You could be gone, maybe even overseas, for a long time. What is something happens?

KRISTA: Then, it happens. Part of the job description.

SETH: As much as I don't like the idea of you doing it, I would be totally happy for you if you did. It sounds like you would be happy, too, with yourself.

KRISTA: Well, you talked to me. I feel a little better just saying it all. What do you want me to say to you?

SETH: First, I have a question: How is she doing? Do you know?

The Lone Actor

Behind black curtains, he waits
scripted and silent.
The winged stage protects
him from the open field
where applauding guns
kills innocent characters.
Five more lines until the cue.
First his. Then hers. Then his again.
Anytime, now, a few more…
He transforms from a golden tiger
sneaking up on the blood
and picking at his skin
in the edge of torn thumbs.
Two more lines until the cue.
his heeled shoes click
as he hovers in the dark.
Sweat salts his upper lips
and his lines repeat,
visible in his head, through his eyes.

~Brad Southerland, (2004:94)

Your Turn.

Write the rest of the scene. How would you film this scene? Decide about lighting and set design. Where does the scene take place?   Who is "she" they are referring to? Which actress and actor   would you cast in the roles?

LESSON 15. THE ENGLISH LANGUAGE—THE "VOICE" OF NATIONS

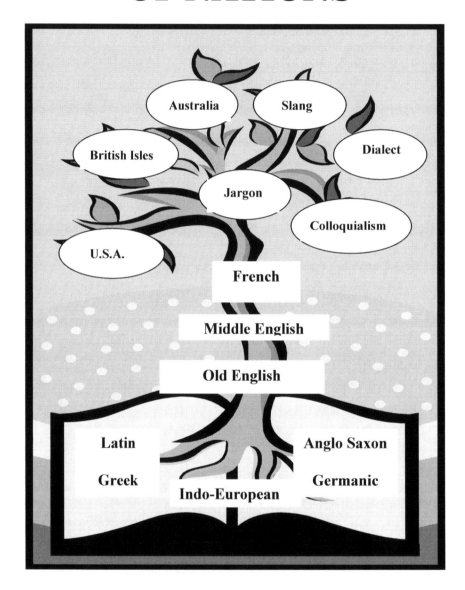

"The English language is nobody's special property.
It is the property of the imagination…"
—Derek Walcott, Interview, 1986

From *Beowulf* to Texting: Why Should I Understand the English Language?

Our English language has many branches; its roots grow deep in world history, and they provide nourishment to the living branches of language today. Like a tree, language lives and continues to grow and adjust to its environment. The English used in our current conversations and writing, embodies many influences from its history. Indo-European, Latin, Greek and German words are still part of our everyday conversation. We continue to add new words to our dictionaries from many different areas of communication, including the impact of technology, and the contributions of immigrants, especially those from Spanish and Italian speaking nations.

The English language, as a formal system of communication, has a set of rules, signs, symbols, sentence structure and grammar, which makes form and structure possible, and this system of conventions in language enables effective communication. Lincoln's Gettysburg Address, just 272 words long, stands as one of our greatest speeches because Lincoln used language gracefully. Who does not recognize the phrase, "Four score and seven years ago, "or "This nation, under God, shall have a new birth of freedom—and that government of the people, by the people, for the people, shall not perish from the earth"? Much of today's language, especially in "talk and conversation," lacks distinction and grace and sounds like loud, unintelligible shouting. Often, it forgoes grammar and structure and makes little effort at achieving style. In other words, "texting," and language used in social media, looks a little like the Olde English found in *Beowulf,* one of the first examples of written English communication.

As writers, we have an obligation to use the English language in creative and inventive ways to continue to make English "new." However, when writers know the rules and respect the history of our language, they have something to push around and something to push against; they know which rules to bend, and which rules to break. Writers should measure their use of language by its artfulness, its ability to "make meaning," its mastery of the rules and its appreciation of the history and traditions of the English language.

Writers Appreciate the Vitality and History of the English Language.

How Has History Influenced English?

(Latin) Celts, Romans 500 B.C.-600 A.D. Myths, Folklore	(German) Saxons, Jutes, Angles, 600-1066 A.D. *Beowulf*	(French) Norman Conquest 1066-1399 Chaucer's *Canterbury Tales*

(English)
Renaissance
1349-1649

Printing press, *King James Bible,* Shakespeare, Milton, Jonson, Donne

American English Develops Personality

→

(Beginnings in America)
1650-1800

Anne Bradstreet, William Bradford, Thomas Jefferson, Benjamin Franklin, Thomas Paine

"Revolutionary English"

(American Romanticism)
1800-1860

Washington Irving, Henry Wadsworth Longfellow, *Webster's Dictionary*

"Standard Rules"

(American Renaissance)
1840-1860

Ralph Waldo Emerson, Henry David Thoreau, Walt Whitman, Emily Dickinson

"A New Poetry"

(Realism, War, Westward Expansion)
1850-1900

Frederick Douglass, Mark Twain, Abraham Lincoln, Stephen Crane

"American Dialects"

(Depression, WWI & WWII)
1900-1950

Harlem Renaissance Hemingway, Steinbeck, Faulkner, Fitzgerald

"American Slang"

(Contemporary)
1950-Present

Maya Angelou, Martin Luther King, Amy Tan, Toni Morrison, Gabriel Garcia Marquez, Ray Bradbury

"Technology & Social Media, Race & Culture"

Your Turn:
Use the Internet to find passages written by authors during each of the time periods above. What differences do you discover in sentence length, word choice, grammar, spelling, use of images and figures of speech? How do their styles compare with "text messaging" and "tweeting?"

How Did English Vocabulary Develop?

Although it may surprise you, English shares a common origin with Russian, Armenian, Latin and Farsi because all these languages can be traced back to north central Europe many centuries ago.[1] Scholars discovered the Indo-European language by noting similarities between the various languages. Read each series of related words from Indo-European languages and the English equivalent below:

Lithuanian	Latin	Persian	Sanskrit	English
tri	tres	thri	tri	three
manen	me	me	me	me
moter	mater	matar	matar	mother
brolis	frater	baradar	bhratar	brother

Many English words still show their Germanic origins. Read each of the following series of related words from Germanic language. Then, discover the English equivalent.

German	Dutch	Swedish	Danish	English
was	wat	vad	hvad	what
fuss	voet	fot	fod	Foot
blut	bloed	blod	blod	blood
kussen	kussen	Kyss	kysse	kiss

Etymology—the history of a word that traces its development and transmission from one language to another. The history of a word is indicated in a dictionary by brackets and the use of the symbols below:

[<L.   < Gr.   <Fr.   <OE.   < ME.]

Your Turn:
In a good dictionary, look up each word below. Then write Old English (OE) if the word existed in English before 1066, or French (Fr), if the English adopted the word from French during the Middle English   (ME) period.

1. Worthy
2. Honor
3. Chivalry
4. Freedom
5. Truth
6. Courtesy

How Has English Changed?

Language constantly changes. Throughout its history, English has proved versatile, innovative, and imaginative. Several hundred years from now, the English your grandchildren will speak and write might be as different from today's English as Modern English differs from Old English. To become the English you recognize today in books, magazines and newspapers, Old English has changed in three major and important ways:

1. Pronunciation. For examples, in Old English the a was pronounced like ah in: "Ah, I see." This changed to an o sounds in Modern English, so the Old English haldan became the Modern English hold.

2. Vocabulary. For example, the Old English word "wiotana," meaning "wise men," is no longer part of the English vocabulary. The Modern English word "computer" was obviously not part of the Old English vocabulary.

3. Sentence Structure. The word order for an Old English sentence might be, "Again, he asked what the nation's name was that they from came." The Modern English sentence would read, "He asked the name of the nation you came from again."

Below, you can see how one verse in the Bible has changed throughout its publishing history: [2]

Matthew 8:24

Old English (Latin & German —500 B.C—600 A.D.) :
> Da weard micel styrung geworden on baere sae,
> swa baet scip weard ofergoten mid ybum;
> with od lice he slep.

Middle English (French—1066-1399 A.D.):
> And loo! A grete steryng was maad in the see,
> so that the litil ship was hilid with
> wawis but he slepte.

Modern English (Shakespeare , King James Bible—1349-1649):
> And behold, there arose a great tempest in the sea,
> in so much that the ship was covered
> with waves; but he was asleep.

Revised English (Contemporary):
> Suddenly a terrible storm came up,
> with waves higher than the boat.
> But Jesus was asleep.

> **Your Turn:**
> Look up each of the following words in a good dictionary. Then, in a few words, explain the word's origins: boondocks, video, blitz, kayak, isotope, khaki, ketchup, tea, mustang, apricot. Where did the word originate? What is its history? What was its original meaning? What does it mean today?

Why Is Shakespeare Important?

The following phrases were composed by an English author: "Love is blind;" "there's a method in his madness;" "he's eaten me out of house and home;" "to thine own self be true;" or "to kill with kindness." William Shakespeare, the Bard of Avon, penned these lines more than 400 years ago, and they have become so much a part of English that they have become clichés. Today, many of us quote Shakespeare without even realizing it.

If you wrote and spoke in the Shakespearean way, others would quite rightly correct you. Of course, if the Elizabethans at Court spoke and wrote like us, the Queen would have banished them from her sight. Language sticks closely to the people who speak it, changing its forms as much as people change their manners and style of dress.

Shakespeare contributed over 2,000 new words to the English language because he did not have a dictionary to guide him with rules, and he often needed to invent a word to fit into the proper meter/rhyme scheme of iambic pentameter, the popular poetic form of the time. Sometimes he also used an apostrophe to indicate he had left out a syllable so the amount of sounds and syllables fit the rhyme pattern.

Your Turn:
Rewrite the following quotations from Shakespearean plays by putting the sentences in today's grammatical form. If the quotation includes an apostrophe, supply the syllable, or sound, omitted in the italicized part of the quotation.
Think to yourself, "How would I say this casually to a friend?"
1. "The king himself is rode to view their battle." (*Henry the Fifth*)
2. "Hast any philosophy in thee, shepherd?" (*As You Like It*)
3. "How come you hither?" (*The Tempest*)
4. "Still keep you o'th windy side of the law?" (*Twelfth Night*)
5. "Here on this molehill will I sit down." (*Henry the Sixth*)
6. "That he is mad, *'tis* true *'tis* pity, and pity *'tis 'tis* true." (*Hamlet*)
7. "Younger than she are happy mothers made." (*Romeo and Juliet*)
8. "A great man, I'll warrant. I know by the picking on's teeth." (*The Winter's Tale*)
9. "Plucking the grass to know where sits the wind."(*The Merchant of Venice*)
10. "What stature is she of?" (*As You Like It*)

Your Turn Again: In this exercise, a word is missing from each quotation. Supply the word you believe comes closest to Shakespeare's original idea. The word must fit the rhythm of the line, maintain the rhyme scheme and make sense.
1. "We the globe can compass soon,
   Swifter than the wandering _____. (*A Midsummer Night's Dream*)
2. "The sun not yet thy sighs from heaven clears,
   Thy old groans ring yet in my ancient _____. (*Romeo and Juliet*)
3. But if the while I think on thee, dear friend,
   All losses are restor'd and sorrows _____. ("Sonnet XXX")

Why Do We Have Slang?

Slang has existed for centuries, and although today's teens use words most of us do not understand, their use of slang is no different from any other generation. Young people have always developed their own language to distinguish themselves from the adults in their lives and to exclude them from teen conversations. Used as an act of rebellion against authority figures, slang also helps to separate teens from others who are not part of their peer group, or part of the "in" crowd. Rarely, do parents or teachers understand slang when teenagers use it—and that, after all, is the purpose!

The chart below shows slang used by young people in two classic stories of teenage relationships in two different eras. You should supply a slang term from today's changing language synonymous with the words in the first two columns.

(1500's—1600's "Romeo and Juliet"	1950's Language "Westside Story"	1980's-2012 Today's Teenagers
1. fray, bandying	rumble, brawl	Throw down
2. prison	can	
3. fist	skin	
4. calm	cool	
5. coz, sirrah (term of familiar address)	Daddy-o	

Your Turn:
Below are some of Shakespeare's proverbs, or general pieces of advice. Explain what each means to you in a literal way and tell of an experience, real or imagined, that illustrates the truth of the proverb. Write your responses in your Writer's Notebook.
1. "The empty vessel makes the greatest sound." ("Henry the Fifth")
2. "Ill blows the wind that profits nobody." ("Henry the Sixth")
3. "The empty vessel makes the greatest sound." ("Henry the Fifth")
4. "Men's evil manners live in brass; their virtues we write in water." ("Henry the Fifth")
5. "What's gone and what's past help should be past grief." ("The Winter's Tale")
6. "Small showers last long, but sudden storms are short." ("Henry the Fifth")
7. "When clouds appear, men put on their cloaks." ("Richard the Third")
8. "A little fire is quickly trodden out." ("Henry the Sixth")

How Are American And British English Different?

From examining word origins, you can see that vocabulary changes with time. It also changes with distance. Although English is spoken in both the United Kingdom and America, British English and American English have many differences in vocabulary.   For example, in America, we talk about the "hood" and "trunk" of a car; in England, these car parts are called the "bonnet" and the "boot." Use context clues (and a dictionary?) to help you figure out the meanings of unfamiliar British words and expressions, or idioms, which are underlined.

1. Because of a lorry accident, there is a diversion on the motorway near the Watney roundabout.
2. While visiting London, we queued up for a train in the underground station.
3. Use the Belgium lace serviettes at dinner tonight.
4. During the interval, many theatergoers leave the stalls.
5. Popular vegetables at an English dinner include: Swedes, courgettes, and sprouts.
6. The mother wheeled the pram on the pavement and stopped to read the boarding.
7. My friends in Britain watch the telly from a settee in their lounge.
8. While staying at Cambridge, we could not decide whether to lease a flat or live   in a caravan.
9. In many English villages the chemist's shop, the ironmonger's and the sweatshop are on the high street.
10. When we stopped for petrol, the attendant washed the windscreen, wiped the headlamps, and looked under the bonnet with a torch.

Words "Borrowed" from Other Languages

French: beige, blouse, breeze, boutique, toast, tart, mobile, office **Spanish**: alligator, barbeque, bonanza **Italian:** ballot, carnival, trio **Aztec:** avocado, chocolate, tomato **Algonquian Indian:** raccoon, squash	**German:** kindergarten, pretzel, waltz **Irish/Gaelic:** bog, clan, plaid **Hebrew:** kosher, Sabbath, schwa **African:** banjo, tote, juke, banana **Arabic:** admiral, alfalfa, alcohol **Hindu:** bandanna, shampoos

Your Turn:
The following is a list of words derived from people's names. Look up each word and write a sentence or two, describing the origin of each. For example,   the word, "panic" comes from the Greek god, Pan, known for his habit of frightening travelers, and today,   "Panic" means "fright."

1. Boycott
2. Teddy bear
3. Mason-Dixon line
4. Cereal
5. Bartlett pear

6. Volcano
7. St. Bernard dog
8. Big Ben
9. Braille
10. Cardigan

How Can Latin "Roots" Build Vocabulary?

The Latin language, even though it has not been spoken for many years, has provided almost 90% of the words that we use in English today, and it formed the basis for vocabulary in other languages such as Spanish, French, Portuguese, and Italian. If you learn the breakdown of these basic Latin prefixes and "root" words, you will hold the master key to a super vocabulary.

Prefix	Its Meaning	Example Words	Latin Root	Its Meaning
Inter-	Between	Intermittent	-mitt, miss-	To send
De-	Down, away from	Detain	-tain, tin-	To have or hold
Pre-	Before	Precept	-cept, capt-	To take, to seize
Trans-	Across, beyond, through	Transcribe	-scribe-	To write
Sub	Under	Subsist	-sist-	To stand
Mono-	One, alone	Monograph	-graph-	To write
Epi-	Not, not any	Epilogue	-log, ology-	Speech, science
Ad-, As-	To or towards	Aspect	-spect-	To look
Ex-	Formerly	extended	-tend-	To stretch
Com-	With, together	Complicated	-plic-	To Bend, twist,
Re-	Back, again	Reproduction	-duct-	To lead, make, shape
In-	Not	Indisposed	-pos-	To put, place
Ob-	Toward, against	Object	-ject-	To throw
Anti-	Against	Anti-social	-sol-	To be alone

Your Turn:
Combine the prefixes and root words below and see how many English words you can create. When you think you have formed a word, check its meaning in a dictionary.

Prefixes	Root Words
Co-, de, dis, inter, non, post, pre, re, sub, trans, out-, over-, under-, pro-,	-dict, -duc, -gress, -pel, -pend, -port, -tract, -ver, -err, -fac-, frag-, frac-, jud-, am-, ben-, brev-,

What Can I Learn From a Dictionary?

The dictionary is the universe organized in alphabetical order."
—Anatole France

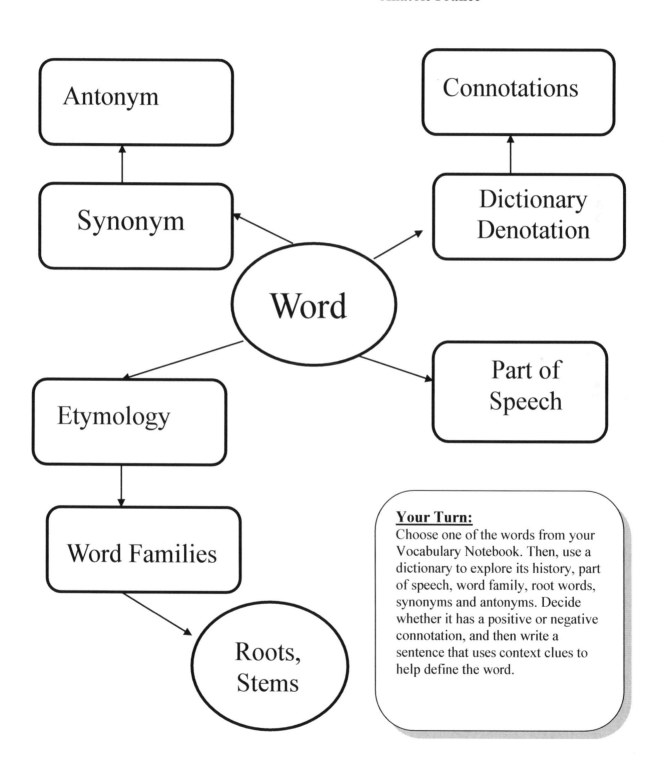

Your Turn:
Choose one of the words from your Vocabulary Notebook. Then, use a dictionary to explore its history, part of speech, word family, root words, synonyms and antonyms. Decide whether it has a positive or negative connotation, and then write a sentence that uses context clues to help define the word.

Antonym

Synonym

Word

Connotations

Dictionary Denotation

Part of Speech

Etymology

Word Families

Roots, Stems

What About Vocabulary Quizzes?

Vocabulary is not an end—it is a tool. Once writers feel power and control over words, then the content of their prose and poetry reaches a new level of maturity. Using the writing process can improve students' vocabularies by giving them responsibility, for, and power over, the words they use as they write. Developing a curiosity about word meanings and reading good books can help too.

All academic disciplines have specialized vocabularies. For instance, to become an accomplished musician, a student should understand and master terms like adagio, allegro, coda, concerto, requiem, and rondo. Mathematicians need to understand factors, quadrants, equations, theorems, postulates and tangents. Economists who guide consumers and Wall Street have mastered terms like supply and demand, budget deficits, gold reserve, trade balance, free market, stock options and dividends.

This lesson of *The Writer's Voice* will provide "tricks" to master the intricacies of our English language—the biggest, most cosmopolitan in the world—and a language that few people would call "user-friendly." First, let's take the vocabulary quiz in this section:

Directions: Identify the correct meaning for each word:

1. **dog**
   a. To hunt or track
   b. An animal
   c. A worthless person
2. **bird**
   a. clay pigeon
   b. To observe wild birds
   c. A feathered vertebrate
3. **cabinet**
   a. A cupboard used for storage
   b. A governmental advisory group
   c. Exhibition room in a museum
4. **model**
   a. A miniature representation
   b. A person who wears designer's clothing
   c. To pattern or imitate
5. **stage**
   a. The height of a river's surface
   b. A part of a theater
   c. To produce for public view

Your Turn:
OK. So, did you get it? All the answers are correct. In order to determine the definitions of each of the words above, you need their context, or words around them, organized into sentences to provide clues. Of course, it helps remember meanings when we write sentences, so choose one of the words and write a sentence for each one of its meanings.

What Are the Clues to Context Clues?

No one can possibly know the definitions of approximately 750,000 words in the English language, so here are a few clues that will help you "guesstimate" meanings by looking   at a word's environment, framework, or <u>context</u>.

1. **<u>Direct definition</u>**, often indicated by the words "is" or "means" :
   Ex. *Sauerkraut* is a food made from fermented cabbage.

2. **<u>Explanation through example:</u>**
   Ex. Mr. Jones has *arthritis*; the joints of his fingers are swollen and painful.

3. **<u>Words in a series of related words:</u>**
   Ex. The fragrance of the flowers filled the garden. There were *kalanchoes*, temple bells, geraniums and violets in bloom.

4. **<u>Synonym or restatement,</u>** often indicated by the words, "that is," "or," or "in other words."
   Ex. The *velocity,* or speed, of the projectile was 15 kilometers per minute.

5. **<u>Comparison/Contrast:</u>**
   Ex. Alva was very *diffident;* however, Bobby was outgoing.

6. **<u>Familiar expressions or figures of speech (similes and metaphors):</u>**
   Ex. No one doubted that our guest was *somnolent.* She slept like a log.

7. **<u>Inference:</u>** making conclusions or "reading between the lines"
   Ex. The monk looked *emaciated* after his long period of fasting.

8. **<u>Mood or tone:</u>** An author reflects a mood by the word used. An unknown word has meaning in harmony with the mood.
   Ex. The carnival noises filled the night with sounds of excitement, happiness and joy. The evening was *felicitous.*

9. **<u>Familiar word parts:</u>** Often we can guess the meaning of a word by recognizing parts of a word we already know.
   Ex. The *acqui*sition of a large amount of money through a gift helped pay our bills.

<u>Your Turn:</u>
 Find ten new words, or words used in unusual ways, in a story, newspaper, or literature that you have been assigned to read. Beside each word, identify the kind of context clue that the author has used to help define the word. Then, write a new sentence for the word that uses it in context.

Why Should I Keep a Vocabulary Notebook?

Developing an academic, sophisticated and mature vocabulary is a lifelong process. Although a teacher can facilitate the process of learning new words through careful word study, modeling and guidance, ultimately, readers and writers have to take responsibility of finding, and using, words that will best communicate meanings and messages. Keeping a notebook of new words, or words used in new ways, and their context will help you develop a more mature vocabulary. [3]

Your Turn:
Reading is the best way to improve vocabulary. As you read, list important, interesting and innovative words in the vocabulary chart in the back pages of your Writer's Notebook .or a separate file on your computer. Make a prediction, based on context clues, and then after you have finished a section or passage, confirm your predicted meaning by finding the word in a dictionary or thesaurus and writing the definition in your Vocabulary Notebook.

New Word, or Word used in an unusual way	My prediction of meaning based on Context Clues	Confirmed or Revised Meaning checked in a dictionary
1. "In the <u>lexicon</u> of the political class, the word sacrifice means that the citizens are supposed to mail even more of their income to Washington so that the published class will not have to sacrifice the pleasure of spending it." — George Will	1. Lexicon means a group of words used by a group of people	1. (1) The collection of words--the internalized dictionary--that every speaker of the language has. (2) A stock of terms used in a particular profession, subject, or style.
2.	2.	2.
3.	3.	3.
4.	4.	4.

What Are Analogies?

Analogies compare two things for the purpose of explanation or clarification based on a partial similarity. Analogies ask us to figure out how things go together and they are related to each other. For example, CAT is to KITTEN as DOG is to PUPPY—the second word in each group names the young, or baby, of the first word. The relationship in analogies generally falls into the following categories:

Type of Relationship	Example
Action to object	Play: Clarinet
Cause to effect	Sun: Sunburn
Item to category	Iguana: Reptile
Object to purpose	Pencil: Writing
Object to its material	Curtains: Cloth
Part to whole	Page: Book
Time Sequence	Recent: Current
Type to Characteristic	Dancer: Agile
Word to Antonym	Assist: Hinder
Word to Synonym	Provisions: Supplies
Worker to Product	Artist: Sketch
Worker to Workplace	Chef: Kitchen
Word to derived Form	Act: Action

Your Turn:

 In the blank, identify the type of relationship implied in the analogy. Then, create original analogies for your Writer's Notebook.

_____ 1. MICROSCOPE: INSTRUMENT:: necktie:

_____ 2. DESIGN: PATTERNS::plan: program

_____ 3. AIRPORT: TERMINAL:: car: automobile

_____ 4. PROMISE: GUARANTEE:: agreement: contra

_____ 5. CONDUCTOR: ORCHESTRA::director: cast

_____ 6. ZENITH: APEX:: base:: foundation

_____ 7. ACCORDION: REED::piano: key

_____ 8. SWORD: SCABBARD:: knife: sheath

LESSON 16:
READING LIKE A WRITER—
THE "VOICE" OF IDEAS

Reading makes us smarter.

The **CORE** of Reading:
Connection, Ownership, Response, Extension

> **"There is, then, creative reading as well as creative writing."**
> Ralph Waldo Emerson
> *Nature* [1836, 1849]. Introduction.

Why Write? Why Read?

All children are language experts. After the need for food and care, they need language. Immediately after birth, they start hearing the sounds around them and they can tell the differences between their mother's and father's voices. By trial and error as they grow, they discover the way language works. In 1985, the Commission of Reading concluded in its report, *Becoming a Nation of Readers*, "The single most important activity for building knowledge required for eventual success in reading is reading aloud."[1] And for this, they do need books, parents and teachers who can challenge their geniuses.

Reading and writing are parallel activities: one reinforces and deepens the power of the other. Reading helps us develop mental warehouses—places where we store images, experiences, language and ideas. Writing becomes the vehicle by which we transmit those pictures and reflections to others and to future generations. As students read from a variety of authors, they will acquire knowledge and discover techniques they can use in their own essays and compositions—knowledge that will give them power.

Specifically, we have many reasons to read and write in today's competitive academic environment and global workplace.

Why We Write:

1. To share thoughts and ideas:
2. To help us think;
3. To help remember facts, details and other information;
4. To influence change;
5. To synthesize great amounts of information;
6. To take messages, fill out applications, succeed on tests, send emails;
7. To learn to express ourselves more clearly in a variety of situations to a variety of people;
8. To earn a living.

Why We Read:

1. To makes us smarter.
2. To improve our vocabulary and language skills;
3. To make us knowledgeable by adding information to our data base;
4. To boost our creativity;
5. To understand other people;
6. To understand mortgages, job applications, legal contracts and other documents;
7. To understand history so we do not repeat it.
8. To provide pleasure and to help us escape from the ordinary, the mediocre and the mundane.

Writers and Readers Have Power!

Essay: "A Reading Autobiography"[1]

Early experiences with reading led to a love affair with words, fostered by a father whose passion for writing letters lasted from my birth to his death. From those early times, I have associated reading with intimacy and comfort, self-esteem and power

By the time I entered first grade, I had a strong appetite for books. I would stop on my way home from school at the library where I could choose from a whole smorgasbord of books. I never earned ribbons for reading "X" amount of books like some kids in my class because even as a seven year old, I insisted on quality instead of quantity; I would rather read two long books instead of four short ones. I especially loved a series of biographies with orange copies that I read in alphabetical order—from Clara Barton to George Washington. I enjoyed also enjoyed another series—the Bobbsey Twins books. A favorite book told the story of how the twins built a houseboat and won a race across a frozen lake. Through the people/characters in these books, I could visit all kinds of places, fight wars, lead nations and save lives. When I had grandchildren, I began to search for original editions of these books in antique stores, and today, on my books shelves, I have several orange biographies and original editions of the Bobbsey Twin books to share with them.

As a child, I never liked mysteries so Nancy Drew, even though she had the same last name as I did, held little fascination. My reading habits as a child and as a teenager, involved reading the first chapter, then the last chapter and then the middle chapters. Doing this allowed me to empathize with characters, to "hiss and boo" or "cheer" knowing the outcome of their actions. In adulthood, I discovered mysteries and so had to stop reading the endings first. I'm not sure why this change occurred—possibly I discovered there are only a few basic plot lines: fish out of water, boy meets girl, the quest, characters interacting within a limited environment—and so mysteries, with their plot "twists and turns" and devious, unsavory characters entertained me. Reading for pleasure, rather than for knowledge or power, came late in my life, and mysteries supplied escape, and no mind was further from my own than a murderer's. For whatever reason, I love mysteries today. A huge thrill happened a few years ago, when I met James Lee Burke, author of *Sunset Limited, Burning Angel* and *Stained White Radiance* at a small neighborhood bookstore. When I asked him where he got his ideas for Dave Robicheaux, the detective he created, he said, "I've lived a lot, listened a lot and learned a lot." Now, I try to listen a little more and live a little more, and my love of words focuses more on writing them than reading them.

Growing up in small, semi-Southern, rural community, dominated by football and "good ole boys," books represented another way of life, a world I wanted to know and experience. I loved the characters; Lady Brett Ashley, Tom Joad and Jett Rink were more real to me than my neighbors. The summer months before I left for college were the longest I ever spent in my life. I spent most of the time dreaming, drawing pictures, reading and writing poetry, copying passages from Hemingway, imitating his sentence structure, replacing his words with my own, eliminating adjectives, finding new verbs, trying to describe people and places with as few words as possible. I kept a diary of conversations, listened to baseball games on the radio and wrote long lists of colloquialisms and idioms. When I left home, I knew I was ready to get on with my life.

When my Dad died, he left a folder in his closet that contained cancelled checks that paid for my education and a copy of his poem:

> Never again, I'll hear him speak,
> Or feel his lips upon my cheek.
> Life seems a barren thing and stark.
> He isn't back, and it's "Oh! So dark."[2]

In those final lines of poetry, typed on his battered Smith Corona typewriter, my father expressed his final good-bye to his favorite reader and writer.

How Do I Explore My Reading History?

It helps to move forward when we look backward—see the paths we have navigated so we can chart a course for the path that lies ahead. Take a few minutes, and respond to the following questions in the Reading Inventory below in your Writer's Notebook:

Questions about Your Life as a Reader:

1. Did your parents read to you/tell you bedtime stories? Did you have favorite childhood stories? What were they?
2. Did you go to a preschool, Head Start center, or local library or bookstore where someone read stories to you? Did you enjoy the stories? Like the reader?
3. What kinds of TV shows did you watch? Did you watch the commercials? Do you remember any of the jingles?
4. Were you encouraged to talk? Did your parents listen to you? Did they look at you when you talked to them? In your family, did one speaker often interrupt another?
5. At school, did your teachers read to you? At a certain grade level, did they stop reading aloud? Why do you think they stopped doing this?
6. Were there classroom libraries in your school? Were there any books written by students? Did your teacher show you how to make your own books? Encourage you to publish your writing on bulletin boards, in hallways and common areas or in contests?
7. Do you recall ever reading aloud in front of the class? How did you feel? Did you do well? Did it make your nervous? Proud? Fearful?
8. Think back to junior and senior high. Did your reading habits change? Did you have a summer vacation that included reading many books? What books were they? Did you have favorite authors? Did you read books that took you away from reality and into another world? Or did you read books about the everyday world and everyday life?
9. Now, do you have friends who read, and with whom you talk about what you read? Have you ever belonged to a book club or reading group?
10. Do you have bookshelves in your home? What kinds of books do you own? Do you read more than one book at a time? Are there books you always wanted to read, but never have. Make a list of them. Do they naturally fall into categories?

Questions about Reading:

1. What is the name of your favorite book? Why is it your favorite?
2. Do you ever read magazines? Newspapers? Comics?
3. How much time do you spend reading online publications? Social media sites?
4. How important do you think it is to read well?
5. What is your favorite school subject? Why?
6. Did you ever keep a Reading Journal or Learning Log?
7. What did you do when you became frustrated with reading a book?
8. What are some things that get you excited about reading?
9. How do you determine whether a book is worth reading or not?
10. Who are your favorite authors and what do they do that makes them special?

> **Your Turn:**
> Use your responses to the questions to generate ideas for an autobiography of your reading interests. Save it for your portfolio—and for your children to read.

How Do I Read for Different Purposes?

Good readers learn to read for different purposes. Sometimes it is all right to skip over an unfamiliar word, or "guess" at an unknown word's meaning, and sometimes we need to read with a dictionary at our fingertips. If you can get the general sense of a sentence or paragraph without knowing every word, there is no need to interrupt your reading by using a dictionary to find the word's meaning. Sometimes you will want to read material quickly, but you will need to read more carefully when reading to learn, especially if it's new information. To see what I mean, try reading the passage below that has been attributed to a study of reading at Cambridge University: [3]

Olny srmat poelpe can raed tihs.

I cdnuolt blveiee taht I cluod aulaclty uesdnatnrd waht I was rdanieg The phaonmneal pweor of the hmuan mnid, aoccdrnig to a rscheearch at Cmabrigde Uinervtisy, it deosn't mttaer in waht oredr the ltteers in a wrod are, the olny iprmoatnt tihng is taht the frist and lsat ltteer be in the rgh it pclae. The rset can be a taotl mses and you can sitll raed it wouthit a porbelm. Tihs is bcuseae the huamn mnid deos not raed ervey lteter by istlef, but the wrod as a wlohe.

Amzanig huh?

To discover different purposes for reading, read   the two different descriptions of an eagle below:

The Eagle
He clasps the crag with crooked hands:
Close to the sun in lonely hands,
Ring'd with the azure world, he stands.

The wrinkled sea beneath him crawls;
He watches from his mountain walls,
And like a thunderbolt he falls.
Alfred Lord Tennyson

"The eagle is one of the largest and most powerful birds in the world. At close range, eagles look fierce and proud. As a result, they are pictured as fierce, courageous hunters. Some eagles soar high in the air hunting for food. Because of this, eagles have long been symbols of grace and power."
World Book Encyclopedia

Your Turn:
Compare the poetic description of an eagle with the prose description. What does the poem express that the prose description does not? What does the prose description express that the poetic description does not? What is the purpose of the poem? What is the   purpose of the prose passage?

What Makes A Good Reader?

Over several years, researchers—and teachers in their own classrooms—have discovered some of the characteristic behaviors that effective and efficient readers share.[4] They have also determined some of the ways   immature and poor readers react when faced with a new, or difficult, piece of text. As you review the chart below, try to determine your own reading strengths and weaknesses. In future sections of this lesson, you will discover strategies to help you become a better, more mature reader—and how to **Connect, Own, Respond** and **Extend** your reading.

Mature/Good Readers	Immature/Poor Readers
Before Reading—Connect with Material • Activate prior knowledge; • Understand reading tasks and set a purpose for reading; • Choose appropriate strategies to use while reading.	**Before Reading—Lack of Connection** • Begin reading without preparation; • Read without knowing, "why;" • Read without considering how to approach the material.
During Reading—Feel Ownership of Information and Ideas in Material • Monitor their understanding and comprehension by knowing it is occurring and that they are understanding; • Anticipate and predict; • Use "fix-up" strategies when they don't understand; • Use context clues to understand new words and words used in new ways; • Understand the structure of a text (essay, argument, story, poetry); • Organize and integrates new information.	**During Reading—Lack of Ownership** • Get distracted easily; • Do not know they do not understand; • Read "to get done"; • Do not know what to do when they don't understand; • Do not recognize important vocabulary words; • Do not see any organizational pattern in what they read; • Add on, rather than integrate new information.
After Reading—Reflect on Ideas and Information and Extend Them To Other Areas: • Take some time to reflect on what they read; • Can summarize main ideas; • Seek additional information from other sources; • Feel success is a result of effort.	**After Reading—Lack of Response** • Stop reading and stops thinking; • Feel success is a result of lack rather than of effort.

> <u>**Your Turn**</u>:
> On the chart, highlight your strengths and circle your weaknesses. Do most of you problems occur before, during, or after you read new material?

How Can I "Connect" With A Text?

Years ago, when I decided to pursue a Master's Degree in Reading, I discovered some tools and strategies that could help students—and my own children and grandchildren—become more effective readers. Today, you can find more than a million "hits" on the Internet that discuss two of them: **QAR** (Question Answer Relationships) and **KWLS** (What I Know, What I Want to Know, What I Learned, What I Still Need to Learn).[5] Below, you can find the versions of these two strategies that I used in my classroom:

QAR: Determining Types of Questions Most Asked About Reading

Level 1: Right There Questions—You can find the answer directly stated in the text, usually in the same sentence.

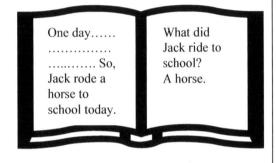

Level 2: Think and Search— Words for the question and words for the answer come from different parts, or sections, of the text.

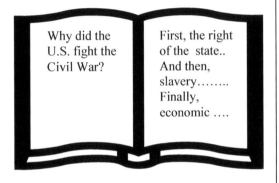

Level 3: The Author and You— The answer is NOT in the text. You have to think about what you know, what the author tells you and how it fits together.

> If you could interview President Lincoln about the events leading up to the Civil War, what would you ask him?

Level 4: On Your Own— The answer is not in the text. You can answer it without even reading because you use your own experience.

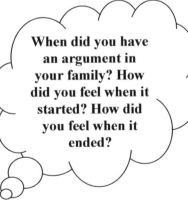

When did you have an argument in your family? How did you feel when it started? How did you feel when it ended?

> **Your Turn:** Create 4 questions about a short story or essay you have read—one for each of the four levels in QAR.

How Does K-W-L-S "Connect" With Text?

Readers who struggle with new material often ask, "How do I know what I need to know before I read this text?" A four column chart, used before, during and after you read can help you determine what you know, what you want to know, what you learned and what you still need to learn.

What I **K**now	What I **W**ant to Know	What I **L**earned	What I **S**till Need to Learn

Another strategy for improving understanding is to "visualize," or illustrate the pictures that the words create in our minds. For practice, choose words from the excerpt from "By the Waters of Babylon" by Stephen Vincent Benet (www.2.esm.vt.edu/~scross/text/babylon.html. that   help readers experience a sense of foreboding in this classic short story.

> "All the same, when I came to the Place of the Gods, I was afraid, afraid. The current of the great river is very strong—it gripped my raft with its hands. That was magic, for the river itself is wide and calm. I could feel evil spirits about me, in the bright morning; I could feel their breath on my neck as I swept down the stream. Never have I been so much alone—I tried to think of my knowledge, but it was a squirrel's heap of winter nuts. There was no strength in my knowledge any more, and I felt small and naked as a new-hatched bird—alone upon the great river, the servant of the gods."

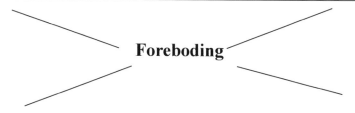

Foreboding

Your Turn:
In your Writer's Notebook, draw a picture of the scene you imagine in Benet's story—or from another story you have read recently.

How Does A Reading Log Help "Own" Text?

A reading log, reading diary, reading journal, reading record—whatever you want to call it—is an important and effective way to help you **OWN** and remember, the important ideas and information you gain from your reading experiences. Often, in conversations and job interviews, someone might ask you about something you have read. When you keep a reading log, you will have a tool that helps record the journey you take through a book so you can engage in a dialogue with people who will understand that you are a thoughtful and intellectual reader.

Use the format, and questions below to start keeping a reading log of the prose and poetry you intend to read during a semester—or even during an entire year.

Date/Class/Time I read:	Page numbers I read:	Teacher's Initials (if required)

Bibliography Information: Title, Author, Date & Place of Publication:

My Ideas/Responses to the Literature I Read

Author: What is the author's name? What is the author's credibility? Background? Experiences?

People/Characters: Who are the major people/characters? Choose a few phrases to describe them.

Events/Plot: What happens? Write a brief summary of the story.

Point of View: Who's telling the story? Why did the author chose this particular point of view?

Setting: Where and when does the book take place?

Themes/Thesis: What is the book, article, poem, play, or essay REALLY about?

Significant Quotations: Copy several significant, important or favorite quotes from the book, and explain their significance.

Style: How would you describe the author's writing style? How does it affect the book?

Evaluation: Record notes about the reading itself. Strengths? Weaknesses? Areas of agreement or disagreements? What other reactions do you have to the events and ideas? Does it remind you of anything else you have read? How? Would you like to read something else the author has written? Why or why not?

> **Your Turn:**
> Read several selections in an anthology and keep a reading log for each of them.
> Add your own comments about the strengths and weaknesses, areas of agreement,
> or disagreement, or any other reactions you might have had to the ideas and events
> that occur or are discussed in the selections you read.

How Does Taking Notes "Own" Text?

Having a conversation with a piece of literature—interacting with the author's words and ideas—provides an important way for students to OWN their experiences with those of a character or author. Taking notes, in a methodical and structured way, helps young writers analyze and evaluate the ways authors use language, structure and literary devices to achieve a purpose and tone, and meet the needs of readers.

Here is a sample of a student's notes, using two columns, taken while reading an essay about Gary Soto's father in the memoir, *Living Up the Street*.

My Summary	My Questions As I Read
Soto's father & a friend prepare a new lawn (par. 1)	Who is his friend? Why are they doing this? Why do people care about their yards? How have I helped my father with a chore?
Narrator's father is teaching him how to water the lawn (par. 2)	Why did the water hiss when it streamed out of the hose? Why did he put his thumb over the hose? What kind of person doesn't know how to water a yard?

Below, is an example a student's notes on Sandra Cisneros' figurative language in *The House On Mango Street:*

Technique	Textual Evidence	My Comments/Interpretation
Use of repetition	"different hair," "Papa's hair," "hair is lazy," "Carlos' hair,"	Repeating the word "hair" emphasizes the differences in hair dependent on culture, and family genes.
Simile	"like little rosettes," "like little candy circles"	The author creates a warm, pleasant description of her mother's hair which reminds her of the safe feeling she felt as a child.

> **Your Turn:**
> Take notes on a passage that you believe is especially well written. Practice asking questions of the author on one page, and then practice identifying, analyzing and commenting on the techniques that you believe made the passage effective.

How Can a Précis "Respond" to a Text?

"Tell me about the movie you saw Friday night."
What did we do in class yesterday?"
Provide a brief overview of the essential ideas in the Monroe Doctrine.
—Questions that require a brief summary, or précis, as an answer.

One-way to make sure you understand, comprehend, and "OWN" a piece of writing when you read is to RESPOND by writing a summary, or condensed version of a larger reading. Your purpose in writing a summary is to provide the basic ideas and most important and relevant details of the original reading. To begin, ask yourself, "What was it about and what did the author want to communicate?"

A précis is an even more precise, concise summary of essential ideas, statements or facts that reproduces the same ideas, mood, and tone as the original piece of writing—but on a much smaller scale. The sole purpose of a précis is to produce a reduced snapshot of the original author's exact and essential meaning, without personal opinions, evaluation or interpretation. The composition of a good précis is difficult because it takes <u>careful reading,</u> <u>critical thinking </u>and an <u>exact writing style</u>. When writing a brief and precise summary, follow these suggestions:

1. Read the selection closely and carefully. Look up, or guess, using context clues, the meaning of all words and phrases you may not know. Look how the author has organized the material; determine what language devices and rhetorical strategies the author has used.

2. **Read the material a second time and this time, take notes. Ask yourself, "Who? What? Where? When? How? and Why?"**

3. Write the précis in your own words from your notes alone. Quoting sentences—topic sentences, for example—result in a sentence outline, not a précis.

4. WRITE TIGHT. Strip your sentences to the bare bones by eliminating filler words, adjectives, adverbs, "be" verbs and abstract, vague nouns.

5. Do not alter ideas contained in the original. Follow a logical order. Do not rearrange ideas or facts. Try to preserve the original purpose, mood and tone as much as possible.

6. Write the précis in Standard English. A précis should be a model of exact diction and clear, correct sentence constructions because it must be intelligible to a reader who has not read the original essay, article or story.

<u>Note:</u> The word, summary, has several synonyms (précis, synopsis, digest, abstract, or abridgement) but all these terms share the same quality of distilling, or condensing, something large into something more easily understood.

Original—
xxxxxxxxx
xxxxxxxxx
xxxxxxxxx

Précis –
xxx

What Does A Précis Look Like?

In personal, academic and business communications, summarization provides an opportunity to communicate what is important, serves as a way to check understanding and provides practice in decision making and sequencing.

Reducing a Paragraph to a Précis

Original Text:

For a hundred years and more the monarchy in France had been absolute and popular. It was beginning to lose both power and prestige. A sinister symptom of what was to follow appeared when the higher ranks of society began to lost their respect for the sovereign. It started when Louis XV selected as his principle mistress a member of the middle class; it continued when he chose her successor from the streets. When the feud between Madame Du Barry and the Due De Choiseul ended in the dismissal of the Minister, the road to Changeloup, his country house, was crowded with carriages, while familiar faces were absent from the court of Versailles. For the first time in French history the followers of fashion flocked to do honor to a fallen favorite. People wondered at the time, but hardly understood the profound significance of the event. The King was no longer the leader of society. Kings and presidents, prime ministers and dictators, provide at all times a target for the criticism of philosophers, satirists, and reformers. Such criticism they can usually afford to neglect, but when time-servers, the sycophants, and the courtiers begin to disregard them, then should the strongest of them tremble on their thrones. (208 words)

Duff Cooper [6]

Précis:

For years, Louis XV ruled France, but when he chose mistresses from the lower class and dismissed his minister, people left his court in protest. This event predicted his downfall. Leaders like Louis XV often ignore critics in media and government, but when they ignore the criticism of friends and followers, they risk failure. (47 words)

A Précis Summarizing a Book:

The Writer's Voice is a compilation of lessons, teacher-written essays, student models, and assignments created, developed and used by a high school teacher who taught language and composition for almost thirty years. The guide provides beginning or "struggling" writers with helpful techniques and strategies in a "reader-friendly" manner that is easy to follow, helpful to use and entertaining to read.

A Précis Summarizing a Film:

The newspaper magnate, Charles Foster Kane, one of the richest and most powerful men in the world, dies in the Oscar Award winning film, "Citizen Kane." A newspaperman tries to discover the meaning of the last word he spoke, "Rosebud," through flashbacks and interviews with people who knew him. Considered the best film ever made, the reporter never learns quite enough to unlock the riddle of Kane's dying breath, but instead, we see the life of a man, who dies alone in his castle, "Xanadu," surrounded by possessions, and whose power, fame and money never brings him happiness.

> **Your Turn:**
> Choose an article in a magazine, a book, story, or film you have read recently, and write a brief summary of its most important ideas and events. Imagine you are writing it for someone who has not read the book, story or seen the film.

Writing About Reading:
Connect, Own, Respond and Extend [6]

Prompt: *In class this semester, we have discussed issues concerning education in a multicultural society. Write a carefully reasoned essay defending or challenging Carol Locust's belief that the "educational system was not designed to honor diverse racial and cultural groups." Cite evidence from the text to support your thesis.*

In her article about American Indian belief systems, "Wounding the Spirit," Carol Locust suggests that American Indians have experienced discrimination because of their traditional beliefs, especially when their beliefs conflict with those of the dominant culture's educational system (Locust, 25). Her purpose is to influence changes in an educational system that "was not designed to honor diverse racial and cultural groups" (25). As she explains the sacred and holy belief systems of the Indian tribes, influenced by their tribe affiliations and memberships, outside religion, and length of time of the reservation (27), readers understand that the inability of the educational system to understand these values promotes discrimination. Her plea, "As Indian people, we ask that educational systems recognize our right to religious freedom and our right, as Sovereign Nations, to live in harmony as were taught" (43) has relevance, not only for the education of Indians, but for the education of other minority cultures. Before teachers change the world, however, we have to meet our own prejudices and change them.

According to Locust, to change education for "Amerindians" and end discrimination, educators must first begin to understand the belief systems among Indian people, fundamental to the "health and spirituality of tribal members" (26). They should learn to identify the ways Indian beliefs in "wellness and unwellness" (28), the spirit world and the connection between mind, spirit and body, manifest themselves in Indian attitudes and behaviors (28). Public and bureau schools can institute several changes that would provide educational and learning benefits for Indian students. For instance, Indian youngsters, often absent to help a sick relative, should have extended opportunities to finish schoolwork, alternative assignments when asked to dissect animals, freedom to express and communicate their views, and protection for their need for privacy. Respect for symbolic objects and significant holidays, avoidance of labeling based on standardized testing, lessons based on modeling, collaboration and sharing among groups. Using nonverbal communication, visualization, imagery, metaphors and storytelling can encourage and teach verbal skills.

Careful and thoughtful reading of Locust's article can help loving, caring educators to see that students, whether they are from minority or majority cultures, are products of their experiences, beliefs and values. They enter our classrooms with the need for understanding, respect and appreciation for their ideas and their uniqueness as individuals. As educators, we need to listen to their stories and provide chances for them to share them with other students. Students, whether they are Caucasian, African-American, Latino, Amerindians, or Asians, are more than percentages or computer ID numbers—or strange sounding names on class rolls. All members work together and contribute to the group, supporting each other in times of stress; for they know that they will find the same network of support for themselves should they require it" (41). Her wisdom applies not only to groups in classrooms, but to all humanity.

I have already made changes and adjustments in my classroom for the students who enter my doors from many different cultures. Whether they come from minority or majority groups, students have many different learning styles; they come from different systems of values and principles established through family relationships and experiences, and they have a variety of strengths and weaknesses. The interactive classroom environment suggests instruction that facilitates, coaches, and models. A teacher's desk sits in the corner, rarely used and mostly neglected. Student tables are organized in four person "pods," an arrangement that reinforces the need for communication and collaboration. Bookcases contain collections of children's poetry and storybooks, paperback classics, mysteries, science fiction, fantasy, romance, adventure and nonfiction. Professional books about creativity, literacy, assessment and adolescent psychology; reference books on American and world literature, art, history and music line the walls. On another wall, bulletin boards, pictures of heroes representing America's "salad bowl" of ethnic and immigrant history establish the theme of our first unit, "Strength from Diversity." The world map contains pins that mark the places where both the teacher and the students have traveled. The portable stereo might play the "Star Wars" soundtrack, Debussy's "Clair Du Lune" or Wagner's "Valkyries" depending on the mood and tone of the literature we will be enjoying.

My first efforts involve finding out who my students are so I can help them advance as far as they can go. Reading and writing journals, letters, memoirs, autobiographies and narrative poetry help us discover each other's unique voices. Students respond to artwork in the textbooks and on overhead transparencies, which encourages discussions, builds background knowledge and shares viewpoints. Soon after school begins, teams explore the Internet to find out more about an author or historical event, design a web page, or participate in an online discussion group. As we read, we will think aloud and connect to the author's experience and add vocabulary words to the word banks in their portfolios. After reading, we might use a graphic organizer to analyze the structure of the text. In discussion groups, we will determine the author's thesis, purpose. We will discover how images, figures of speech and connotations help achieve the purpose, convey an attitude and provoke a mood.

Together, we can assess their understanding by writing another version, designing an advertisement, travel brochure or power point presentation. We can create a poem, write a play based on a piece of literature and perform it in class or participate in a guided writing lesson based on selections as model. The learning process may take more time, but "at completion, the students know what a task is done a certain way, not just how to do it, for they have seen the completion of the circle (41). Giving up prejudices is easier when we do not have too many to start with—it becomes harder and more of a challenge when prejudices have made up a large part of the fabric of our lives. However, for the United States to survive, parents, teachers, and representative adults in our institutions need to give up the ideas and stereotypes that govern our actions. If we do not, it will be too late.

Your Turn:

Underline the thesis in this essay and highlight evidence cited from the essay, "Wounding the Spirit." How does this essay differ from the essays you read—and wrote—earlier in this book? Next, try to understand the CORE of writing about a piece of literature by responding to these questions:

1. How does the writer show a CONNECTION to the essay she read by Carol Locust? Where?
2. How does the writer show OWNERSHIP and understanding of the purpose and main ideas expressed in Ms. Locust's essay?
3. Where does the writer RESPOND intellectually and emotionally to the ideas in the essay she read?
4. How does the writer EXTEND the ideas into other areas of her life especially to her classroom?

Why Should I Read "Classics?"

Over the years, many students have asked me, "Why should I tackle the classics, the books on a teacher's reading list? Why not just see the movie? Read the Cliff Notes? Study the Spark notes?" I usually answer, "Because you don't want to remain uninformed, stupid and alliterate   for the rest of your life. And, when having dinner with your boss, it's nice to be able to talk about something other than football scores." Do I have some valid reasons for encouraging writers to read the classics? Of course. Let's consider my answers to some other questions from students over the years:

What Is A Classic Book?
- A book that has remained in print more than one generation and invites reading decade after decade.
- A book that I'm glad I didn't miss reading during my lifetime.
- A book that other intellectual, well-read, thoughtful and educated people have read.
- A book, like   senior citizens, that are   loved not because they're old, but because their wisdom and experiences have a timeless quality.

How do authors of "best seller" books differ from authors of "classic" books?
Commercial writers confirm their readers' prejudices, endorse their opinions, appeal to their feelings and satisfy their wishes for quick, easy entertainment. We read their books in airplanes and doctor's offices. Classic authors, thoughtful observers of life, question our beliefs, challenge our ideas, and force us to enter new worlds of experience and enlightenment. We read their books at home and in classrooms, and when we are finished we put them on our bookshelves as a reminder of our accomplishments.

Testimony: Famous Authors Discuss Classic Books

"A book is a mirror: if an ass peers into it, he can't expect an apostle to look out."
~G.C. Lichtenberg

"A great book should leave you with many   experiences, and slightly exhausted at the end."
~William Styron

"When you read a classic, you do not see more in the book than you did before; you see more in you than there was before."

~Alfred Kazin

The man who does not read good books has no advantage over the man who can't read them.
~Mark Twain, attributed

Books can be dangerous. The best ones should be labeled "This could change your life."
~Helen Exley

Your Turn:
 Make a trip to a library or bookstore in your area or search "Literature" online. Check out the titles in the "Literature" Section, and list titles of books you want to read immediately, books you would like to read someday and books you will never read.

What Books Should I Read Before I'm 30?

Many people and organizations, including the American Library Association, *Time* Magazine and even Wikipedia, have lists of "must reads" for people, So, not to be outdone, I'm including in *The Writer's Voice,* my own list of books whose authors provided the "voices" of writing that I listened to over the years. The list is not meant to be all inclusive, but reading these books helped me to become a lover of words—a lexophile—and they took me to places I never dreamed of visiting while meeting characters I never thought I'd meet.

Today, I am a grandmother, and my shelves at home contain favorite books from my youth as well as today's favorites. I know it is a cliché to say that a good book is a trusted friend, but I can place my hands on a particular book and know that in this age of throwaways and disposables, a well-written book will have something to say to generation after generation. The greatest legacy we can leave for children is the love of a good book, so below you will find my choices of favorite books I read before my thirtieth birthday.

Top 10 Nonfiction	Top 10 Memoirs, Biographies
1. *In Cold Blood*, Truman Capote	1. *My Life*, Helen Keller
2. *Roots,* Alex Haley	2. *I Know Why the Caged Bird Sings*, Maya Angelou
3. *Silent Spring,* Rachel Carson	
4. *All the President's Men*, Carl Bernstein and Bob Woodward	3. *Anne Frank: Diary of a Young Girl*, Anne Frank
5. *A Day At Appomattox*, Bruce Catton	4. *Autobiography of Mark Twain*, Mark Twain
6. *The Right Stuff*, Tom Wolfe	5. *House on Mango Street*, Sandra Cisneros
7. *The Elements of Style*, E.B. White & William Strunk	6. *A Moveable Feast*, Ernest Hemingway
8. *The Making of a President, 1960,* Theodore H. White	7. *John Adams*, David McCulloch
	8. *Walden*, Henry David Thoreau
9. *Working*, Studs Terkel	9. *Profiles in Courage*, J.F. Kennedy
10. *Blue Highways*, William Least Heat Moon	10. *Narrative of a Slave*, Frederick Douglass

Top 10 American Fiction	Top 10 World Fiction
1. *Gone With the Wind*, Margaret Mitchell	1. *Nineteen Eighty-Four*, George Orwell
2. *A Farewell to Arms,* Ernest Hemingway	2. *Portrait Of An Artist As a Young Man,* James Joyce
3. *Grapes of Wrath*, John Steinbeck	3. *Lord of the Flies*, William Golding
4. *Huckleberry Finn*, Mark Twain	4. *Brave New World,* Aldous Huxley
5. *Fahrenheit 451*, Ray Bradbury	5. *Heart of Darkness*, Joseph Conrad
6. *Atlas Shrugged,* Ayn Rand	6. *Animal Farm*, George Orwell
7. *The Great Gatsby*, F. Scott Fitzgerald	7. *Women in Love*, D. H. Lawrence
8. *The Naked and the Dead,* Norman Mailer	8. *War and Peace,* Leo Tolstoy
9. *Lonesome Dove,* Larry McMurtry	9. *Kim*, Rudyard Kipling
10. *The Robe,* Lloyd C. Douglas	10. *Darkness At Noon*, Arthur Koestler.

Student Voices: Books and Reading

Censorship

The books cuddle in the depths
of every shelf,
from *Gone With the Wind*
to *Horton Hears a Who.*
Invisible heroes and kittens lay
without movement.
When the door opens,
the pictures quiver and rats scurry.
The outline of the fireman
comes into view
and the wave of fire
yearns to burn every zenith into nothing.
                    —**Nishi Sarda (1995:5)**

Fahrenheit

Stories never brought to life
die only in substance.
Burning down the years,
sound of fire embedded in their souls.
Each man beneath a mask
an image of every other.
Fire, the protector and destroyer,
transforms pages of a book
into black butterflies.
            ~**Archana Dave (2000:93)**

Mark Twain

Last night at a convenience store
I saw Mark Twain
wearing a cap with a Navy patch on it
and a dark jean jacket.
He leaned against a brick wall,
and talked on a pay phone.
Drawing a small cigar to his lips
and lighting it with a plastic lighter,
he eyed his eighteen wheeler
parked by the gas pumps.
A couple of times, he nodded yes
or chuckled into the phone.
Then, he hung up.
From his pocket,
he pulled out jingling keys
and climbed into the cab of his truck.
I went inside the store,
said hello to Mr. Hawthorne
reading a paper and sipping coffee.
I put a six-pack of Coke on the counter
and Walt handed me change.
I smiled and left,
walking to the passenger's side of the car.
I let Ernest drive,
because he knows the way.
            ~**Justin Cone (1995:3)**

Your Turn:
Write about a memory you have of reading—either pleasant or unpleasant. Tell a story about that memory in either prose or poetry. Use all of the best writing skills you have learned by writing your way through *The Writer's Voice.*

LESSON 17:
WRITING ACROSS THE CURRICULUM—THE "VOICE" OF COLLEGE/CAREER READINESS

Writing in English Language Arts	Writing in History/Social Studies Classes
Writing in Science Classes	Writing in Math/Technical Classes

> **"If we did all the things we are capable of doing, we would astound ourselves."**
>
> ---Thomas A. Edison -

What Is Writing Across the Curriculum?

In the last several years, the complex role of educational challenges in the United States has made it clear that the language arts is not just the responsibility of English teachers. Two changes happened to motivate the need for changes in writing instruction. First, professions became more specialized. Technology influenced the need for a whole assortment of engineers: chemical, civil, electrical, aeronautical, petroleum, nautical, environmental, geotechnical, etc. Doctors began to specialize in pediatrics, podiatry, obstetrics, hematology, dermatology, and gastroenterology, and even English teachers became specialists in English as a Second Language, Bi-lingual Education, Literacy and Media.

Secondly, high schools reflected a diversity of social and economic backgrounds, ethnicity and culture —and not all college students grew up speaking "academic" language. Earlier in the twentieth century, our education system served a very different function; it was designed to educate the elite few who were wealthy and showed potential for leadership. Other students were trained to work long hours in fields and factories; schools patterned themselves after an industrial model of assembly-line production. When factories and farms began to disappear, the need for college degrees increased; high school diplomas could no longer guarantee that jobs waited for students after they graduated.

Teaching students how to diagram sentences, read Shakespeare and write literary analysis no longer served the needs of a changing world and a changing economy. Students needed to learn how to communicate effectively and clearly, the knowledge they gained from their studies of history, social studies, science, mathematics and technical courses. Whether the writing in all classes took the shape of short "quick writes," and warmups or longer reports and essays, writing had become a way to learn, a way to think, and a way to respond to the challenges of an economy based on information and communicating with the world.

Writers Find Meaning in a Changing World.

Why Write Across the Curriculum?

Colleges, businesses and industry demand that students learn to write beyond typical essays in a high school English class. The Texas Higher Education Coordinating Board and the Common Core standards have proposed cross-disciplinary writing and reading standards to help students develop the skills they will need when they complete high school graduation requirements. College instructors expect first year college students to use a wide range of subject-specific reading and writing strategies in all of their courses. Business leaders emphasize applying these skills across a variety of contexts and subject matter.

Writing is clearly linked to thinking and learning, and students who can clearly comprehend and write about a subject effectively on a given subject learn the material much more effectively and thoroughly. The National Council of Teachers of English, in a "Policy Brief" in 2008,[1] recommended that schools, in order to improve writing proficiency, should:

1. Develop authentic writing assignments that bridge the gaps between school and workplace writing;
2. Include multiple measures of writing proficiency, including portfolios;
3. Create curricula that fosters writing in every subject at every grade level;
4. Build a technological infrastructure to support new media writing;
5. Invest in professional development for writing instruction.[1]

"Real World" writing shares the same characteristics of effective writing that student writers who have used *The Writer's Voice* consistently should have acquired through the instruction, practice, evaluation and performance emphasized in the lessons and "Your Turn" assignments. To prepare for writing in college and in a career, writers should:

1. Use clear, concise and error-free word choice, sentence structure and paragraphing (25-39);
2. Avoid overly technical phrases and "fancy" stylistic choices (133-150);
3. Make the subject matter and purpose explicitly clear (46-47);
4. Show a keen awareness of an audience's knowledge, biases, opinions; backgrounds (17);
5. Stress proper usage of documents design and layout, including font size, bullet points, bold and italic text, images and diagrams (examples contained throughout *The Writer's Voice*).

The purpose of *The Writer's Voice*, to help "students discover how to write from a position of strength,"(2) includes Learning to Write as well as Writing to Learn in many academic subjects across the curriculum.

What Assignments Cross the Curriculum?

Warm-Ups ("entrance" tickets) and Cool Down ("exit" tickets) encourage students to make connections, engage and evaluate their own learning in writing. While these "low-stakes/formative" assignments are less rigorous than "high-stakes-summative" assignments, they are a good place to begin.

General Warm-ups:
1. What did you learn the last time we had class?
2. What do you already know about…."
3. Where have you heard this term, word, phrase before?
4. What do you want to learn about……today?
5. Imagine you are---protoplasm, Abe Lincoln, Hamlet, quadratic equation…

General Cool Downs:
1. What questions do you have about today's lesson?
2. Summarize in 3-5 words what you learned today.
3. Persuade me that you understand…
4. What were the causes of….?
5. How is what you learned today relevant to your own life? To another class?

Example Prompts on Math Content and Process
1. Describe square root.
2. When do you use fractions at home?
3. Compare the terms we learned today.
4. Explain the difference between parallel and perpendicular.
5. Tell everything you know about prime numbers.
6. What do you know about imaginary numbers?
7. What is the difference between area and perimeter?
8. Write a word problem that involves measuring square feet.
9. What does it mean to solve an equation?
10. Describe today's math concept to a young child.

Writing Prompts on Attitudes Regarding Mathematics
1. Describe things you find difficult in math.
2. How do you apply math in your life?
3. What are your personal goals for this quarter/semester in math?
4. Write a children's story that explains using fractions.
5. Choose an occupation and describe ways that workers use math concepts.
6. Write a letter of advice to a student who will take this class next year.
7. What famous mathematician do you admire? Why?
8. I would be better in math if I …
9. Describe how you feel when you are unable to solve a math problem.
10. Describe the math process you know best.

Writing Prompts for Science Writing

1. How does science enter into your life?
2. What scientific concepts regarding the weather do you wonder about?
3. What is the greatest scientific discovery in the world, and why?
4. What scientific invention would you like to make that would help the most people?
5. Which is the better choice—paper or plastic?

Writing Prompts on Heredity

1. What common traits (hair color, eye color, etc.) do you share with other members of your family?
2. What traits did your grandparents have that were handed down to your generation?
3. Write what you know about your family's ethnic roots.
4. What would you change about your physical traits if you could?

Writing Prompts on the Ecosystem

1. Describe how you feel about protecting the ecosystem in our area.
2. How can the average person or household make a change in the ecosystem?
3. Where do you see dangerous practices regarding the environment?
4. Describe the environment/ecosystem that you interact with directly.
5. What steps are you taking personally to protect the environment?

Writing Prompts on Body Systems

1. Describe what would happen if your inner ear became infected with a virus?
2. Sit quietly and listen to your body. What systems are you aware of and how do you know they are working?
3. What was the last thing you ate that upset your digestive system?
4. In a moment of fear or stress, what do you notice about your body's reactions?

Writing Prompts for Social Studies

1. If you lived in one of the original thirteen colonies, which one would you choose? Why?
2. What Constitutional Amendment do you think will be added in the next 20 years? Why?
3. What important figure in American/World History would you like to invite to dinner? What questions would you ask?
4. What do you know, or think you know, about the Amazon river?

Your Turn:

Choose one of the assignments from math, science or social studies and write a response. Use the Grammar/Style Checker to check it for style and mechanics. Then, take your composition to a teacher in each subject so they can check for your use of correct information.

What Skills Do I Need for Career Success?

Based on surveys of several corporations here is a summary of skills most often deemed important and reported by a variety of organizations and employers[2]:

1.	**VERBAL COMMUNICATION**	Able to express ideas clearly and confidently in speech
2.	**WRITTEN COMMUNICATION**	Able to express yourself clearly in writing
3.	**COMMERCIAL AWARENESS**	Understand the commercial realities affecting the organization
4.	**ANALYZING AND INVESTIGATING**	Gather information systematically to establish facts & principles. Problem solving
5.	**INITIATIVE/SELF-MOTIVATION**	Able to act on initiative, identify opportunities & be proactive in putting together ideas and solutions
6.	**DRIVE**	Determination to get things done, make things happen & constantly looking for better ways of doing things.
7.	**TEAMWORK**	Work confidently within a group
8.	**PLANNING/ORGANIZING**	Able to plan activities & carry them through effectively
9.	**FLEXIBILITY**	Adapt successfully to changing situations and environments
10.	**TIME MANAGEMENT**	Manage time effectively, prioritize tasks and work towards deadlines

Your Turn:
Would you hire yourself as an employee? Review the list of Top Ten Skills and decide which ones are your strongest? Then provide an example for each one of your strengths from your classes, extracurricular and volunteer activities or work experiences. Decide where you have weaknesses and devise a plan for turning them into strengths.

What Skills Do I Need for College?

Many students graduate from high school without the tools they need for college. Estimates as high as 50% of students who enter their first year of college need to take remedial classes to help them develop the skills, especially in writing, to succeed in college. The purpose of this section of *The Writer's Voice* is not to try to determine the reasons that this happened, but to make you aware that it is never too late to improve writing proficiency when you know what colleges expect.

A brief summary of Common Core Standards for English Language Arts,[3] authored by the National Governors Association Center for Best Practices follows:

Writing Standard 1: Text Types and Purposes—Argumentation

W1. Write arguments to support claims in an analysis of substantive topics or texts using valid reasoning and relevant and sufficient evidence.

Writing Standard 2: Text Types and Purposes—Exposition

W2. Write informative/explanatory texts to examine and convey complex ideas and information clearly and accurately through the effective selection, organization, and analysis of content.

Writing Standard 3: Text Types and Purposes—Narration

W3. Write narratives to develop real or imagined experiences or events using effective technique, well-chosen details and well-structured event sequences.

Writing Standard 4-6: Production and Distribution of Writing

W4. Produce clear and coherent writing in which the development, organization, and style are appropriate to task, purpose and audience.

W5. Develop and strengthen writing as needed by planning, revising, editing, rewriting, or trying a new approach, focusing on addressing what is most significant for a specific purpose and audience.

W6. Use technology, including the Internet to produce, publish and update individual or shared writing, taking advantage of technology's capacity to link to other information and to display information flexibly and dynamically.

Writing Standard 7-9: Research to Build and Present Knowledge

W7. Conduct short as well as more sustained research projects based on focused questions, demonstrating understanding of the subject under investigation.

W8. Gather relevant information from multiple print and digital sources, assess the credibility and accuracy of each source, and integrate the information while avoiding plagiarism.

W9. Draw evidence from literary or informational texts to support analysis, reflection, and research.

Writing Standard 10: Range of Writing

W10. Write routinely over extended time frames (time for research, reflection, and revision) and shorter time frames (a single sitting or a day or two) for a range of tasks, purposes, and audiences.

Many states, including Texas, have focused on making sure students are prepared for a changing and complex future by adopting their own College and Career Readiness Standards.[4]

Writing

A. Compose a variety of texts that demonstrate clear focus, the logical development of ideas in well-organized paragraphs, and the use of appropriate language that advances the author's purpose.

1. Determine effective approaches, forms, and rhetorical techniques that demonstrate understanding of the writer's purpose and audience.

2. Generate ideas and gather information relevant to the topic and purpose, keeping careful records of outside sources.

3. Evaluate relevance, quality, sufficiency, and depth of preliminary ideas and information, organize material generated, and formulate a thesis.

4. Recognize the importance of revision as the key to effective writing. Each draft should refine key ideas and organize them more logically and fluidly, use language more precisely and effectively, and draw the reader to the author's purpose.

5. Edit writing for proper voice, tense, and syntax, assuring that it conforms to standard English, when appropriate.

B. Understand new vocabulary and concepts and use them accurately in reading, speaking, and writing.

1. Identify new words and concepts acquired through study of their relationships to other words and concepts.

2. Apply knowledge of roots and affixes to infer the meanings of new words.

3. Use reference guides to confirm the meanings of new words or concepts.

Research

A. Formulate, explore and refine research topic and questions and devise a timeline for completing work.

B. Select information from a variety of sources.
1. Gather relevant sources.
2. Evaluate the validity and reliability of sources.
3. Synthesize and organize information effectively.

C. Produce and design a document.
1. Design and present an effective product.
2. Use source material ethically.

The national and state standards share many objectives. Generally, the more standards students can demonstrate successfully, the more likely they are to be prepared for college.

LESSON 18: PORTFOLIOS— THE "VOICE" OF SELF-APPRAISAL

Top Ten Questions Writers Ask Teachers

10. Is this for grade?
9. Do you take off for spelling?
8. Do I need to write drafts?
7. How long does it have to be?
6. When is it due?
5. Can I write on both sides?
4. Can I write in pencil?
3. Does grammar count?
2. What is a "be" verb, anyway?
1. Do you really read all these compositions?

The answers: 10. Maybe, 9. Sometimes, 8. Yes, 7. It depends, 6. On the due date, 5. No, 4. Yes—think in ink, 3. Yes, 2. You'll find out soon, and 1. "Oh, yes."

> **"If there is a special Hell for writers it would be in the forced contemplation of their own works."**
> —John Dos Passos

What Is A Portfolio?

A portfolio is a collection of samples that communicate your interests and give evidence of your skills, talents and abilities. You will use your portfolio to show others what you have accomplished and produced. When you began writing using the "Your Turn" assignments in this book, you kept your responses in a Writer's Notebook. Now, it is time to prepare final copies for possible publication, and to organize them into a portfolio to share with others.

A portfolio helps you inventory who you are and the story you tell; the ideas and information you provide in a portfolio show what you have learned and discovered and help determine where you want to go next. Increasingly, colleges and professions require portfolios for admission, graduation, and job application requirements. There are many different types of portfolios; the final product depends on the requirements of a school, teacher or employer. A portfolio should grow, develop and change as it becomes a "living" document that reflects your work ethic, integrity and willingness to "learn to learn" as you continue your education and grow as a writer.

What can you include in a Writer's Portfolio?

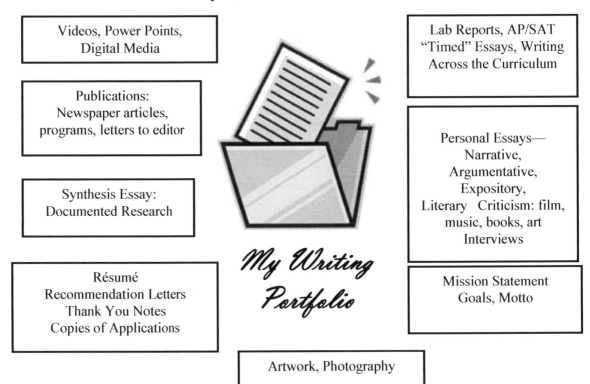

Videos, Power Points, Digital Media

Publications:
Newspaper articles, programs, letters to editor

Synthesis Essay:
Documented Research

Résumé
Recommendation Letters
Thank You Notes
Copies of Applications

My Writing Portfolio

Artwork, Photography

Lab Reports, AP/SAT "Timed" Essays, Writing Across the Curriculum

Personal Essays—
Narrative,
Argumentative,
Expository,
Literary Criticism: film, music, books, art
Interviews

Mission Statement
Goals, Motto

Writers who practice their craft find a way to publish and share their words and ideas.

How Are Portfolios a Pathway to Progress?[1]

Readers and writers vary in how well they write from assignment to assignment, topic to topic and day by day. Although this is normal and natural, teachers often forget that this happens when judging how well a student reads or writes. To offer a well-grounded evaluation of a student's reading and writing skills, it helps to examine a broad sample of that writer's compositions and essays.

Portfolios provide a cumulative collection of the work students have completed. They are an ideal way to illustrate how a student's work has developed over time, and can give students, parents, administrators and colleges a strong sense of what students can do. Portfolios encourage students to reflect upon their own progress as writers when they include self-evaluations of writing included in their portfolios. Such reflection can help students become aware of, and take control over, their own growth as readers and writers. When responses and evaluation become a responsibility shared by students and their instructors, assessment complements the process of learning to read and write.

The use of portfolios cause schools to reconsider how they use their time and require teachers to rethink the way they teach and the way they assess students. As teachers incorporate portfolios, they will need training in how to use them. When principals declare, "This year, you will use portfolios," they invite frustration and failure. The purpose of a staff development workshop, is to provide guidelines, information and research on methods, materials, and answers to most frequently asked questions as students and teachers prepare to use "Portfolios—Pathway to Progress."

1. What purposes do Portfolios have in the classroom?

In order to circumnavigate the often-muddy waters of written text, students have to accomplish many tasks. Developing literacy skills is a complex process that involves many attributes: making sense of the alphabet system, understanding and acquiring vocabulary, manipulating syntax, constructing a schema, and building background knowledge. To make meaning from a text, learners have to form pictures in their minds, secure, or have at their disposal, resources of knowledge; they have to understand the conventions, patterns and structures of a first language. Readers and writers need to discuss, predict, question, reread and rethink. They have to find the stamina needed to pursue the pleasure, and sometimes, the pain of becoming literate, feel   motivated to take the journey offered by text, and have the fortitude to stay on the path when they run into roadblocks. Above all, they have to engage in a fundamental need of social interaction—the human need for TALK.

The ability to choose writing pieces to be graded—rather than being graded on everything—can be a powerful motivating device for students who also need time to reflect, set and reset future goals. Portfolios allow students the opportunity to assess processes as well as products and analyze patterns of errors in their own reading and writing—and correct them. Portfolios make assessment an ongoing part of everyday reading and writing opportunities and instruction. Portfolios can help teachers identify strengths and weaknesses of students; understand their development, discover the power of their instruction, sharpen confidence in their ability to create lessons and have information to share with others when assessing the curriculum of a writing program.

2. What do Portfolios look like?

Portfolios should be discipline and purpose specific. However, they should also be as individual as the students who create them. Generally, however, there are four types of portfolios: project, expert, professional and personal. In graduate school, portfolios might consist of research, case studies, observations, learning logs. Businesses might require expert or professional portfolios that demonstrate ability to create, design, or analyze problems. They might include multi-media projects, drawings, proposals or showcase special accomplishments connected to a specific job. Portfolios, no matter what they look like, should demonstrate critical thinking and the ability to solve problems in creative, innovative ways.

A common misconception about portfolios is that they should include only a student or job applicant's best work. In secondary schools and universities, student achievement is more clearly documented when first drafts and other learning products such as learning logs, reader-response journals, student-generated vocabulary lists, artwork related to lesson topics, graphic organizers ("mind maps"), and outlines accompany finished products. The samples should represent a wide range of presentation formats. Students might want to experiment with many different formats before deciding which one best document the skills and learning they want to communicate. The most popular forms include:
- Traditional "manila folder" where students keep their work;
- Bound notebook with separate sections kept for "work in progress" and final drafts;
- Published collection of carefully selected, revised and bound work;
- e-portfolio format that uses technology including the Internet, CD-ROM, video, animation or audio.

There is no one "right" way to build a portfolio. In the past, most portfolios came in binders, leather carrying cases, or scrapbooks. Today, electronic portfolios have become a popular alternative to traditional paper-based portfolios because they offer teachers, administrators and employers the ability to review, communicate and assess portfolios online. A word of warning, however: technology changes so fast that a portfolio kept on a CD-Rom or a "flash drive" yesterday may not work on next year's version of a computer! After all, how many of us can play an 8-track tape or watch a movie on a VCR?

3. What questions can help students choose pieces of writing for their portfolios?

Portfolios should emphasize the potential for learning by helping writers see themselves capable of taking risks and becoming confident in their own capabilities. Helping readers/writers know about their worlds, to use a range of techniques and strategies as they make decisions and put their reading and writing to work in the "real world" can provide perspectives on how to assess their progress and success. When choosing samples for their portfolios, students might ask these questions:

A. **Self-Efficacy:** What samples show a willingness to take risks? Participate in conversations about writing and reading? Show improvement?

B. **World Knowledge:** What samples show evidence of student's experiences? The cultural and ethnic diversity of their lives? Knowledge beyond school tasks?

C. **Reading/Writing Strategies:** What samples show an understanding of syntax, language and text structure? Are there illustrations? Graphs? Mind Maps? Outlines? Is there evidence of enjoyment and passion? Integration of new information? Questioning? Evidence of the writing process: planning, drafting, revising, editing, manuscript form?

D. **Reflection:** Are there samples that show an ability to discuss reading and writing? Logs and journals? Summaries and self-evaluations?

. E. **Functional and Critical Thinking**: Are there samples that show the student has put writing to work in the real world? Letters, memos, notes? Instructions? Research projects?

Stories, poems, songs, plays, artwork? Reviews of films, books, music and/or art? Technology forms such as web pages, Power Point presentations, Excel spread sheets, videos, proposals or position papers?

4. Can you provide some suggestions for building a portfolio based on reading Jonathan Edwards' "Sinners in the Hands of an Angry God"?

> **A. Diary entry.** You are a devout member of the Enfield, Connecticut church congregation. In a diary entry, describe your feelings after listening to six hours of an Edwards' sermon.
>
> **B. Newscast.** Edwards was dismissed as pastor of the Northampton congregation after he publicly named members who he believed had lapsed in their devotion. Write a newscast announcing the dismissal and the reasons for it.
>
> **C. Public Letter.** Imagine you are Edwards, and write an open letter defending the actions that led to your dismissal. Explain why you publicly denounced members of the congregation.
>
> **D. Oral Interpretation.** Create a video of your reading an excerpt from the sermon in your choice of dramatic style.
>
> **E. Oral Report.** Sermons like those of Dr. Martin Luther King still have the power to inspire us. Research Dr. King's sermons and their role in the Civil Rights Movement. Give a brief report on your discoveries. Record it on audio or video.
>
> **F. Television commercial.** Create a commercial to persuade people to adopt a healthier lifestyle. Include music or sound effects and share your commercial with your friends.
>
> **G. Puritan Handbook.** Gather information about the Puritan beliefs and famous "work ethic." Create a handbook, or "blog" that includes guidelines and rules for living and working as a proper Puritan.

As we can see from the examples provided, a Writer's Portfolio can contain a wide variety of writing assignments that include information from a wide variety of reading experiences. A portfolio should reflect the spectrum of a writer's use of language and composition skills in a variety of situations, both academic and extracurricular. What is the greatest danger threatening a final portfolio? Procrastination! Writers should not put off collecting samples, and revising and editing final pieces of writing until the last minute. How useful and important a portfolio is for a pathway to success will depend on what time and effort student writers put into building it.

What Other Assignments Can I Include?

If you are still searching for writing assignments to include in your final portfolio, you might try some of the favorites of students in my classes in the past several years below:

Personal Narrative Essays:

1. Letter of Introduction—Write a letter to put in a time capsule and read in the year 2300 that preserves information about some influences on you and your life in the early part of the 21st century.

2. "Show Not Tell" College Admissions Essay—write an essay about a "hallmark" or trademark experience in your life so that a college admissions officer understands what makes you "tick."

3. In the tradition of Native Americans, choose an Indian name for yourself, and write a narrative poem, or a brief anecdote, that shows how you earned, or received, your name.

4. Search your life for an event that lasted six minutes or five or seven—the point is for it to cover a brief moment in time. Think about a moment that seemed to last forever (the moment you stood at the foot of a hospital bed; the moment before a car accident; the moment before you went on stage, the moment you realized you were smarter than other people), then use it! A flashback might help readers visit the event with you.

Descriptive Analysis Essay: Objective vs. Subjective Description

1. Choose one (1) topic from the list below and write a short composition, which objectively describes the person, place of object. Then, write another composition, which subjectively describes the same topic. If you're brave and want to reach "outside the box," combine and blend the two types of description. Then, illustrate it with your own drawing.

Person	Place	Object
Musician	Your bedroom	A musical instrument
Artist	Your old neighborhood	A locker or desk
Minister	A foggy day	A season of the year
Athlete	A practice field	A pair of shoes
Dancer	A favorite city	A car
An older relative	A view from a window	A childhood toy

Exposition— "I –Search" Reports
1. Write an essay that uses a variety of strategies (description, anecdote, testimony, process, cause-effect, persuasion, definition, examples, metaphors, compare/contrast and classification) to write a definition of a common object—chocolate.
2. Explore the Internet for sources that provide information about a current events problem. Then, compile an "Annotated Bibliography" to serve as a reading record of your research. You will use the information you discover to write an argumentative essay later in the year.

Argumentation— "A Modest Proposal" Satire
Write a modest proposal for solving one of the following problems: eliminating welfare dependence, making affordable health care, improving public education or another problem that concerns you.
Be sure to incorporate elements of satire like irony, hyperbole, and understatement.

Argumentation: "Declaration of Independence" Parody

Write an imitation of this famous document. Choose a topic for your declaration that you can treat humorously (sport, technology, job, parents, teacher, a particular class or teacher (change names to protect the innocent—and yourself). As you write, imitate Jefferson's style and structure, use of parallelism, repetition, anaphora and lofty, dignified language.

Analysis: The Ad & The Ego

Choose an ad in a magazine or on the Internet. Then, write a description of the ad—size, color, product/logo placement, spacing, numbers, web sites, etc. Describe the kind of person the ad tells its viewers they can become if they purchase the product. Analyze the l language for colloquialism, jargon, emotionally loaded words, figures of speech and imagery. Identify the ad's emotional, logical and ethical appeals. Discuss inaccurate or incomplete information. Finally, interpret the ad's social, philosophical, political or religious agenda—the subliminal message presented below the level of awareness.

Compare/Contrast Authors:

Create a dialogue between two different authors in which they express their opinions about current issues of today. Imagine they've been invited to appear on CNN, MSNBC, or Fox News. Imagine Martin Luther King talking to Thomas Jefferson, Ernest Hemingway talking to Stephen Crane, Ayn Rand talking with John Steinbeck.

Student Choice:

William Stafford, professor and former poet laureate of the United States, wrote the following poem in his book of poetry, *An Oregon Message:*

Final Exam: American Renaissance

Fill in the blanks: Your name is

_____ _____ldo Emerson. Your friend

Thor_____ lives at _____ Pond; he owes

You rent and an axe. Your neighbor

In a house with _____gables

Won't respond to another neighbor, Herman

_____, who broods about a whale colored _____.

You think it is time for America to _____.

In a few choice words, tell why.

Fill in the blanks and follow the directions in the poem. (I actually used this poem as a final exam. I owe many of my writing and thinking skills to reading poets like Dr. Stafford.)

> ### Your Turn:
> Choose several of these additional "suggested" assignments and follow the directions in each of them. Remember to think about the subject, the occasion, audience, purpose and tone as you draft, revise, edit and proofread.

Student Voices:

I Want

I want a rabbit's foot
And a four leaf clover
And that penny I found in fourth grade.
I want that rubber band I wore around my wrist
When I won the track meet two years ago
And that picture I snapped of Madonna
At her concert in Floriday
And I want that silly cat fact
I made out of modeling clay in preschool
(my mom said it's the best cat sculpture
She'd ever seen)
But most of all
I just want an A+ on my Physics test.
                    ~-Lexie Koenig (2006:32)

Fairy Tales

I remember when writing was fun.
I'd come home
With a paper behind my back,
Smiling at my mother,
Proud of my hard work.

She'd smile back,
Read it slowly out loud'
And notice my artwork.
"You're so creative," she'd say.
Then she would post it on the refrigerator
For everyone to see—
Her little author in the making.

That was a time when writing was fun.
I wrote my own fairy tales
And expected them to be published.
A time when my only critic
Was my mom,
The only opinion that mattered.
                    ~-Demeeka Rogers (2003: 86)

Major Findings from NAEP Reading Assessment, "The Nation's Report Card"

- Students whose teachers reported using multiple choice tests on a weekly basis had lower reading/writing scores than students whose teachers reported less than yearly use of this type of assessment;
- Using projects or presentations for assessment purposes were associated with higher reading/writing scores; students whose teacher reported using such methods monthly had higher scores than students whose teachers hardly ever used them;
- Students who reported saving, or whose teachers saved, their writing pieces in folders or portfolios had higher average scores than students whose work was not saved;
- Student asked to write more than one draft of a paper had higher average scores than their peers who were "sometimes" or "never asked" to do so.

http://nces.ed.gov/nationsreportcard/reading

What Are General Evaluation Guidelines?

After many years of evaluating and assigning grades to more than 25,000 essays and compositions (6 pieces of writing x 135 students x 30 years), I formulated some general guidelines to help students understand the criteria for effective, and interesting writing. I hope they will help you set standards and continue to grow, learn and mature as a writer, reader, and most importantly, as a "thinker."

Grade "A" —Exceeds Expectations

- Provides illuminating, instructive, and informative insights and ideas;
- Avoids the obvious, seeks originality of expression;
- Develops ideas with a variety of sentences, word choices, rhetorical strategies and language devices;
- Uses punctuation for effect as well as clarity;
- Contains richness of detail, content and vocabulary;
- Demonstrates an active sense of style, fluency and purpose;
- Shows a keen awareness of audience;
- *Readers respond, "Wow! This piece deserves publication."*

Grade "B"—Contains Some Strengths

- Contains some interesting ideas and information;
- Develops ideas with a sense of order and organization;
- Uses words adequate enough to express writer's thoughts and affect readers' emotions;
- Uses punctuation to aid meaning and affect tone;
- Makes some stylistic choices and shows signs of revision;
- *Readers respond, "If I had more time, I might reread this piece."*

Grade "C" —Average

- Depends on the self-evident and cliché;
- Writes uninteresting and/or uninformative communication and discussion;
- Uses an obvious pattern of organization **or** writes without a plan;
- Contains limited vocabulary and ability to control sentence structure, paragraphing, grammar usage and mechanics;
- Shows a general unawareness of strategies, choices and techniques;
- Needs at least one or more thoughtful revision;
- *Readers respond, "O.K. but I'll forget it in five minutes."*

Grade "D"—Shows Ineffectiveness

- Shows lack of understanding of the writing task and/or lack of interest in the topic;
- Wanders aimlessly without an organizational plan, pattern or purpose;
- Fails to vary words, phrases, or sentence patterns and structures;
- Needs several more revisions and more careful proofreading;
- Contains isolated hints at what the writer has in mind;
- *Readers respond, "I'm sorry that you did not succeed in your attempt to communicate your ideas."*

(+) excellent proofreading

(-) unsatisfactory proofreading

How Do I Evaluate Personal Narratives?

A "rubric," or checklist of certain criteria for different kinds of composition, s can help you understand how your writing will be judged. When you know the criteria **before** you start to plan, write, revise and edit, you will know what you need to do to achieve your purpose and reach your audience. "Rubrics" provide focus, emphasis, and attention to particular details when studying models and examples of good writing. For example, a rubric for a narrative essay—memoir, anecdote, college admissions essay—might contain the criteria listed below:

Criteria: Personal Narrative	Average	Good	Excellent
1. **Ideas:** Focuses on a single event, or a series of closely related experiences; includes facts and details that add to a sense of time, place and people;			
2. **Organization:** Sustains a narrative structure that depends on chronological order; begins with an interesting first line that "hooks" readers, and comes to a satisfying conclusion;			
3. **Voice:** Relies on action verbs, dialogue and concrete details to "SHOW" not tell; shows attitude— humorous, sarcastic, bragging, pensive, thoughtful, ironic			
4. **Diction**: Avoids overworked "be" verbs, worn out adjectives, flabby adverbs and clichés;			
5. **Syntax:** Use a variety of sentence types and structure, including a sentence fragment used for effect and as an element of style;			
6. **Conventions:** Demonstrates control of spelling, capitalization and punctuation;			
+1: **Presentation:** Uses a "grammar/style checker to indicate word count, reading level, paragraphing and margins.			

Your Turn:
Find a draft of a personal narrative you wrote in your Writer's Notebook, and use the "rubric," to revise, edit and proofread it for your final portfolio. Review "Lesson 5: Narration—The 'Voice' of Story Telling" when you need help.

How Do I Evaluate Essays and Reports?

On the next few pages, you will find different criteria and different rubrics for different types, forms and methods of writing. Using these checklists can guide you through the writing process more efficiently and make your writing more interesting for your readers. "One size does not fit all" when it comes to communicating ideas and experiences!

Criteria: Descriptive Essay	Average	Good	Excellent
1. **Ideas:** Contains details that work together to create a dominant impression of a person, place or object;			
2. **Organization:** Contains a thesis that clearly states the main idea; presents consistent, logical and effective spatial or order of importance;			
3. **Voice:** Uses sensory details, creative figures of speech and interesting comparisons in subjective paragraphs; provides appropriate facts and information in objective paragraphs;			
4. **Diction**: Avoids overworked "be" verbs, vague, abstract nouns, weak adjectives, flabby adverbs and clichés;			
5. **Syntax:** Use a variety of sentence types and structure to achieve style, grace and rhythm;			
6. **Conventions:** Demonstrates control of spelling, capitalization and punctuation;			
+1: **Presentation:** Uses two columns to show different types of descriptions			

Your Turn:
Find a draft of a essay, report, or oral presentation you wrote in your Writer's Notebook, and use the "rubrics," to revise, edit and proofread pieces for your final portfolio.

Criteria: "I-Search" Report (Exposition)	Average	Good	Excellent
1. **Ideas:** Presents accurate information, integrates quotations correctly, uses information from a variety of credible sources;			
2. **Organization:** Contains a thesis that clearly states the main idea; ends with a conclusion that summarizes importance;			
3. **Voice:** Develops ideas with a variety of methods, rhetorical strategies and techniques of language; uses 3rd person, avoids "I" pronoun;			
4. **Diction:** Avoids overworked "be" verbs, vague, abstract nouns, weak adjectives, flabby adverbs and clichés;			
5. **Syntax:** Use a variety of sentence types and structures that provide coherence;			
6. **Conventions:** Demonstrates control of spelling, capitalization and punctuation;			
+1: **Presentation:** Creates an appropriate, and informative publication—a brochure, newsletter or website.			
Criteria: Oral Presentation	Average	Good	Excellent
1. **Ideas:** Answers all questions with elaboration and details;			
2. **Organization:** Presents all information in logical, interesting sequence;			
3. **Voice:** speaks clearly, pronouns all terms correctly, modulates tone, maintains direct eye contact;			
4. **Graphics:** reinforce and explain screen text and presentation;			
5. **Conventions:** Demonstrates control of spelling, capitalization and punctuation in written portion.			

Criteria: Argument/Problem-Solution Essays/ Proposals/Literary Criticism	Average	Good	Excellent
1. **Ideas:** Provides adequate background so readers understand cultural and historical significance, uses evidence from several sources that is knowledgeable, accurate and specific, shows an understanding of the problem, interprets information, determines purpose for reading;			
2. **Organization:** Begins with a compelling "lead," contains a clearly stated thesis that states an opinion, states purpose, and addresses task in assignment, uses transitional words and phrases to help readers follow the organizational pattern, clearly comes to a conclusion by offering a course of action or summary statements;			
3. **Voice:** Establishes the writer as a credible sensible and sincere person through the use of a variety of ethical, logical and emotional appeals; develops paragraphs gracefully— "little bits of textual evidence" documented correctly and smoothly;			
4, 5, 6: Diction/Syntax/Conventions: : Incorporates language/poetic devices as an element of style; uses a variety of sentence structures, a robust vocabulary and mature control of grammar and mechanics;			
+1: Presentation: Includes correct in-text and parenthetical documentation and a "Works Cited" that indicates sources.			

Your Turn:
Find drafts of essays that used analysis, synthesis and evaluation to develop and argue a position that you wrote your Writer's Notebook. Use the "rubric," above to revise, edit and proofread them for your final portfolio. Review "Lesson 8: Argumentation— the "Voice of Opinion," and Lessons 12, 13 and 14 when you need help.

How Do I Evaluate Fiction and Poetry?

Criteria: Short Story	Average	Good	Excellent
1. **Ideas:** Conveys a dominate impression of setting, conflict, characters and theme;			
2. **Organization:** Sustains a consistent point of view, "hooks" readers in the beginning and leads them to a satisfying conclusion that resolves conflicts; uses past tense throughout the story;			
3. **Voice:** combines elements of descriptive and narration, language techniques, details, imagery to create a consistent mood and tone;			
4. **Diction:** Avoids overworked "be" verbs, vague, abstract nouns, weak adjectives, flabby adverbs and clichés;			
5. **Syntax:** Use a variety of sentence types and structures so reading is a pleasure;			
6. **Conventions:** Observes language conventions and punctuates for effect and meaning;			
+1: **Presentation:** Manuscript format—double spacing, page numbers, paragraphing, word count, and reading level.			
Criteria: Poetry	**Average**	**Good**	**Excellent**
1. Appeals to readers' senses and imagination through the use of figures of speech and sound devices as appropriate;			
2. Brings readers fresh, universal insights into the human experience—does not just entertain;			
3. Contains details, action verbs, specific nouns— Shows rather than Tells; eliminates "fillers" and unnecessary words;			
4. Observes conventions of grammar, spelling and punctuation.			

Final Portfolio Evaluation Rubric

Criteria	Needs Work (75-79)	Good (80-89)	Excellent (90-100)
Development: (Contains a Variety of Assignments and Evidence of Process)	5-10 samples	10-15 samples	15+ samples
Organization: (Includes Cover, Table of Contents, Résumé, Self-Evaluation)	Incomplete, gaps, lacks a pattern, page numbers	Follows a pattern, page numbers, section dividers, cover/resume/self-evaluation	Interesting cover, complete table of contents, well-written résumé
Visual Appeal: (Cover Design, Graphics, Layout, Neatness)	Messy, sloppy, haphazard presentation Fragmented or piecemeal design	Includes all sections, clean, easy to view	Effective use of colors, space, balance, proportion, thematic elements
Self-Evaluation, "Voice"/Individuality	Brief, sketchy self-appraisal	Self-appraisal	Thoughtful, reflective and insightful self-appraisal.
Format: (Control of Syntax and Mechanics)	Shows little revision, editing and proofreading of assignments	Shows some revision, editing and proofreading of assignments	Shows careful revision, editing and editing of all assignments
Interview	Hesitant, awkward, little eye contact	Cooperative, interactive, some eye contact	Confident, eager to contribute, enthusiastic

Teacher/ Appraiser's Comments:

Your Turn:
Preparing a Writer's Portfolio

"What do you want to be when you grow up?"
—Parents to their children
"The best part of human language, properly so called, is derived from
reflections on the acts of the mind itself."
--Samuel Taylor Coleridge, _Biographia Literaria [1817]_

Assignment: Mastering the process of self-evaluation and goal setting is essential for success in the next century when most people will likely change jobs and careers many times. The last "Your Turn" assignment in _The Writer's Voice_ invites you to prepare for success in the future by creating a portfolio today. You can think of your portfolio as a special purpose autobiography; how important it is depends on what you decide to put into it. I believe you will feel very proud of your accomplishments and your writing when it is completed.

You should organize your samples into a notebook with sheet protectors (to make it easy to change samples in the future). If you choose to create a digital, or e-portfolio, you should organize your writing onto a flash drive, disk or website.

Prepare your portfolio to present to a college admissions officer, scholarship committee chair, possible employer, or any other adult you want to impress.

Since the primary purpose is to demonstrate what you have learned as you have written your way through this book, or a certain part of your school or academic career, your portfolio should have examples that show the writing "voices" you have developed. Your should include finished, publishable final drafts of the following sections indicated by a Table of Contents:

Part I.

- The Writing Process: Letter of Introduction
- Personal Essay: Narration: A Memoir
- Personal Essay: Objective/Subjective Description—People or Places
- Expository Paragraphs that Define, tell "How to," Discuss or Explain
- Argument—Take a Stand on a Controversial Issue
- Analysis—The Role of Media, Advertising
- The Research Process: Annotated Bibliography on Current Topic
- Synthesis: Problem-Solution on Current Topic
- Evaluation: Literary Criticism of film, book, short story or poem
- Literary/Imaginative Writing: Short Story, Poetry
- History of English: Most important influence

Part II.

Publications, programs, newspaper clippings, letters of recommendation
Your Choice from journal entries, class assignments, lab reports, computer
graphics, spread sheets, speeches, etc.

Part III. An Up-to-date Résumé

Your resume will be the first page of your portfolio and will serve as an
introduction, not only to you, but to the unique skills and abilities illustrated in your
portfolio. Review "Lesson 1: Getting Started" to update your résumé.

Part IV. A Self-Evaluation Essay

Write an essay that shows a mature, thoughtful evaluation of your reading/writing
processes. The questions below will generate ideas to include in a self-evaluation.
Do not just answer the questions. Use your best writing skills. Write tight. Your
word limit is 500. Reading level should be 10-12.

A. Learning Goals:
1. What were your reading/writing goals at the beginning of this year?
2. What problems did you encounter as you tried to reach those goals?
    How did you solve them?
3. What are your reading/writing goals for next year?

B. The Portfolio's Content
1. Who else has seen your portfolio? Describe their reactions
2. What surprises you about your portfolio? Why?
3. Choose the piece of writing most satisfying to you and explain why.
4. Choose the piece of writing least satisfying to you and explain why.
5. How does your writing show you are willing to take risks?

C. Your Style
1. If asked to describe the person represented in your portfolio, what
    words, phrases and sentences would you use?
2. Assume you keep adding to your portfolio. What might it contain
    five years from now? Ten years? Twenty years?
3. What did you discover about yourself as you completed this project?
4. What grade would you assign to this portfolio? Justify your
    decision.

Portfolio Self Evaluation
Chris Miller

Over the course of my junior year in high school, I experienced pitfalls in organization and success in completing my assignments. This year my English teacher furthered my education by forcing a college-ready mindset on me. The assignments that acted as progressive obstacles gradually increased my writing literacy and helped me reach the ultimate goal of reading like a writer.

When I first began my junior year, the main obstacle I faced was absent-mindedness. I had a nasty habit of relying on my "stream-of-consciousness" writing to get me through the most challenging tests, quizzes and essays. As time progressed, and with help from AP writing "prompts," my mind was unlocked. I began to use every dark facet of my brain to create intellectual, creative and stimulating works of literature. My first assignment, to create an "Annotated Bibliography," challenged my skills of analysis. In the past, I would write a cushy, adjective-filled review but after that experience, I can now write insightful, thought-provoking criticism. My writing because of AP English gained a foundation for future writing and reading.

The portfolio that I created from many of these essays, labs and tests, contains the essence of a mature writer. The only thing that surprised me in creating this anthology was the intricateness of designing it. Anyone can create an "OK" portfolio, but it takes a process of deep planning to put that "wow" factor in our work. A portfolio should contain a color scheme, a consistent organizational format, and a well-trained mind to fill its pages. If an anthology contains all these elements, it can become a "professional" portfolio that an employer, educator, or community member would gladly read—the main reason I chose the quote from David Thoreau for my front cover, "If you have built castles in the air, your work will not be lost. That is where they should be. Now, put the foundations under them.

Out of my entire portfolio, the subjective and objective essays definitely take the gold. When these two papers, very different in their techniques and usage, come together, they form an exciting essay filled with both vivid details and facts. Originally, the objective essay, "Rutland, MA" contained only solid facts that provided information for the reader. Its counterpart and subjective essay, "A Winter's Nightmare" contained details and images that entertained the reader. With a bit of encouragement, the two combined to form, "Rutland—A Winter's Nightmare" which both informs and entertains readers at the same time. The key to a well-written piece of prose is to break it down into objective and subjective parts. This procedure guarantees that writing will contain the best of both worlds.

An outstanding portfolio requires a balanced writer. An author (or students) should always evaluate their own work. Then it comes to performance demonstrated in this portfolio, I feel a grade of a ninety or above is very fitting. With over twenty pieces of prose (and counting) as well as an online version "in progress," what more can I say? The progression of my writing is clearly seen as the portfolio opens page by page.

Word Count: 516   Reading Level: 10.2

Portfolio Self-Evaluation:
"At   The End of The Road"
Angie Pratcher

A man lies on a burgundy couch. Under dim, fluorescent lights, a sweaty thumb and forefinger fidget with a silk designer necktie as he talks about his childhood. Every day, people pay thousands of dollars for a medically trained, professional "mind adjusting." Or, simply put, therapy. Each patient wants to discover something about themselves, and because they have regrets of the past and doubts of the present and because they have worries about their futures, the share their stories of accomplishment; they talk of their inner thoughts; they revisit a jumbled past in hope they can create a path for an organized future.

Producing this writer's portfolio was my therapy. For the cost of a leather bound binder, and a package of sheet protectors, I have physical proof that I have been constructive with my life; I have been challenged and succeeded, and because of this, I have a brighter future ahead.

Traveling down the road that created the material for this portfolio, I have found my voice—my style of writing and communicating with the world. Henry David Thoreau once said, "All I know in life, I have learned from borrowing." Tools and techniques of classic American writers have influenced my "voice." I have borrowed their styles and methods and churned them together into my own writing sample.   Through editing and re-editing an expository paper, I learned to sculpt like Ernest Hemingway. I discovered the satisfaction of cutting and rearranging words and clauses until they form a perfect Sentence. And for this, I am a better writer. F. Scott Fitzgerald should be credited with showing me how to describe a human gesture and capture an action with a moviemaker's detail. And for this, I am a better writer. Through Ayn Rand's *Anthem* and Sandra Cisneros' *The House on Mango Street,* I can see the importance of the individual in whatever I do, and much life it can bring to a piece of writing. And for this, I am a better writer. Flipping through the plastic pages of this portfolio, I don't see a one-dimensional, mass producing writer or person. I see someone with the ability to express herself through many activities and moods that challenge and bring new insights to any old situation or story.

Originally, I developed this portfolio solely to impress a college admissions committee.   I included a section of my writings from this past year because I wanted them to see my diversity as a writer, to see my ability to write well in many different categories. I developed sections devoted to my words after school on the staff of our school's award winning literary magazine, and as a member of the color guard because I wanted them to see my work ethic and passion for artistic activities outside of school. I developed this portfolio for the wrong reasons. I had the idea that I would walk into an interview, confident that my interviewer would learn all there is to know about me. Instead, I will walk into any situation, anywhere, confident, with a new knowledge of myself, a true therapeutically meaningful accomplishment.

Word Count: 517   Reading level: 10.7

FINAL LESSON: ADVICE FROM STUDENT WRITERS —THE "VOICE" OF EXPERIENCE

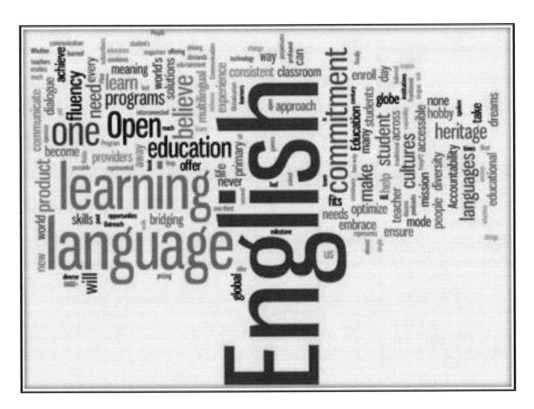

Wordle.com

"The classroom should be an entrance into the world, not an escape from it."

— John Ciardi, poet, translator and etymologist

What Do Student "Voices" Say About Writing?

A few years ago, a district curriculum assessment director asked me for suggestions of comments teachers could use when they scored essays student written essays for the newest series of high stakes standardized testing. My friend and journalism teacher in the classroom next to me, Sue Blackmon, and I put our heads together and submitted the comments we most often used in conferences with students about their compositions:

1. How do you "hook" your readers? Is there another way to do it?
2. What are you trying to say here? At this point, what is the character thinking? What are you thinking?
3. Read this aloud to me, and tell me how it sounds to you.
4. What else can you add here? Something seems to be missing.
5. Circle your transition words. Are they working to help tie ideas together?
6. Can you think of a stronger action verb to use in place of this "be" verb?
7. I know what you're trying to tell your readers. But, how can you show them?
8. Haven't you heard this phrase before? Can you think of a more creative way to say the same thing?
9. Some of these words are unnecessary. Which ones can you eliminate without changing the meaning?
10. In other words, what do you think this composition is really about?

When students in my Creative Writing class had a few minutes to spare, I also asked them to suggest some comments teachers might use students in conferences and on final drafts, and they submitted the following ideas:

1. Thanks for your essay. I needed more paper to finish my papier-mâché duck.
2. Maybe English shouldn't be your language, after all.
3. At least, you're handsome, pretty, etc. You will have a future!
4. I'll be perfectly honest. I read past your name, and then gave up.
5. I can't believe I missed watching "Desperate Housewives" to read your composition.
6. Hang in there. Six more revisions and you might have something to say.
7. Good work. Even the Leaning Tower of Pisa stood upright at one time.
8. And to think, I got a paper cut from this, too.
9. When I wrote B.S. on your essay, I meant "Be Specific."
10. See me after class. Bring scissors.

I appreciate the students in the literary magazine whose "voices" I heard as they worked on publishing our school's nationally recognized student anthology. In this last section of *The Writer's Voice,* you will hear their "voices" in their own words, as they discuss the art and craft of writing. With any luck at all, their ideas will keep students' essays and compositions from becoming part of an endangered species.

Writers can still find their "voices" in a multiple-choice world.

Student Voices: "Literary Cuisine"
Emily Caulfield (2003:12)

I never really saw a difference in writing and cooking. Perhaps this explains why experienced critics of my work would rather peruse a poem than savor a stew. However, I truly believe that a rich sauce and a striking syntax, or toasted croissant and a tantalizing cadence, differ simply by their textures and tangibility, not their warmth and effect. In truth, only raw thought, diced and kneaded into words and sentences mattered over a flame of unrelenting revision, produces a veracity of expression worthy of a sprig of parsley and a reader's palate.

I remember my first writing assignment. I remember the smell of Play Dough and glue as my first grade teacher passed out tablet paper she held in her apron. The sheet stretched before me, a veritable ocean of lines and spaces that meant as much to me as the "Golf War." (I never understood why they didn't just play eighteen holes and be done with it.) And so, as grubby fingers and stubby pencils flew all around me, I experienced my first cases of Writer's Block. In that Lilliputian orange chair I swung my dingy Keds and searched my brain for some sort, any sort, of inspiration; the muted whisk of my classmates' instant ingenuity taunted me as ruthlessly as any of the boys at recess. At last, as writing time ended and the apron began weaving up and down the aisles once more, I introduced my first scribbled thoughts into the world. Though Keats and Milton may not have appreciated the complexity of Toby, the purple pterodactyl I had just created, my ascent into the realm of literature was victorious. I had created a masterpiece.

The subjects of my work have evolved since days of tablet paper and banana clips. The scope of human emotion, mirrored explicitly by the very act of writing, demands a diversity of genres in the literary world. In pursuit of such variety of style and verity of thought, writers developed a menu, a range of literary dishes that expresses the sweet, the sour, and the salty of all that embodies the human experience. The simple act of stirring and spreading thoughts along a one-inch margin cleanses and soothes the brain like a long drink of herbal tea. Though, as in kitchens around the world, stories sometimes emerge undercooked, failed metaphors must be scraped from the bottom of the pan, and the occasional experiment results in disaster, there is not greater joy than this creation of recipes for the human soul. The moral experience entails a range of dishes, a buffet to tantalize the palate and tease the mind. Writing is creation. Cultivation. Cuisine.

Your Turn:
What do you remember about the first story or poem you ever wrote? Can you compare that experience to something else? How have your ideas about writing changed since working through *The Writer's Voice?*

Student Voices: "To Write: An Evaluation"
Julianne Wilson (2008:23)

Sometimes being a writer is a more difficult task than I would like, and writing is almost as easy to put off tomorrow as that new diet and exercise program—and housekeeping. I am not a disciplined writer and it disappoints me when I happen to equate lack of discipline with not being a passionate or committed writer. The blinking cursor stares at me from behind a screen, glaringly accusing me of not having anything worth saying, of not pulling something from the depths of my consciousness and making a statement.

My perfectionism strangles my creativity and fingertips lie motionless over the keyboard. I do not know how to say what I want to say, and sometimes I cave into the feeling of not wanting to take the time to find out. The entire process of writing is difficult or Hemingway wouldn't have related it to cutting open your own flesh. People are perpetually expecting writers to say something profound, something that echoes within them, and writers are constantly slaving to say the same thing in a new way over and over.

I will never know what anyone learns from my writing as I have not made reading the minds of those I have never met a common practice, strictly limiting myself to only those people I know personally. At the same time, I do hope that if nothing else my readers (how strange to possessively claim them as my own) will learn something about themselves because that, of course, is just what we all know to little about. My greatest improvement happened when I realized an idea had died, and then, letting it go, only to pray that someday the time will be right for a resurrection. When writing, I generally try to imagine myself just as I imagine a professional author would, with an audience of humdrum human beings who have a general appreciation for literature but who don't ogle over the subtle complexity of a Shakespearean character's development.

How can writers ever be completely satisfied with something that came from their own hands? In the face of literary giants of this world, however, I have accepted my own mediocrity. If it were possible, I would change everything about my writing and end up as one of those writers who write one piece during their entire lives and never really finishing it. But I kind of think those sort of authors are saps; there is no perfection in writing so we should just put something down and write, "The End," already. To improve with each piece that I write would be a wonderful goal, but it is altogether more likely that I will at some point in the future create a piece of writing that will be usurped by a junior year English assignment. That's just life, though, and I am okay with that.

> **Your Turn:**
> So, it's okay for an assignment, or topic, to frustrate writers who believe they have something to say, but can't always find the words to say it. Is there such a thing as "Writer's Block?" If so, why do you believe it occurs? How can writers avoid it?

What Final Advice Do Students Have?

Several years ago, I asked students in my classes to write letters to future students that offered advice on ways to improve their writing. Below are some of the best responses I received on that assignment. Enjoy and profit from their advice. [1]

"I would suggest that you use paragraphs to separate the body, introduction and conclusion. I think your teacher will be impressed by this, mine was...If you ever get stuck, or have trouble, never hesitate to ask your teacher or even a friend sitting next to you. They often can come up with good ideas...Remember, writing is a very important tool in life. When you get a job in the real world, and your manager asks you to write a summary of your high school life, will you be able to do it correctly?"

~Stephen Anthis,

"Make sure to be spontaneous and creative with your writing. Let's think about this for a second. For instance, if you and Spot (your dog) were playing outside, you might interpret this story from a bird's point of view. You also need to become part of the composition. Try to feel things that go on in your reader's life and try to understand their problems and emotions, too.

Finally, when you are finished with your paper, you can relax and enjoy the sunset on the horizon. You know you tried 150% instead of your normal 70%, and when 'try, try, try' comes into your mind, you know for sure that it works and you can store that little word for future use, or pass it on to someone else."

~Sally Trussell,

"By writing a little each day, you can make improvements on your grammar and writing style. You can prove this by comparing recent writings to stories that you wrote six months ago. The next writing assignment you do, make it your best one yet. And the assignment after that, make it better than the first, if not for you, do it for me."

~Gary Wilson,

"First, a writer must work in a relaxing atmosphere in order to produce a piece of the highest quality. I have a plastic, green beanbag chair that I love to sit in while writing a rough draft. Sitting upright in a sold oak chair makes me feel like I'm in a desk at school, and that's the last place I want to be. Create pictures that place your reader "in" your writing instead of being a mere onlooker holding a paper. Remember that the reader taking pleasure in your writing is your number one goal."

~Nick Ondrasek,

A Writing Teacher's "Voice" of Appreciation

I retired after thirty years of teaching students to write. Shortly afterwards, I learned that the AAUW (American Association of University Women) had selected me to receive their Woman of Achievement Award in recognition of my career as an educator. In my Acceptance Speech, I had an opportunity to thank people who had influenced me, but I also wanted to share some thoughts about the state of writing in education today. Below, you can read the speech I gave to my family, friends and leaders in education and community: [2]

AAUW: Thank you for your generous introduction. I'm honored to accept the AAUW award on behalf of educators who I represent here today.

To Fr. Rob Price: Thank you for your prayers. Your words remind us that the greatest teacher of all, Jesus Christ, told stories, and He never used worksheets to teach His lessons.

KISD School Board & Administrators:
You have provided resources and training that have helped teachers keep up with changing needs in a changing world—even when they were met with reluctance. After my friend, Roberta Sajda, Klein Forest's amazing art teacher, and I wrote the first grant for computers at Klein Forest, our principal, asked me if I would become a T.I.M.—a technology integration mentor—"teachers teaching teachers," a concept that became a component of our grant application. I said, "Mr. Spencer, you know I don't know anything about using computers except word processing." He replied, "Yes, Mrs. Dozier. We know. We think if we can teach you how to use computers, we can teach anybody." Technology enhanced my relationship with students---but never replaced it.

Klein Forest Principals and Colleagues: My heart stayed with Klein Forest because of your support. When I had an idea, you often said, "I don't know about that, Mrs. Dozier, but try it and let me know how it turns out." If my idea worked, I told them; if it didn't, they never heard another word about it. Thank you for empowering me to become the "instructional specialist" as an English department chair, and as a teacher in my own classroom.

Parents of my students—many of whom are here today: Thank for you for sharing your teenagers with me. You provided the DNA they needed to succeed. However, you should know that I never taught your kids to write. I only gave them permission.

My Students: I did some quick math (and for an English teacher that's a challenge) —in thirty years, almost 4,000 kids entered the doors of my classroom—reluctant, nervous and apprehensive because many had heard that I was *The Teacher From the Black Lagoon,* the children's book I read to students on their first day in my classes. They learned quickly that they shouldn't ask, "Is this for a grade?" or "How long does it have to be?" or "What do I have to do to pass this class?" Instead, they learned to ask, "How do I improve my writing?" "Can I use my imagination? Write my own opinions?"

I usually answered: "Avoid the obvious. Think outside the box. Be specific. Think about your audience. Remember the 3 C's: Clear, Correct, and Concise. Edit most of your "be" verbs and all of your adverbs—they're the sign of a weak minds." And, yes, you have to use your imaginations, ideas and opinions." And when they finished revising and editing a piece, they often asked, "Do you think it's good enough to be published, now?"

To all my student writers, especially those I worked with on our beloved *Aquilae Stilus*. Klein Forest's nationally recognized student art/literature anthology: You were such talented writers that you made me look good.

Our children, their husbands and wives, and our grandchildren. I told a friend that I was receiving this award because the AAUW thought I could fill up two whole tables with just our family. All sixteen of our children and grandchildren are sitting there watching timers on their cell phones to make sure I don't exceed the time limit. Thank you for being here on this special day and for helping me develop the principles that guided lessons in my classroom:

- One size does not fit all—whether it's a shoe, a lesson or a curriculum because every youngster learns and develops in a unique and individual way;
- Filling in bubbles on a scantron does not build skills for college, careers or a lifetime of learning. Reading and writing every day does.
- And, lastly, all children—<u>all children</u>—have special gifts and talents, and it's up to us as parents, educators and community leaders to help them discover those abilities and provide opportunities for young people to use them.

My husband, Don, for most of our almost fifty years together, you have called me "Mrs. Dozier" in public (and sometimes in private), and you never objected to students calling you, "The Don." So, thank you for buying my first computer—when I really wanted a new kitchen floor—and for buying my cell phone, laptop, and tablet computer. Thank you for learning to cook so I had more time to grade papers, write grants and work on a book and its digital version. And thank you for understanding that teaching kids to write was more than a job—it was—and it still is—my ministry and mission.

My mother. Who left school after the eighth grade to help at home during the Depression to help with the cooking, cleaning and laundry for two brothers and three sisters who worked to support the family. She knew I would become a teacher, when, at four years old, I set up a classroom for my brothers, my dolls and our dog in our living room. "She WILL go to college," she said to my Dad, "so she can always take care of her family—no matter what happens." I am not sure what she would say if she could be here, but I know what I would say to her, "Dear Mom, thank you for your sacrifices. I hope I made you proud."

Conclusion:
A few years ago, an eighty-two year old tour guide drove us through Glacier National Park. After our tour ended, he planned to take a group to Antarctica. At the end of every day's adventure into Glacier Park, he said, "Tomorrow, the best is yet to come."

And, so thank you, American Association of University Women for 130 years of believing in "advocacy, education and research" that make a difference in the lives of young women. And, thank you for honoring me as an educator. "Tomorrow, the best is yet to come."

Featured Student "Voices"

PREFACE
LESSON 1: GETTING STARTED
1. Dozier, Lynne. (1993). "Setting SMART Goals." Professional Staff Development In-Service.Klein ISD.

LESSON 2: THE PROCESS OF REVISION
1. Lynne Dozier. (1993). "A Teaching Philosophy." Teacher of the Year Essay. Revised, 2012.

LESSON 3: GRAMMAR AND MECHANICS
1. I first used the "Parts of Speech" poem as a teaching tool in my classroom in 1993. I read it to a "rap" beat and have performed it in several staff development in-services since then. Variations of the poem can be found in many places on the Internet.

2. The original version of this poem was written by Jerrod H. Zar in 1992. It has appeared on the Internet thousands of times, on web pages, in emails, and in books and articles about writing. http://www.bios.niu.edu/zar/poem.html

LESSON 4: THE ESSAY OR "I-SAY"
1. Dozier, Lynne. (1998). "Flying With Words." Autobiography of Reading. University of Houston. Revised, 2012.

2. Nataraj, Shanthi. (1993). "Gastronomically Speaking—One Sunday Afternoon In Argentina." College Admissions Essay: Northwestern University.

LESSON 5: NARRATION
1. Lynne Dozier. (1999). "Hallmark Stories." Essay. University of Houston. Revised, 2012.

LESSON 6: DESCRIPTION
1. Dozier, Lynne. (2003). "Hayti, Missouri 2003." Journal. Revised, 2013.

2. Dozier, Lynne. (2003). "The Town Square 1959." Journal. Revised, 2013.

3. Dozier, Lynne. (2005). "Berlin—A Place." Journal. Revised, 2013.

4. Dozier, Lynne. (2005). "France—The People." Journal. Revised, 2013.

LESSON 7: EXPOSITION
1. Dozier, Lynne. (1997). "Explaining Values." Essay. University of Houston. Revised, 2007.

2. More examples of graphic organizers used as teaching tools for reading, writing and research can be found at: http://www.educationoasis.com/curriculum/graphicorganizers.htm.
3. Payne, Ruby. (2004). "The Role of Language and Story." *A Framework: Understanding and Working with Students and Adults From Poverty.* Aha Press, 3rd Edition.

4. In 1956, Benjamin Bloom headed a group of educational psychologists who developed a classification of levels of intellectual behavior important in learning. During the 1990's a new group of cognitive psychologists, lead by Lorin Anderson (a former student of Bloom), updated the taxonomy to reflect relevance to 21st century work. The two graphics show the revised and original Taxonomy. Note the change from nouns to verbs associated with each level. For more information, see http://ww2.odu.edu/educ/roverbau/Bloom/blooms_taxonomy.htm

LESSON 8: ARGUMENTATION
1. Dozier, Lynne. (1999). "An Argument: Character Education." Essay. University of Houston. revised in 2012.

2. The use of the Rhetorical Triangle to explain the organization of an argument can be found in many places and is a standard teaching strategy. For more information about Rhetorical Triangles, please visit: http://www.iupui.edu/~uwc/pdf/Rhetorical%Triangle.pdf

3. King, Martin Luther. (28 August, 1963). "I Have a Dream." March on Washington for Jobs and Freedom.Washington, D.C. .

4. Montano-Harmon, M.R. (1990). *Developing English For Academic Purposes. Dissertation.* California State University. Fullerton, California.

5. Gardner, Howard. (2004). *Changing Minds.* Harvard Business School Press. Harvard University. Cambridge, Massachusetts.

LESSON 9: POETRY
1. Nayak, Megan. William Nestor. Steve Matthew. (1998). "A Few Poetic Definitions." Writer's Notebooks. Klein Forest High School. Houston, Texas.

2. Dozier, Lynne. (1995). "Oh, Teacher. My Teacher: Creating a Live Poets' Society." *Poet Magazine.* Vol. 5. Oklahoma City, Oklahoma. 56-57.

3. Boye, Alison. (1995). "Poetry Personified." *Poet Magazine.* Vol. 5. Oklahoma City, Oklahoma. 58.

4. Dozier, Lynne. (1993). "Hayti, Missouri 1959." *Getting the Knack: 20 Poetry Writing Exercises.* Stephen Dunning and William Stafford, eds. NCTE. 52.

5. Ibid.

LESSON 10: STYLE
1. Dozier, Lynne. (1995). "The 3 P's: Prose, Poetry and Profits. *English Journal.* NCTE. 37-42. Revised, 2012.

2. "Levels of Diction." (3 August 2012). http://www.pnc.edu/engl/writingcenter/dict.html

LESSON 11: SATIRE
1. Chance, Joey. (2002). "How many students…?" Klein Forest High School. Writer's Notebook. Klein Forest High School. Houston, Texas.

LESSON 12: MEDIA LITERACY

1. Dozier, Lynne. (1999). Research Paper. "Idioms, Idiots and Ideas." University of Houston. Revised, 2011. Sources included in the Works Cited for the text.

2. Orwell, George. (1946). *Nineteen Eighty-Four.* New York: Harcourt, Brace, Jovanich.

3. Lutz, William. (1987). *Doublespeak: From "Revenue Enhancement" to Terminal Living. How Government, Business, Advertisers, and Others Use Language to Deceive You.* New York: Harper & Row:

3. Ibid.

4. Maslow's Hierarchy of Needs has been a part of educational training and pedagogy for many years and aspiring teachers, writers and students can find more information in various places on the Internet.

LESSON 13: RESEARCH

1. Dozier, Lynne. (1993). "Teaching Johnny to Spell." *English in Texas.* Texas Council of Teachers of English. 1993: 6-9. Revised, 2012. Sources included in the Works Cited for the text.

LESSON 14: MEDIA CRITICISM

1. Dozier, Lynne. (1994). "Lessons From Loo Ten Tant's Journal." *English Journal.* National Council of Teachers of English. 1994: 34-38. Revised, 2012. Sources included in Works Cited for the text.

2. History of Computing Project. "Biographies of Key Figures in the History of Computing." (2 April 2012.) http://www.thocp.net/biographies/aristoteles.html.

3. The American Film Institute (http://www.afi.com/tvevents/100yearslist.aspx) provides a complete source of information about film history, criticism, a bibliography of awards and honors that pay tribute to the art of film.

LESSON 15: THE ENGLISH LANGUAGE

1. Crum, Robert. (1986). *The Story of English.* New York: Viking Press.

2. Ibid.

3. Adapted for high school classes from *Framing Literacy: Teaching/Learning in K-8 Classrooms* by Frances Mallow and Leslie Patterson. Norwood, Massachusetts: Christopher Gordon. 1999.

LESSON 16: READING LIKE A WRITER

1. Trelease, Jim. (2006). *The Read-Aloud Handbook.* Penquin. 6th edition.1.

2. Dozier, Lynne. (1998). "Autobiography of Reading." Essay. University of Houston. revised, August 2012.

3. Drew, Dan. (1981). "Poem for Daughter." Personal Letter.

4. Chart adapted for high school readers from "Metacognitive Behaviors of Good and Poor Readers." w.acesc.k12.oh.us (Cook 1989). http://ww2.youresc.k12.oh.us/cos/lang_arts/files/res_readers.pdf

5. This text circulated on the internet in September 2003. I first became aware of it when a colleague, trying to track down the original source, sent it to me. It's been passed on many times, and in the way of most Internet memes, has mutated along the way.

6. QAR, KWL and KWLS are common strategies used to help students use questions to activate prior knowledge. Variations of these strategies can be found in many different places on the Internet.

7. Cooper, Duff. (2001). *Talleyrand.* New York: Grove Press, 2001.

8. Dozier, Lynne. 1998). "Educational System—Races." Essay. University of Houston. Revised, 2012.

LESSON 17: WRITING ACROSS THE CURRICULUM

1. "Research-Based Recommendations for Effective Writing Instruction and Assessment." National Council of Teachers of English. September, 2008. www.ncte.org/library/NCTEFiles/Resources/Magazine/Chron0908Policy_Writing_Now.pdf

2. Companies and organizations, including Forbes magazine, Kent University, Fox Business, Target, and Microsoft list these qualities as necessary for successful careers after college.

3. National Governors Association Center for Best Practices, Council of Chief State School Officers Title: Common Core State Standards for English Language Arts. Publisher: National Governors Association Center for Best Practices, Council of Chief State School Officers, Washington D.C. Copyright Date: 2010

4. Standards for Ensuring Student Success from Kindergarten to College and Career, prepared by the Texas Education System in 2009. http://www.thecb.state.tx.us/collegereadiness.pdf.

LESSON 18: PORTFOLIOS

1. Dozier, Lynne. (2000). "Portfolios: Pathways to Success." Klein ISD Staff Development In-Service. Revised 2012.

2. The National Assessment of Educational Progress (NAEP) is the largest nationally representative and continuing assessment of what America's students know and can do in various subject areas. Learn more about "The Nation's Report Card" at: http://nces.ed.gov/nationsreportcard/reading

FINAL LESSON: STUDENT ADVICE

1. Anthis, (1995). Stephen. Gary Wilson. Sally Trussel. Nick Ondrasek. Advice for Student Writers. Writer's Notebooks. Klein Forest High School. Houston, Texas.

2. Dozier, Lynne. (18 February 2012). "A Teacher's Appreciation."American Association of University Women Educator of Achievement Award Speech

—Index: "Your Turn" Assignments—

Note: I developed the "Your Turn" assignments included in *The Writer's Voice* to meet the objectives of the Advanced Placement Language & Composition course in my syllabus, submitted and approved by the College Board in 2007. The assignments also meet Common Core Standards (www.corestandards.org/ELA-Literacy) and Texas Standards for College Readiness (ccrs@thecb.state.tx.us). The AP English Language and Composition course objectives are listed below:

- analyze and interpret samples of good writing, identifying and explaining an author's use of rhetorical strategies and techniques;
- apply effective strategies and techniques in their own writing;
- create and sustain arguments based on readings, research and/or personal experience;
- write for a variety of purposes;
- produce expository, analytical and argumentative compositions that introduce a complex central idea and develop it with appropriate evidence drawn from primary and/or secondary sources, cogent explanations and clear transitions;
- demonstrate understanding and mastery of standard written English as well as stylistic maturity in their own writings;
- demonstrate understanding of the conventions of citing primary and secondary sources;
- move effectively through the stages of the writing process, with careful attention to inquiry and research, drafting, revising, editing and review;
- write thoughtfully about their own process of composition;
- revise a work to make it suitable for a different audience;
- analyze image as text; and evaluate and incorporate reference documents into researched papers.

Lesson 16. Reading Like a Writer: The "Voice" of Ideas

Lesson 17. Writing Across the Curriculum: The "Voice" of College and Career Readiness

Lesson 18. Portfolios: The "Voice" of Self-Evaluation

Lesson 18: Advice from Student Writers: The "Voice" of Experience

Guiding Question: How have your ideas about writing changed since
working through the assignments in *The Writer's Voice?*
Guiding Question: How can writers avoid "Writer's Block?"

-----*About the Author*------

For thirty years, Lynne Dozier taught English Language Arts, Advanced Placement Language and Composition, Creative and Practical Writing at Klein Forest High School in Houston, Texas. She also served as ELA Department Chair for thirteen years. During the last five years of her teaching career, she coordinated Grants, Community Relations and Advanced Placement Programs. She earned a Bachelor's Degree with majors in English, Art and Psychology at Southeast Missouri State and a Master's Degree in Literacy Education at University of Houston. Throughout her career as an educator/teacher/writer/researcher, she received several awards:

- Klein ISD 75th Anniversary "Diamond" Award (2013)
- AAUW (American Association of University Women) Outstanding Woman—Education Honoree (2012)
- Bob Costas/College Board Grant for Excellence in Teaching Writing (2010)
- Klein ISD Superintendent's Initiative Award (2010)
- Susan O'Connor Teaching Excellence Award (2008)
- The Scholastic Art & Writing Award (1998, 2004, and 2007)
- KISD and Region IV State "Teacher of the Year" (1994-95)
- Excellence in Education, University of Texas (1991-92, 1993-94, 1995-96),
- "Who's Who in American Education" (1994-2011)

Her publications include:
1. *The Writer's Voice: 18 Lesson to Improve Writing,* 2013.
2. "Teacher to Teacher: One True Sentence." *The Elements of Literature: Annotated Teacher's Edition.* Holt, Rinehart & Winston. 2009
3. The 3 P's: Prose, Poetry and Profits." *English Journal.* November, 1995.
4. "Oh, Teacher, My Teacher: Creating Live Poets' Society." *Poet* magazine, 1995.
5. "Dances With Wolves: Lessons from Loo Ten Tant's Journal." *English Journal.* . January, 1994.
6. "Hayti, Missouri—1959." *Getting the Knack: 20 Poetry Writing Exercises,* edited by William Stafford and Stephen Dunning, 1992.
7. "Teaching Johnny to Spell." *English in Texas.* Summer, 1990.

Lynne retired in June 2011, but continues to serve teachers and students as a member of the Klein Education Foundation Board of Directors and as a writing consultant with D&L Global, Inc. In between visits with her eight grandchildren, and travels throughout the world with her husband of fifty years, Lynne still finds time to write and edit several projects including a history of her church and her next book, *The Last Assignment: Students Remember an English Class.*

Made in the USA
Lexington, KY
22 June 2016